T0306070

"…this is a unique story of a woman's journey from a fatherless child at the age of two, to a precocious child and a trailblazing student in her formative years through college, to a successful STEM professional and global technology leader, to a blissful life as a wife, mother, and grandmother. She is now at the pinnacle of her purpose and destiny. Having been there from her years in advanced education, I have watched her blossom into a remarkable force to be reckoned with.

I strongly recommend anyone interested in pursuing a career in STEM, and/or anyone who needs inspiration or encouragement when faced with what may seem like insurmountable obstacles, to read her story. It will be medicinal for your spirit as you aspire to live on purpose in this life!"

Fayè A. Briggs, Ph.D.
Founder & CEO, Afristec International,
Inc. & Niminq, Inc.
Intel Fellow Emeritus

"For anyone who harbors self-doubt possibly triggered by "imposter syndrome" or by being a "first and only" (what some describe as "Jackie Robinson syndrome"), this book can be directly and compassionately relatable and helpful to them. For anyone from the broader community and readership who may wish to understand better and more intimately what persons who experience either or both of the two aforementioned syndromes might at times face and have to deal with in their lives and careers, this story can effectively speak directly and informatively to them as well. And for all who aspire to attain success at the highest levels to fulfill their innate potential for accomplishment and achievement, no matter their past or current economic and/or social status, this book can motivate and be a north star for them in striving for and reaching their goals."

Timothy M. Pinkston, Ph.D.
Professor and Vice Dean, USC Viterbi
School of Engineering
University of Southern California

"This book is an inspiring tale of how to overcome seeming insurmountable obstacles."

Calvin Lawrence
IBM CTO and author of bestselling book,
Hidden in White Sight: How AI Empowers
and Deepens Systemic Racism

Soft Power for the Journey

This is a story of an African American woman working at the highest levels in STEM. Dr. Sandra K. Johnson earned a Ph.D. in electrical and computer engineering from Rice University, Houston, Texas, in May 1988, the first Black woman to do so. She then became a successful global technology leader and an IBM Chief Technology Officer (CTO). The story narrates the inextricable human dimension of dealing with various personal and familial challenges that people naturally encounter—with the highs and lows, and exhilarations and disappointments. It portrays her inner strength, persistence, dedication, boldness, quiet resilience, wisdom, strong faith, and this *soft power* she leverages throughout her life. It is a heartwarming, compelling story designed to encourage, be aspirational and awe-inspiring, and uplift the spirits of a broad and diverse readership.

From tragically losing her father at the age of two, to being raised by a single mother of four children, Sandra showed promise in math and science, and discipline and unrelenting drive at a young age. Raised in the deep south, she exhibited leadership even while in kindergarten and blazed trails in leadership while in junior high and high schools. Her early education was in segregated schools, with integration coming to her hometown as she started the fifth grade. Dr. Johnson's innate abilities led her to a summer engineering program for high school students, then on to college and graduate school.

Dr. Johnson has made innovative contributions in high-performance computing—supercomputers—and other areas of computer engineering. She has dozens of technical publications, over 45 pending and issued patents, and a plethora of recognition and honors in her field. The book is a fascinating and intriguing story that conveys in captivating and relatable ways the remarkable life arc of a resilient person from an underprivileged background who persistently overcomes whatever odds and challenges are encountered in her life. It is a riveting human tale of a triumphant spirit, moving forward with *soft power* to celebrate achievements and handle obstacles with steel willpower, influential support, and faith.

Sandra K. Johnson's 26-year career at IBM included roles as Chief Technology Officer, Research Staff Member, WebSphere Database Development Manager, and Linux Performance Architect and Manager. Dr. Johnson was a member of the IBM Academy of Technology and an IBM Master Inventor, she is the author of over 80 technical publications and books, and she is a Fellow of the Institute of Electrical and Electronics Engineers.

Soft Power for the Journey
The Life of a STEM Trailblazer

Sandra K. Johnson, Ph.D.

CRC Press
Taylor & Francis Group
Boca Raton London New York

CRC Press is an imprint of the
Taylor & Francis Group, an **informa** business

First edition published 2024
by CRC Press
2385 NW Executive Center Drive, Suite 320, Boca Raton FL 33431

and by CRC Press
4 Park Square, Milton Park, Abingdon, Oxon, OX14 4RN

CRC Press is an imprint of Taylor & Francis Group, LLC

© 2024 Sandra K. Johnson

ISBN: 978-1-032-72428-7 (hbk)
ISBN: 978-1-032-72425-6 (pbk)
ISBN: 978-1-032-72427-0 (ebk)

DOI: 10.1201/9781032724270

Typeset in Palatino
by Apex CoVantage, LLC

In memory of my mother, Gloria Dean Johnson, whose sheer determination, strength, love, and support were, and still are, my constant inspiration throughout my life's journey.

To Black women, and all who have been marginalized, ostracized, minimized, and underestimated; may we continue to draw on our inner strength and steadfast collective support as we traverse this maze we call life!

Contents

Foreword, xi

Preface, xiii

Acknowledgments, xv

PART 1 **The Early Years**

CHAPTER 1 ▪ The Beginning		3
CHAPTER 2 ▪ Junior High School		12
CHAPTER 3 ▪ High School		24

PART 2 **The College Years**

CHAPTER 4 ▪ Early College		47
CHAPTER 5 ▪ The Upperclassman		67

PART 3 **Graduate School**

CHAPTER 6 ▪ Stanford University		91
CHAPTER 7 ▪ Rice University		109

PART 4 **Blazing the Trail**

CHAPTER 8 ▪ A New Life in Westchester		129
CHAPTER 9 ▪ Moving on Up		140
CHAPTER 10 ▪ Rough Waters Ahead		151

PART 5 **The Awakening**

CHAPTER 11 ■ I Didn't Know That   165

CHAPTER 12 ■ California and Texas   171

CHAPTER 13 ■ More Enlightenment—Why Are
              You Not a DE?   189

PART 6 **The Move**

CHAPTER 14 ■ Technology in Africa?   207

CHAPTER 15 ■ The Middle East and Africa   222

CHAPTER 16 ■ What's Next?   243

PART 7 **Amazing Opportunities**

CHAPTER 17 ■ Entrepreneurship   251

CHAPTER 18 ■ Ups and Downs   263

PART 8 **Keep Rising**

CHAPTER 19 ■ New Opportunities   281

CHAPTER 20 ■ A New Life   287

INDEX   303

Foreword

I WAS A COLLEGE PROFESSOR in the early 1980s and very interested in encouraging and guiding some of my Black students, or other Blacks around the country, to pursue STEM graduate degrees. This was particularly the case for my chosen discipline, electrical and computer engineering (ECE). There were so few undergraduate Blacks in ECE, and I shared with some the advantages and lifestyles of STEM professionals with graduate degrees. I was unable to convince any. It was sheer joy to see Sandra's graduate school (Ph.D.) application submitted to the ECE department at Rice University. I called her to discuss her candidacy, excited that her technical interests aligned with mine.

I was her Ph.D. thesis advisor, and she was steadfast and persistent in her work. In fact, about mid-way through her studies, I left Rice University and moved to Silicon Valley to work in industry, including founding my own technology company. Dr. Johnson completed her work on her own, with minimal input from me! In fact, I was unaware of many of the obstacles she faced at Rice. I learned about them decades later. I share this to emphasize her inner strength, determination, and perseverance, her innate *soft power* that has driven her to overcome many obstacles in her life.

Her story is a story of inspiration, joy, sadness, and ultimate success in defining her own path in life. You will learn about her stellar career as a STEM professional, as well as the times of joy and sadness, peace, and grief that we as humans experience. From coming face to face with shocking negativism, to comedic scenes at funerals—of all things—this is a unique story of a woman's journey from being a fatherless child at the age of two, to a precocious child and a trailblazing student in her formative years through college, to a successful STEM professional and global technology leader, to a blissful life as a wife, mother, and grandmother. She is now at the pinnacle of her purpose and destiny. Having been there from her years in advanced education, I have watched her blossom into a remarkable force to be reckoned with.

I strongly recommend anyone interested in pursuing a career in STEM, and anyone who needs inspiration or encouragement when faced with what may seem like insurmountable obstacles to read her story. It will be medicinal for your spirit as you aspire to live with purpose in this life!

Fayè A. Briggs, Ph.D.
Founder and CEO, Afristec International,
Inc. and Niminq, Inc.
Intel Fellow Emeritus

Preface

SCIENCE, TECHNOLOGY, ENGINEERING, AND MATH (STEM) FIELDS of endeavor are a critical part of economic infrastructures. In fact, STEM fields are significant drivers of successful economies. STEM fields train individuals to be innovative, solve problems and think critically. However, while STEM workers are compensated well for their skills and abilities—in the United States and worldwide— workers in STEM disciplines are generally in short supply. The issue is more acute for women and people of color. There is a critical need for people representing such groups to be visible and recognized, thus encouraging and inspiring a new generation of people—and existing professionals—from multifarious backgrounds to consider and pursue careers in STEM.

Soft Power for the Journey: The Life of a STEM Trailblazer is my story, an African American woman working at the highest levels in STEM. I've had many firsts in my life, including being the first African American woman to earn a Ph.D. in electrical and computer engineering in the United States. When I graduated from Rice University in May 1988, I went on to become a successful global technology leader. At some point in my career, a good friend said a few words to me that were enlightening regarding a component of my purpose. She asked me why I was trying to blend in like everyone else. She told me I am not like the typical person. She said, "you are exceptional". There are few people like you, with your background, who do what you do. You need to be visible to encourage and inspire others to follow in your footsteps.

In addition, I recall listening to a newscast of a panel many years ago. There was a discussion on the dearth of women and people of color in STEM disciplines. One of the panelists said there are so many young Black children who aspire to be professional athletes.

They see the success of these professionals and aspire to be like them because they are visible. Many of these young people do not fully understand that from a practical perspective; they are unlikely to reach this level of play, independent of the sport. However, they have a greater chance of success in STEM, one that could enable a very rewarding, lifelong career and possibly a happy life. But there are relatively few people who have the level of visibility to inspire them. We need more STEM people of color visible in our society, where young people can learn about their life's story and aspire to the same level of success, or greater.

I took these two experiences to heart and buried them in my consciousness. I was eventually convinced that one of the people this panelist was describing was me. As I reached a mid-level point in my career, I began to write down some of my experiences, with the intention of including them in a future memoir.

This memoir includes the triumphs and disappointments we all encounter in this journey we call life. I share this story to encourage and inspire all people who at some point in their lives have felt marginalized or unheard—those who have reached a crossroad in their journey and are questioning or searching for the next path or journey to take. I share to show that highly successful people also experience mountaintop and valley experiences, like all humans. However, it is through drive, inner strength, perseverance, boldness, determination, and faith, through *soft power* that I have successfully taken the journey less traveled.

If I, who after tragically losing my father at the age of two and being raised by a single mother with meager beginnings, can make it, then so can you. Be encouraged and inspired, my sister, my brother!

Acknowledgments

ONE'S LIFE JOURNEY IS FULL of hills and valleys, joys, and sorrows. Along the way are many who provide encouragement and support as one aspires to reach their goals. This is critical for those who are trailblazers who face a multitude of obstacles along the way. There have been many who have helped me with encouragement, kind words, words of wisdom, strategies, planning, and other necessary deeds. I thank the many family members, mentors, colleagues, and friends who have been an integral part of my life's journey and success, both professionally and personally. Some of them include Gloria D. Johnson, Leonard P. Hango, Fayè A. Briggs, Sidney Burrus, Rodney Adkins, Mark Dean, Fran Allen, Nancy Stewart, Joan Mitchell, Lew Terman, Angela Archon, Calvin Lawrence, Colin Parris, Al Zollar, Ted Childs, Sharon Coleman, Tamara Golden, Linda Roach, Linda Scott, Caroline Benveniste, Mae Ruth Johnson, Edward M. Johnson, Roy Lee McKinley, Edward J. McKinley, Rosa Bea Lewis, Noah Lewis, Lela Hagger, George W. Johnson, James Curtis Johnson, Dora Russell, Claude Russell, Audrey Winey, Joanne Wilson, Leola Washington, Shirley Hinton, Mary Ann Cobbs, Pat Holder, Dr. Charles Moody, Dr. Dana Carson, Sid Ahuja, Harlin Hill, and His Royal Majesty, King Adamtey I.

I also thank a host of people who helped me remember some of the events of my life as I drafted this memoir; those events that made the cut for the book and those that did not. They include Schirrell J. Lewis, Theryl A. Johnson, Ricky J. August, Charlie McLaughlin, Linda D. Brooks, my Delta line sisters (DD36), Richard Holland, Leslie Feinzaig, and Joanne Wilson.

I thank the editors who diligently worked with me to refine the memoir to facilitate an enjoyable, heartwarming, heartbreaking, and sometimes comedic read. My memoir journey has been a little lighter because of your gifted input and feedback.

1

The Early Years

CHAPTER 1

The Beginning

I WAS BORN ON SEPTEMBER 19, 1960, in Fukuoka, Japan. My father served as an enlisted airman in the US Air Force, stationed at Itazuke Air Base (now known as Fukuoka Airport). He was an aircraft mechanic, one of few Black men who served in this capacity. My mother was a housewife who took care of me and my older sister, Darlene. I was born around 5:30 AM, which in fact was September 18 in the United States. Since I conducted the research to learn this fact, I have celebrated my birthday on both September 18 and 19.

My father and mother were both high school graduates. He graduated from Halifax Training High School, a public school in Halifax County, Virginia. My mother graduated from W.O. Boston High School, also a public school, in Lake Charles, Louisiana. My mother always took pride in being a high school graduate. During that time (1956), it was a major accomplishment for a Black person to do so.

My parents met in Lake Charles, Louisiana, at the Chennault Air Force Base in 1955. They fell in love, married, and my oldest sister, Darlene, was born in 1957. They soon moved to Japan when my father was relocated there. While I was born in Japan of American parents, I do not have the same type of birth certificate as Americans born in the United States. My birth certificate is provided by the US Department of State. Having been born in Japan results in interesting conversations when I travel internationally. Immigration officials at various locations throughout the world cannot believe I was born in Japan. For some reason they cannot tell just by looking at me.

DOI: 10.1201/9781032724270-2

Darlene is three years older than me. Our mother, MaMe, has told us that Darlene was doing a good job learning Japanese during our tenure there. MaMe also made sure we had custom-made kimonos. We returned to the United States when I was nine months old. MaMe went home to her mother, and my grandmother, to have her third child. Gregory was born 15 months after me in Lake Charles. Our father had already made his way to Bourne, Massachusetts, on Cape Cod, Massachusetts, and his next assignment at Otis Air Force Base.

My father was promoted to Staff Sergeant early in 1963. Again, he was one of a few Blacks reaching this level at the time. A few months later, he went to work, carpooling with a friend and coworker. Early on the morning of July 3, the authorities knocked on our door. My father had been in a terrible car accident. He and his coworker and friend who was driving were on their way home from work late that night. A drunk driver in another car hit them. My father's coworker walked away with a few scratches. My father was critically injured and taken to the hospital. He passed away a few hours later. By the time the police knocked on our door, he was dead. My father was 29, my mother was 26, Darlene was 5 years old, I was 2, Gregory was 1, and my mother was 3 months' pregnant with my younger sister, Kimberly. While the drunk driver was detained and spent a few nights in jail, he was never convicted of any crime.

My earliest memory is that of playing in my grandmother's lap. I recall playing with her, then looking out the window. I remember being really scared after looking out because we appeared to be in the air, way above the ground. This memory replayed in my head for many years. I finally asked my mother some questions based on this memory. Did MaMa, what we affectionately called my grandmother, come to be with us when my father was killed? Yes was the answer. Another question, "Did we fly from Massachusetts to Virginia for the funeral?". Again, yes was her response. So, while I have no memory of my father, or his funeral, I do remember the flight to Virginia for the funeral.

My father grew up in Nathalie, Virginia, a small unincorporated community in the south-central part of the state. In fact, it is so small there are no traffic lights and a couple of stop signs. The funeral was held in Nathalie at a small family church, Sunflower Baptist Church. He is buried in the church cemetery adjacent to the church.

MaMe had to endure the tragic loss of a husband while pregnant, taking care of three small children, and moving. She moved back to her hometown, Lake Charles, after the funeral. We temporarily lived in a public housing project while MaMe went through the administrative and other processes to secure VA and social security benefits as the family of a deceased veteran. During this time, six months after the death of our father, Kimberly was born. MaMe remained a "housewife" when we were growing up. Her full-time job was raising us.

Our apartment was conveniently located just a block from one of MaMe's sisters, Aunt Mae Ruth, and her family. We spent time going back and forth between our apartment and the home of Aunt Mae Ruth, her husband, Uncle Edward, and our cousins. In addition to MaMa and Aunt Mae Ruth, MaMe had two sisters, and their families, living in Lake Charles. We therefore had a large and supportive extended family to help us adjust to our new life.

After a few months in the projects, one of the contacts in the front office suggested to MaMe that she investigate buying a house. The woman informed her that she was paying more in rent than most tenants, and it was likely she could find a house with a mortgage that was in line with her current rent. MaMe went searching for a house to buy. Her sisters helped her in this process, as MaMe did not have a car. (In fact, she has never owned a car or obtained a driver's license.) She also learned how to use public transit to get around.

MaMe found a small three-bedroom wood-framed house in a nice neighborhood. It also had a two-room structure with an old, rundown carport in the back of the house that we called the garage. The property had a big yard with six pecan trees, three on each side of the house in the front, middle, and back. There were also 2 pear trees and 16 fig trees in the back of the property. It was walking distance from the home of Aunt Roy Lee, another one of MaMe's sisters, and her family. MaMe bought this house, and we moved in. I shared a bedroom with Darlene while Kimberly and Gregory shared a bedroom.

Our house was a short walking distance to New Emmanuel Baptist Church, the one MaMe attended while growing up, and it was her home church. My siblings and I attended New Emmanuel regularly, along with MaMe. We would walk to church every Sunday morning to attend Sunday School. MaMe would join us later for the morning service. This was an activity we practiced every Sunday until I left for college. As children, my siblings and I always sat next to MaMe on her favorite church pew. I recall always having to sit behind a lady with a wide-brimmed hat. It was irritating to me because I could not see anything due to the hat. Even to this day I do not like hats as a result.

MaMe was a no-nonsense disciplinarian who laid down the law. We knew better than to act up during church service. When we did, MaMe, MaMa, my aunts, and all who sat close by, would give us the evil eye. Aunt Mae Ruth, who had the gift of rolling her eyes to indicate her displeasure with our behavior, would do so with great effect, and we would straighten up. After service, they would give us a tongue lashing for bad behavior. Some of them would also call us on the telephone once we made it home to have a discussion.

I had a happy childhood. We had everything we needed and some things we wanted. As I grew older, I realized that was a blessing. I remember how I would place a recently lost tooth under my pillow with great anticipation of a visit from the tooth fairy overnight. I would wake up all excited to see a quarter under my pillow. During the Christmas holidays, I would be excited about a potential visit from Santa Claus on Christmas Eve. By the way, I was always good and nice when adults would ask if I have been naughty or nice. I would also watch all the popular Christmas programs of the season on television, from Charlie Brown to Rudolph and Frosty the Snowman. I would go to bed very early with great anticipation of Santa's arrival through the night. I was utterly exuberant when I woke up very early on Christmas morning to see all the presents.

As children, Gregory and I were assigned the chore of raking the pecan tree leaves in the fall. Raking was a delightful entertainment activity. The trees produced leaves that covered our entire large lawn when they fell. We raked them into huge piles, then put down the rakes, and jumped in the piles and played. We did this repeatedly until we got tired. We also picked many bags of pecans, which fell in the yard from the trees. We had plenty so we gave much away. I ate so many pecans as a child that I grew tired of them. However, MaMe would make pralines with them, which I enjoy to this day.

When the figs were ripe on the trees, we picked them. With so many trees, it seemed like a never-ending chore. We used ladders, as most of the figs were in places we could not reach as children. MaMe would join us from time to time, and MaMa would come regularly to pick figs. MaMe would give the figs away to anyone who wanted them. So did MaMa. We would eat them not only fresh but also as a preserve. MaMe made fig preserves and placed them in mason jars to be used in the coming months. She did the same thing with the pears from the pear trees, although there were not as many of them. Like the pecans, I have eaten enough figs and pears for a lifetime.

We never used the garage's carport, as it was just some concrete with cracks filled with grass and weeds. However, we turned the two-room garage building into a play space, especially as we got older. We positioned old used furniture in the garage, including an old television. It was our place for storage and leisure.

MaMe had two brothers, Uncle Morris and Uncle Ernest, who were both in the US Merchant Marine. Most of the time they were at sea; however, every now and then they would come home to visit MaMa. Uncle Ernest, MaMe's youngest sibling, came home more frequently. He would always give his nieces and nephews money. We would get excited when we learned Uncle Ernest was in town, because we knew we would get a few quarters. Most of the time, we used the money to buy candy at Red's, the liquor store located a block from the church. We could not wait to go to Red's on the way to church when we had money. Uncle Ernest would also tell us of his experiences traveling throughout the world. He planted the seeds which became a catalyst for my love of travel. I lived vicariously through his stories of lands far away, and it was such a joy for me as a young child.

I was extremely shy as a child. This comes through clearly when seeing pictures of me as a child. I started kindergarten at the age of four at the New Sunlight Baptist Church school. Two of my cousins, Theryl and Schirrell, are the same age as me, and they also attended the kindergarten at Sunlight. We graduated in the Spring 1966 when we were five. It was a formal graduation program where the graduates wore a white cap and gown, including a white tassel (which I still have). I recall my mother describing her astonishment at my actions while my fellow graduates and I were preparing for the graduation ceremony. She said I was instructing the graduates to get in line and pay attention. Here I was, taking a leadership role at an early age, something that is innate. My mother was astonished to see me coming out of my shell. In her mind she asked the question, "Is that *my* daughter taking over?".

MaMe was intentional about ensuring that we knew our paternal grandparents. As early as I can remember, we wrote to them regularly. I remember getting excited every time I received a letter from them in the mail, and we wrote back to them. Following my kindergarten graduation, in the Summer 1966, we visited our paternal grandparents for the first time since our father's death. Three years had passed, and they were anxious to see us. We rode the train from Lake Charles to Nathalie to visit them. This was a time in the history of our country when it was challenging for a Black family to travel. However, there were many who helped MaMe take care of us during the journey.

We finally arrived in Nathalie after a three-day trip and were happy to see our grandparents, Big Daddy and Big Mama, aunts, uncles, and cousins. They lived in "the bottom", that part of Nathalie where the descendants of slaves lived for decades. The bottom really lived up to its name. It was at the bottom of a steep hill on a dead-end road made of red clay. There was no electricity or running water in their house. They did have a wood-burning stove, a well, a vegetable garden, chickens everywhere, and an outhouse.

Both Big Daddy and Big Mama were shy and reserved. I fondly recall the one-on-one time I had with Big Daddy. He was a chef in the navy, and he still cooked regularly, everything from scratch. To this day, I have never had lima beans as good as Big Daddy's. He loved to bake sweets, and I loved eating whatever he baked. In fact, he baked a cake every day. There were times when he would get up early to bake something. I somehow sensed those times and would get up and watch him bake. He would always bake something special for me during those times. For example, one time when he was baking a cake, he separately made a single cupcake with icing just for me. He was very quiet, didn't say much. I didn't even know he was making me a cupcake until he gave it to me. I was so excited to be with Big Daddy!

Big Daddy and Big Mama lived in the country. Once a week they would go to Halifax or South Boston to buy groceries, shop for other items, and run errands. Big Daddy would dress up to go shopping. He was always well dressed, and he loved to wear hats. Sometimes

MaMe would go with them, but there were few times when we were allowed to go. We were so excited when we did! We looked forward to their return because they always bought us something special.

We enjoyed spending time with Big Daddy and Big Mama during that summer vacation. But soon we were on the train going back to Lake Charles. In the Fall 1966, at the age of five, I started first grade. I attended Jackson Street Elementary School, a segregated school just a few blocks from my house. Later, Gregory and I would walk to school, and we could not understand why we had to pass another school, Opelousas Street Elementary School, to get to our school that was about two blocks further away. Opelousas Street was a segregated White school but try telling that to a child. We did not understand.

By the time I reached the fifth grade, integration had come to schools in Lake Charles. It was a bitter battle that included Black integration advocates being chased out of town with burning crosses on their lawns. I had no recollection of this, just stories from MaMe years later. For my fifth and sixth grades I attended Opelousas Street Elementary School. Yes, the same school we had passed for years on our way to our segregated school. Opelousas Street had a different type of integration during my tenure. While the students were all Black, and so was the principal, many of the teachers were White. At Jackson Street, everyone was Black. This was not an issue for me.

I noticed one thing that changed. One of my teachers in the fifth grade, a young White woman, seemed to have problems with the class. She appeared to quickly lose patience with some of the students who would act up. This never happened at Jackson Street, as the teachers were no-nonsense disciplinarians. We were too afraid to even think about acting up with most of them. However, on several occasions, this White teacher would get a colleague, another White woman, to come in and softly talk to the students to get them to behave. They were quiet for a few minutes until she left. I had never witnessed a teacher, or for that matter an adult, who was visibly flabbergasted about connecting with children. She did not come back the next year. My sixth-grade teacher was a White male, Mr. Enicks. He was also a minister and rode a motorcycle to work every day. He was a good teacher, and I enjoyed his classes.

One of the organizations I participated in at the church while in elementary school was the Junior Choir. Once MaMe and her sisters thought we were the right age to join the Junior Choir, they devised a plan. To join the Junior Choir, we had to join the church. One Sunday in June 1967, MaMe encouraged me to join the church during the alter call so I could be in the Junior Choir. Little did she know but Gregory followed me, even though she thought he was too young. We were baptized on June 18, 1967. That is how I became an official member of New Emmanuel Baptist Church and its Junior Choir. I became a Christian later.

The Junior Choir rehearsed on Saturday afternoons. Every Saturday Gregory and I, and later our cousin Arnold, would walk to the church for rehearsal. Of course, if we had any money, we would stop by Red's for some candy. The choir directors were Mrs. Gilliam and Mrs. Washington. They both had good hearts but mean streaks. If we did anything they did not like, they would say unpleasant things about our parents. Every third Sunday of the month was the youth day at New Emmanuel. The Junior Choir and Youth Choir would sing in our choir robes, and the young people participated in other aspects of the program. This included reading the scriptures and ushering. On special days, we also had a young person as the main speaker for the service.

We participated in special programs for Mother's Day, Father's Day, Easter, Thanksgiving, and Christmas, and we had special songs to learn. Mrs. Gilliam and Mrs. Washington would give us lines to recite for the program. I really liked getting positive feedback from reciting my lines. In fact, I wanted to perfect the recitation, so I practiced over and over until I was satisfied with my delivery. MaMe and others told me I had a gift for this. I was just having fun.

MaMe would go all out and buy us new outfits for Easter, a tradition in our area. The new clothes represented the resurrection of Jesus and new life. At the time, I was not aware of the meaning behind this tradition, I was just excited about wearing new clothes for Easter.

It was during this time that I also started taking piano lessons. So did my sisters, Darlene and later Kimberly. Our teacher, Mrs. Winey, lived in our neighborhood. Initially she taught us the basics, and then we graduated to more sophisticated techniques. Mrs. Winey noticed early that I had a gift for playing. She encouraged MaMe to buy a piano so we could practice regularly. Mrs. Winey also encouraged MaMe to purchase the *International Library of Piano Music*.

MaMe bought the whole set of those green and white books. They included music from the classical and romantic periods, the 20th century, and material on techniques.

Once the piano was in place, I was maniacal about correctly playing the songs. I practiced pieces repeatedly, to the point where MaMe would force me to stop practicing. Most of the time she would be in the kitchen cooking while she struggled to hear the television program she watched while I practiced. I would stop for a little while, then get back on the piano to practice some more. She would get frustrated with me. I was just laser focused on getting as close to perfection as I could with the songs. I took piano lessons for 12 years. I enjoyed it and could have pursued a career in music, but my passion was elsewhere.

MaMe had a long-time beau while we grew up. Dave was a chef at the Lake Charles Country Club and other notable restaurants in Lake Charles over the years. He was a master Creole/Cajun chef, and I loved it when he would bring that fabulous food home to us from time to time, or when he would prepare a meal for us. Sometimes he would bring us his chef's hat, and we loved pretending to be cooks with it. As a result, I developed a taste for exquisitely good food. I grew up eating some of the best food in the world, thanks primarily to Dave. However, I did not know this until I left Lake Charles and traveled the world searching for similar foods. I did not think of Dave as a father figure, as MaMe made it very clear to Dave or anyone else that we were her children. However, I grew to love and respect Dave as an adult. He was a kindhearted man who was part of our family for many years.

CHAPTER 2

Junior High School

W^E HAD A FEW PETS GROWING UP. Initially, we had a couple of cats and dogs. However, in a short time span, all pets left our abode for various reasons, leaving one of the dogs. Brownie was the typical, temperamental chihuahua. We had him for 13 years. He was a house dog who made his rounds with my siblings and me. As we got older, we would take him on rides, first on our bicycles, then in the car. I recall several times when we took him to the beach. Brownie did not like the sand or the water, but he enjoyed the afternoon breezes and riding while sticking his head out of the car window.

Our house was the place to be for the neighborhood children. They were drawn to MaMe because she was a lot of fun to them. There were many days when Lisa, Michelle, and Renee Garriett, who lived across the street, played with Kimberly. Lisa, the oldest, was Kimberly's age. Cathleen Pete, also Kimberly's age, and her sisters, Renee, and Sonja, also spent time at our house. They lived on the corner of the block. LaVerne Griffin was Darlene's age, and her younger brother, Paul Wayne, was Gregory's age. They had a developmentally challenged brother, Lionel, who also played with us from time to time. I played jacks, jump rope, and hopscotch on the sidewalk with the girls as well as other hand games like "Miss Mary Mack, Mack, Mack". In addition, I played marbles with my brother and other boys. We had a few cousins who would stop by from time to time. MaMe had a small basketball goal installed in the backyard. It wasn't long before Gregory was playing with Paul Wayne, Arnold, and others from the neighborhood.

DOI: 10.1201/9781032724270-3

MaMe tried not to show favoritism with her children. However, I remember a couple of times when she demonstrated that I was her favorite. First, one Christmas we all received bicycles, as well as other presents. My bicycle had a nice basket attached. I used it to bring Brownie along when we rode through the neighborhood. The only other time I recall MaMe showing favoritism was during Christmas a few years later. All of us received nice presents. In addition, MaMe gave me a black and white television. My siblings didn't seem to mind this, which was a relief for me. In fact, Darlene did not have an issue with this because we shared a bedroom, so she was able to take advantage of the television.

Growing up, we participated in few entertainment activities outside of our home. Money was limited so there were few times in my childhood and teenage years when I went to the movies. I recall seeing *The Towering Inferno, Jaws, Let's Do it Again*, and, later in high school, *Star Wars*. I recall Uncle Edward would stop by the house with my cousins on the way to the movies and ask us if we wanted to come. Of course, we said yes!

I and my siblings were very close to our cousins, they were more like siblings. All our birthdays were celebrated at parties attended by my siblings and cousins at either our house or that of one of my aunts and uncles. We were a close-knit family. The only other times I recall participating in social events were when attending church-related events. There were few times when we dined out. I went out for lunch or dinner less than a handful of times during my childhood. This was not something with which I was familiar, and I did not consider it to be an issue.

In the Summer 1972, Darlene went with Aunt Mae Ruth and her family on a vacation to Los Angeles (LA). (Darlene was Uncle Edward's and Aunt Mae Ruth's goddaughter.) Nine of them packed into one car and made the drive west to the city. Uncle Noah—Aunt Rosa Bea's husband—drove them because Uncle Edward was still working before his summer break. He joined them later in the summer. They rented a house on Figueroa Street and spent the entire summer there. From time to time, we would get letters and postcards in the mail from them. I lived vicariously through their tales of going to Disneyland, Hollywood, Beverly Hills, and other parts of the metropolitan area.

Uncle Noah and Schirrell—his daughter—flew back home shortly after arriving in Los Angeles. I listened with excitement and admiration as she told me the story of their drive along I-10 West to Los Angeles, their adventure in the city, and the flight from LAX to Houston on a 747 airplane. She told me all about the flight and the plane, at the time the largest commercial airplane flying. I was just taken away by the thought of travel and flying. Although I had been on planes by this time, having traveled to the United States from Japan as a nine-month-old, and from Massachusetts as a two-year-old, I had little or no recollection of those flights. I began to stand outside in our backyard in the evenings, look up at the beautiful dark sky and bright stars, and dream. I spent many summer nights imagining traveling to new places, meeting new people, exploring new and different things, and flying on planes. At the time, my dreams were limited to traveling in the United States. At ages 11–17, I dreamed of a world of travel, saying to myself, "one day". Little did I know what was to come in the following decades.

In August 1972, at the age of 11 (and a month before my 12th birthday), I started Jr. High School, attending Pearl Watson Jr. High. My tenure at Jr. High was from August 1972 to May 1975 and included the seventh, eighth, and ninth grades. This is because the high school we fed into, Lake Charles High School, did not have the capacity to handle the ninth grade. Pearl Watson was one of the three integrated feeder schools for Lake Charles High School. My first year marked the beginning of the third year of integrated schools in Lake Charles. The first few weeks and months were a very new and different experience for me. I started riding a school bus, and I was going to school with White classmates. I interacted with them in class on a regular basis. It was an adjustment.

While I was in Jr. High School, Brownie was in an accident. It was early on a Sunday morning when he managed to go exploring off on his own. He attempted to cross a busy street when he was hit by a car. Gregory had gone to look for him since he had not returned home. He came back with Brownie in his arms looking as though he was near death. The whole family started crying for Brownie, including me. MaMe called one of our older cousins, Bryan, to come and take him to the vet, which he did. In the meantime, MaMe made us get ready to go to Sunday School, as we did every Sunday morning. During this class, each student was asked to stand and read part of the lesson for the day. That morning, our teacher asked me to stand and read the lesson. I just could not get through it. I was trembling and crying as I tried hard but stumbled through. The teacher had no idea what was going on. However, my brother and cousins, who were aware of Brownie's situation, were laughing to their hearts' content. It's funny now as I look back on this, but it was not funny to me then. Pets are an integral part of the family. When they hurt themselves, the family hurts. It turned out Brownie was alright. He lived an additional decade.

I was an athlete in Jr. High. I was on the track team in the seventh grade. I ran the 4 × 100 meter relay. This was before Title IX, a gender equity law in the United States that enables an equal opportunity for women and girls in federally funded education programs, was implemented. There were limited opportunities for women to participate in sports in Jr. High and High School. In fact, the women's track team was cut by the eighth grade, and my high school did not have a women's track team. However, I really loved track practice and preparing for our track meet—we only had one. Our coach placed the fastest runner at the anchor (final) position and the second fastest as the starter (first leg). I was the starter. I recall being in the innermost lane and therefore the farthest back on the track. We practiced the baton handoff repeatedly until we perfected it. With the recitation of one word, "blue", our school color, I would reach forward and hand the baton, which was in my right hand, to my teammate in her left hand. At the same time, she would reach back for the baton without looking back.

On the day of the event, we were excited and ready. I was anxiously waiting for the sound, signaling the start of the race. When it came, I took off. It was hard for me to tell how I was doing because I seemed so far back. However, I was the first to hand the baton off to my teammate, and she took off. When she reached the next runner on our team for the handoff and third leg, she was ahead of everyone. By the third and final handoff, we were way ahead of everyone else. We won the relay. So, I can honestly say I was on a track team with a winning record, even though we only ran one race.

In the Summer 1973, we again visited Big Mama and Bid Daddy, and our paternal aunts, uncles, and cousins in Nathalie, Virginia. This time, we took the Greyhound bus from Lake Charles to Danville, Virginia. I have fond memories of this summer vacation.

I learned how to use a well, which was on Big Daddy's back porch. I took a liking to it. I was enamored by taking this long cylindrical container and letting it fall down this well while guiding it slightly with the rope until I could hear it splash in the water below. I would then pull it up by turning the turnstile slowly until the crystal clear, cold, and refreshing water made it to the top. My elders noticed how embroiled I was with this process. They assigned me the chore of drawing water from the well at least once a day. We used this water to drink, clean up, cook, etc.

I also recall using the outhouse during the day and the pot, which we kept under the bed, at night. These were my least favorite activities during our vacation. Big Daddy and Big Mama also had chickens. The chickens would lay eggs that we used in meals. We also had these chickens for meals. The first time I saw Big Mama wring a chicken's neck, I was crushed. I could not keep that image out of my mind and refused to eat that chicken for dinner. My aunts and uncles tried to convince me that all the meat we ate were previously live animals. I was not to be convinced, and I did not eat that chicken. In my mind, if I did not see the animal slaughtered, I would be fine with having it for a meal.

Twice a day, Big Daddy would walk up the hill to the post office to check the mail. Eventually, he allowed us to walk with him, at least once a day. It was our time to spend with Big Daddy going and coming. We were so excited about getting out of the bottom to check the mail. He eventually gave us the combination to the box and would let us check the mail while he watched. We just knew we were grown!

At one point in the past, there was an active train depot in Nathalie. During our 1973 vacation, it had long closed. However, one day during a visit to the post office, I remember playing with my siblings on the property of this long-closed depot. It was directly across the street from the post office. We were playing catch with a ball. I recall running for the ball, which I caught. It was right in front of a door with cracking and fading paint. However, I could still read the message, "COLORED ONLY". This is my earliest memory of how society treated someone who looked like me differently. I was 12. I was stunned into silence for the rest of the day.

We regularly attended the Sunflower Baptist Church that summer when they had service. It started out being once a month, then twice a month. While we were there, the youth planned their annual trip to Kings Dominion, an amusement park just outside Richmond, Virginia. We were so excited to travel with the youth on this field trip and had a great time.

During this vacation, we also traveled to Washington, DC, to visit more paternal aunts and uncles, as well as many cousins. They lived throughout the Washington Metro area, including Washington, DC, Maryland, and Virginia. Not only did we visit relatives, but we toured our nation's historic monuments and museums as well. I vividly recall visiting the Washington Monument, Lincoln Memorial, and the US Capitol. MaMe bought daily passes for us on the Tourmobile. This enabled us to get on and off this trolley throughout the day while visiting historic sites. It was a wonderful vacation that I still remember to this day.

Soon the summer came to an end, and we were on the bus heading back to Lake Charles. Once we arrived home, we learned of a shocking event that happened while we were away. Our bicycles, which we had stored in the garage behind our house, were stolen while we were away. My aunt, who was responsible for checking on our house while we were away, noticed this during one of her visits to the property. She called the police while we were away, but we never learned what happened to our bikes. This was a hard lesson for my siblings and me about thievery. We moved on to prepare for the pending school year when I started grade eight.

Once I became a teenager, I moved from the Junior Choir to the Youth Choir, singing as a soprano. We also rehearsed on Saturday afternoons, after Junior Choir rehearsal. The Youth Choir directors rotated from one month to the next. We also participated in the third Sunday program every month. It was during this time that I began to stand out as a speaker at the church. I gave short inspirational messages from time to time during our youth Sunday program.

MaMa loved listening to organ music. She began paying for me to have organ lessons. I started lessons with Ms. Hines, a White lady who lived across town. I had lessons on the organ in her apartment. I used the organ at New Emmanuel to practice. After a couple of years with Ms. Hines, she felt she had reached her limit in what she could teach me. She introduced me to the organist at a local Presbyterian Church in Lake Charles. This church had a large pipe organ. My new teacher taught me how to play the pipe organ through numerous lessons. I was really broadening my skill set on different types of instruments.

Also, when I was 14, I became one of the two musicians for the youth Sunday services. My cousin, Schirrell (also 14), played the piano, and I played the organ. We played for every third Sunday service for about three years, until we left to go to college. We were paid $14 a month for this service. I was so excited to have graduated from receiving a few coins from Uncle Ernest every now and then to earning several dollars a month using my skills. I was also intentional about how I spent this money. I saved some of it and exercised caution when spending any of it. This was second nature to me.

Shortly after starting this gig, the minister of music at New Emmanuel decided she no longer wanted to play for funerals. She therefore delegated this task to Schirrell and me. She may have gotten this idea when I played the organ for my maternal great Aunt Gertie's funeral, while she played the piano. So, during my high school years, for every funeral at New Emmanuel for two years, Schirrell and I were the musicians. Most of them were the typical type of funeral; however, two stand out. One I will discuss now. The other one later, when I elaborate on my high school graduation weekend.

One of the large families at New Emmanuel was the Guillory family. The parents had about nine children. One of them was very sick most of his life and was confined to staying at home. He died while I was a teenager. Schirrell and I played for his funeral. The New Emmanuel church building is large compared to the average physical church size in America. It was standing room only at this funeral. Schirrell and I were playing the typical funeral song as the family walked in. As the funeral progressed, one of the young man's sisters was overcome with grief. She began to holler and wail in a large voice. She was wearing black and then jumped up and ran to the front of the church close to the organ where I was seated, and to the side of her brother's casket. I had the best seat in the house for what came next.

She never stopped wailing and eventually fell on the floor and began to roll over. In the process her dress came up, and I noticed she was not wearing any underwear! I could not believe what I was seeing. I was dumbfounded. Most of the funeral attendees could not see her, as she was on the floor in the front. I have no doubt they saw my reaction to what was happening. Now while this woman was just wailing and moving around, no one came to her to try and comfort her. However, the minute her dress went up, and the men around her saw that she was not wearing underwear, several of them jumped up and ran to her aid. They were able to slowly get her dress down and then lift her over their heads to take her out. She never stopped wailing, and I did not see her come back into the church for the remainder of the funeral. The image of her rolling around the floor, with her dress flying up to expose no underwear is one that has remained with me.

I did mischievous things during my youth. However, it was probably not the typical type of child mischief. Both Gregory and Kimberly were in the school band. Gregory played the trombone and Kimberly the flute. Being musically inclined, I decided to teach myself to play their instruments. I remember learning by trial and error how to play "Taps" outside on Gregory's trombone when he was not home. The neighbors would call MaMe to complain, and she would always come out with a few words commanding me to stop. Also, Gregory always seemed to know when I used his trombone. Likewise, I tried to teach myself how to use Kimberly's flute a little later, although I did this inside the house. It was a little more difficult to learn, but I managed to learn some songs over time. Again, Kimberly always knew from examining her instrument when I used it.

While Darlene took piano lessons for a couple of years early on, she was not in the school band and did not play an instrument. However, she was very good at typing. In fact, she was so good that MaMe bought her a typewriter for encouragement. I took Darlene's typing book when she was not home and taught myself how to type on her typewriter. I was as dedicated to practicing my typing skills as I was with the piano. In the long run, this serviced me well. I was so good at it that when I took typing in high school, my teacher did not believe I never took a typing class. I think I finally convinced her that I taught myself. I went on to a regional and state competition in typing. In the summers after high school and during my early college years, I worked as a typist. Later, I was no stranger to the computer keyboard based on my typing experience.

I learned how to use the ukulele in Jr. High School. Our music teacher taught us how to play one song, "Sweet Georgia Brown". I believe I must have been talking about that ukulele quite a bit at home because one day MaMe brought home a ukulele for me. From that day to now, I can honestly say I know how to play the ukulele, although I can still only play "Sweet Georgia Brown".

We all had chores to do while living as preteens and teenagers. In addition to raking the leaves, Gregory and I would cut the grass. This was more Gregory than me. He would also take out the trash. The girls were responsible for washing the dishes and cleaning the house. This was especially true on Saturdays when MaMe would go shopping for groceries, clothing, or other things. One of her sisters, usually Aunt Rosa Bea, would pick her up and take her. MaMe would instruct us to clean up and make sure the house was clean when she returned. We preferred to watch cartoons on TV but tried to be obedient. The exception was Kimberly. She would do nothing but watch us work hard cleaning up the house and washing dishes while she sat on the sofa watching cartoons. We tried to get her to help but she refused. I usually washed the dishes as the last chore before MaMe returned home.

Many times, when I finished with the dishes, Kimberly would come behind me and deliberately dirty up all the dishes just before MaMe came home. MaMe would blame and punish me for not washing the dishes. I don't think she ever believed the truth no matter how many times she heard it from me. Kimberly would just laugh at the situation. It eventually reached the point where I retaliated against Kimberly when this happened. My thinking was I was going to get in trouble anyway. This set the tone early on for my somewhat distant relationship with Kimberly over the years and my sheer disdain for washing dishes.

By the end of the eighth grade, I was about to complete two full years of attending an integrated school. The election for Student Council officers was coming up. I decided to run for Student Council President. I do not recall how this came about, as I was a very shy person and I kept to myself. I also had little leadership training and no idea what was required as a Student Council President or what I would do if elected. However, the title sounded good. One thing I did have going for me was the fact that I was a gifted orator. I was born with this God-given talent, and it was honed during my years giving speeches at my church and acting in church plays.

I knew running for Student Council President meant giving a campaign speech to the entire student body. I knew I would do well with that. However, I did not know anything else about running a presidential campaign, including having a platform, soliciting votes, wheeling, dealing, and so on. I was not even a people person. Somehow, I let someone convince me to do this, simply because I knew how to give a good speech.

There were teachers and others who helped me put together a campaign platform and other things. My mother even participated in soliciting votes for me; I couldn't believe it. I gave a campaign speech that was very well received, and I won. At the time, Pearl Watson was about 65% White and 35% Black. I therefore had to have some White votes to win as I had one opponent. During the time this happened, I did not think about its historic implications or the fact that it was happening at all. It was not my focus. I also could not fully understand why my mother appeared to be so excited about this. She was more excited than I was. It was many years later that I thought of this as the historic, trailblazing event it was. It was the catalyst for years of moving forward as a trailblazer without an understanding of the significance of my journey. It was ordered steps.

During my last year in Jr. High School, as a ninth grader, I started my tenure as the Student Council President. I did well in school, and I had a wonderful term as student body president. I was not driven to get the best grades possible. I was just enjoying my courses and doing well. It was only at the end of the year, when Aunt Mae Ruth asked to see my final grades, that I learned about what it meant to graduate at the top of the class in high school. Aunt Mae Ruth saw that I had As and Bs. Then she told me I was unlikely to graduate as valedictorian in high school. I was just happy to be moving on to high school. I did not know that my grades in ninth grade were going to be a factor. I made the mental note to not spend every waking moment trying to get the best grades in high school. I had already missed the opportunity to graduate at the top. I therefore focused on learning as a joyful, pleasant experience with no pressure to get the best grades possible. I did not focus on graduating at the top until college.

I also learned about some shocking news in ninth grade. Darlene was a high school senior at the time. We both learned that as children of a veteran killed while on active duty, we were eligible to receive VA and social security benefits coming directly to us. This would happen once we turned 18 and were enrolled in college. We also learned that the checks were sent to MaMe but would come to each of us at 18. This meant MaMe would not be receiving Darlene's portion of MaMe's monthly income once Darlene went to college. As part of the college application process, MaMe took Darlene to the relevant government office downtown so she could complete the proper applications to receive her monthly checks while attending college. I went along with them.

In miliary records, the veteran is referred to as "A" in the government system. Dependents are referred to as "B", "C", "D", etc. "B" is typically the veteran's spouse, and "C", "D", etc., are the first, second, etc., offspring. While we were waiting in the office for Darlene's paperwork to be reviewed, an office worker kept coming to the waiting room asking if Darlene was the oldest child. MaMe kept responding in the affirmative to her. This woman seemed to be confused because according to the records she was reviewing, Darlene was in the system as "D", but according to MaMe telling her Darlene is the oldest, she should have been "C". Finally, the woman came back out and asked us "who is Wanda?". Darlene and I had no idea what she was talking about. However, MaMe got up and tried to convince this woman to go to another room so the two of them could talk alone. But she kept asking "who is Wanda?".

This is how Darlene and I learned from MaMe that we have a half-sister named Wanda January. She was born prior to MaMe marrying our father. She is about a year older than Darlene. In fact, she and Darlene were friends in school. MaMe reminded Darlene of this, as Darlene would come home sometimes and mention Wanda. MaMe never told Darlene that Wanda was her sister. We asked her why did she keep this from us? Did our father know this?

MaMe told us Wanda's mother filed for benefits for Wanda after our father's death. Apparently, our father was dating both MaMe and Wanda's mother at the same time. While MaMe knew of our father's past girlfriend, she did not know the woman had his child. When Wanda's mother tried to get the benefits, my mother fought against it, and they went to court. Wanda's mother was able to prove our father was also Wanda's father. She therefore received benefits. MaMe informed us on the way home that the judge asked her not to tell any of us, MaMe's children, that they had another sister. She said that's why she kept it from us. It is also why she tried to inform the government worker about this in another room. That story was just not believable to me. However, I was so astounded by this news that I did not challenge my mother on this, and I never have.

MaMe also informed us that she did not know if our father knew about Wanda before his death. She did not tell his relatives about Wanda until we learned about her. Again, she said she was following the judge's orders. Once the news came out, MaMe contacted Big Mama and Big Daddy and informed them their oldest grandchild is not Darlene but Wanda. We met Wanda shortly after this. It was shocking and surreal. This woman's facial features were the spitting image of our father. She looked just like him. Neither me nor my siblings have such a striking resemblance to our father.

CHAPTER 3

High School

I STARTED HIGH SCHOOL IN AUGUST 1975. I went from being a top dog as a student at Pearl Watson Jr. High School, to being just another sophomore at Lake Charles High School. I was still my shy, quiet, unassuming self, and life as a high school student was good. I really enjoyed the math and science courses and thought about professions that required these skills. In addition, I had the overwhelming desire to have the type of profession that enabled me to own a dishwasher, given my dislike of handwashing dishes. My mother's sisters, especially Aunt Mae Ruth, the high school math teacher, began to seriously talk to me about what I would do when I grew up. They started the conversation when I was a ninth grader, but it became much more pronounced when I started high school. Mrs. Winey also participated in the discussion. She encouraged me to pursue medicine and become a medical doctor. However, I get wheezy and light-headed at the sight of too much blood so that was not an option for me. While I began to think about what I would do, I also spent most of my time enjoying my classes and school in general.

In the Summer 1976, MaMe informed me of an unexpected trip early one morning. Uncle Noah and Aunt Rosa Bea planned a trip up the east coast with their daughter and my cousin, Schirrell. They wanted me to come so Schirrell would have a traveling buddy. I quickly packed my bags and was ready to go. We traveled to New Orleans, Louisiana, Atlanta, Georgia, Washington, DC, Philadelphia, Pennsylvania, and New York City by car. It was my first time visiting each of these cities except Washington. I was

 DOI: 10.1201/9781032724270-4

amazed and awestruck by the sights and sounds of these cities. In Philadelphia, we saw the Liberty Bell and all things about the country's founding. New York was at another level. The Empire State Building, Broadway, etc., I just soaked it all in.

We got back to Lake Charles just in time for me to take my last vacation to visit Big Mama and Big Daddy as a teenager. We took the bus to Nathalie. This time they had moved out of the bottom and into a house a couple of miles away. During the time since our last visit, one of my aunts, Yvonne, lost her husband, Leon, in a car accident. She met and married a new husband and moved out of the house she shared with Leon. She gave this house to her parents.

We were so happy to be out of the bottom and living in a house with running water and electricity! We had a great time that summer doing our usual activities. This included the regular visits to Halifax and South Boston for weekly grocery, etc. We were older now and even traveled to Lynchburg, Virginia, a couple of times for shopping. Once again, we participated with the youth at Sunflower Baptist Church in their annual field trip to the Kings Dominion amusement park. We visited our father's grave a few times while being there. The summer soon came to an end, and we went back to Lake Charles on the bus. I prepared to start my junior year in high school that fall.

In addition to academics, I learned a few skills while being in high school. For years Aunt Rosa Bea, a licensed beautician who at the time had stopped practicing, used to do my hair. She would perm my hair as well as my sisters'. After watching her do this multiple times, I decided to try it myself. I bought a perm kit and tried it out one Saturday. It worked just fine and from then on, I did my own hair.

I also watched my mother as she would sew from time to time. I eventually felt comfortable enough to try this out myself. I taught myself how to sew basic seams as well as the zigzag seam. I found instructions on how to sew in zippers in fabric stores, and I taught myself how to do that. My motivation for making my first outfit came from Aunt Rosa Bea. I remember a special event the family was planning to attend. I wanted to wear a specific kind of skirt, but I could not find one I liked and could afford. I also could not find a skirt pattern I liked. I remember Darlene had a similar skirt.

I examined it closely and thought I could make one for me, with a different fabric. Aunt Rosa Bea emphatically informed me there was no way I could make my own skirt from an existing one, with no pattern. I thought it was easy.

I had the mind to make a believer out of her. I found the fabric I liked. I then bought the zipper, thread, measuring tape, and other needed tools. I used newspaper to make a pattern from Darlene's skirt. I placed the pattern on my fabric and went to work using my mother's sewing machine, iron, and ironing board. The skirt turned out to be a replica of Darlene's skirt and a perfect fit for me. I was happy to show off my new skirt, especially to Aunt Rosa Bea. I made a believer out of her. This trait of turning one's lack of confidence in me to their believing in me has been repeated many times throughout my life.

I also watched my mother crochet. There were times when she would dedicate hours to crocheting something for us or as a gift for others. She would make tops, shawls, and the like. She taught me how to do the single and double stiches. After observing her do this, I tried my hand at it. I obtained instructions for crocheting a shawl, bought some yarn, and went to work. I made that shawl and over time made other things. I became creative, and over the years made potholders, throw pillows, and other items. In later years, as an adult, I used this skill to make items that I sold in arts and crafts fairs (e.g., during the Christmas holidays).

MaMe would not allow me to wear makeup early in my teenage years. She eventually enrolled me in a charm school that was offered by the local Sears Roebuck & Co. store in downtown Lake Charles. There, many young ladies my age learned how to apply makeup, fix our hair, walk properly, including the proper catwalk for performing on a runway, and model clothes. This was a very interesting experience for me, as I learned about something that was not high on my priority list. However, in my mind, one never knows how one can benefit from such a skill, so I kept my mind open. Our charm school graduation included an official fashion show where we modeled some of the clothes in the store on a runway. MaMe allowed me to wear makeup after finishing charm school.

An important teenage rite of passage was learning how to drive a car and getting a driver's license. I was no different in this regard. One of the requirements for high school graduation was completing a driver's education class. This included lectures as well as driving lessons on the road. This culminated in crossing the large bridge coming into Lake Charles—traveling east. I was excited and elated to have taken and passed the class. However, with no family car, I was at the mercy of others who wanted to help.

Other than high school driver's education, Dave was one of the first to give me driving lessons. He had a stick shift car, and I didn't learn much more than how to enable the car to jump back and forth while I tried to drive forward. When I visited my family in Virginia, my last summer as a teenager, one of my aunts let me drive her car once. When I returned, it was Aunt Mae Ruth who from time to time would let me drive her car. Finally, one day out of the blue, she came to our house and told me she was ready to take me to go get my driver's license. I was elated and off we went. I took and passed both the written and driving tests, coming home with a license. I was 16 years old and excited.

My junior year started in August 1976. Lake Charles High School's mascot was the wildcats. The Fall 1976 was also the height of a US presidential election, with Jimmy Carter running as a Democrat and Gerald Ford, the incumbent, as a Republican. Every four years at my high school, during the US presidential elections, we had Wildcat Nation. This was an opportunity for the student body to learn about the US presidential election and politics. The student body was split into two political parties: the Nationalists and the Federalists. I was a Federalist. Each party was to select candidates for President and Vice-President of Wildcat Nation. This occurred during the same time as the US presidential election cycle.

Each party held its own political convention where it elected its candidates to run for each of these offices. During my party's political convention, there was quite a bit of wheeling and dealing, as is done by political parties. The Federalists eventually nominated a candidate for each position, and each accepted. I became my party's Vice-Presidential candidate for Wildcat Nation, with Jimmy Plauche as the Presidential candidate. We were the ticket for the Federalists. I was 16 years old.

Keep in mind again the historical nature of this situation. This was the seventh year of integrated schools in Lake Charles but the first Wildcat Nation activity since integration. The school officials had decided not to have Wildcat Nation during the 1972 US Presidential election cycle because it was the third year of an integrated Lake Charles High School. They decided to focus on ensuring things continued to go smoothly during the first few years of school integration. Here I was, the Federalist Party's Vice-Presidential nominee for Wildcat Nation. I was the only Black and female candidate nominated out of all four candidates.

We had a campaign season where both the Nationalists and the Federalists had candidates seeking their party's nomination for President and Vice-President of Wildcat Nation. It was each party's nomination period. We had campaign slogans, paraphernalia, and all the bells and whistles associated with an actual nomination period. MaMe was really into this campaign. She was excited, yet again, about her daughter running for an elective office at school. She was more aware of the implications of this than I was. As far as I was concerned, I was just running for Vice-President of Wildcat Nation, and I do not recall who put me up for it. MaMe even wrote a campaign song for me. Here are the words:

All the way with Sandra J
She will help your school today
So get with her and vote that way
Vote Sandra John-ahn-son today!

There was a final "pep rally" before the vote on election day, also the same day as the US presidential election. Candidates from each party were to make their case with a campaign speech to the entire Wildcat Nation. I had written my speech a couple of days earlier in the bathroom at home, and my mother reviewed it and approved. It was also reviewed and approved by the teachers counseling the candidates. Then the day arrived. It was an exciting time, with the Nationalists and the Federalists all fired up about their candidates. The Vice-Presidential candidates spoke, followed by the Presidential candidates. The Vice-Presidential candidate for the Nationalists, Paul Honsinger, spoke first. He spent most of his time talking about what he would do as President in the event of the unlikely and untimely death of the President. This was the substance of his speech, and he hammered this home so much that my party began to laugh at him.

I was up next. I was very tempted to make a comment about my opponent's focus on being President, as opposed to Vice-President, even thinking about suggesting he may want to have the President killed so he could be President. However, I resisted this temptation and stuck to the script. I delivered my speech with such a passionate, powerful oratory, that the entire gymnasium leaped to their feet in an enthusiastic outpouring like I had never witnessed before in that gym. This included the Nationalists, the Federalists, the teachers, and the administrators. It was unbelievable, and I was taken aback. I was happy to have completed my speech without a snafu, but the Federalist leadership, all White except me, ran to me, grabbed me, and gave me a big hug.

Let me enlighten you on the implications of this moment. Lake Charles High School was about 60–65% White, 35–40% Black. The White students kept to themselves and so did the Blacks. It was a harmonious coexistence. To have the entire student body, teachers, and administrators, majority being White, stand up and cheer for a Black female student was unprecedented. To have several White students run over and give a bear hug to a Black student for an exciting, exuberating speech she delivered was jaw dropping. For a split second I did not know what to do, as I had never experienced this before. I was in a different place mentally (*e.g.*, I'm so glad this speech is over, what a weight off my shoulders). However, I quickly recovered and was in the moment too. I hugged back just as hard, and we were excited!

It took a while for the students to calm down for the Presidential speeches, but we did. The two candidates delivered good speeches, but it did not result in the excitement of the previous speech. It was pretty much a done deal, but I did not think of it that way. This was still Lake Charles, Louisiana, the deep south. I had learned in my few years not to take anything like this for granted.

Once the ballots were cast and counted, our school principal announced the results. Wildcat Nation President-Elect: Jimmy Plauche; Wildcat Nation Vice-President-Elect: Sandra K. Johnson. It was done. The Federalists had defeated the Nationalists and won control of Wildcat Nation! I had blazed a new trail of elective office and made history. (It would be decades later before I thought about these events in this manner.) We had an Inaugural Ball on January 15, 1977, at the Lake Charles Civic Center. It was held a few days before

US President-Elect Jimmy Carter would be inaugurated as the 39th President of the United States of America.

Several weeks later, I arrived early to my Algebra II class. A few students had also arrived before the bell rang to start class. A couple of my female classmates were talking about the upcoming Inaugural Ball and who they were going with as dates. Another class member, some would argue was the class clown, had also arrived early. Mr. Gray, our teacher, had him sit in the front of the class to keep an eye on him. He was seated in the front and to my right. We were both listening to these two girls talk. One of them turned to me and asked me who was my date for the Inaugural Ball. I told them I did not know; I did not have a date. She then raised her voice and asked the question, as more students were arriving to class, "you mean the Vice-President of Wildcat Nation doesn't have a date to the Inaugural Ball?". I was thinking to myself in embarrassment, *could you say it a little louder*?

Then the other classmate said in a very soft voice, which was unusual for him, "I'll take you". I heard him, but I believe I was the only one who heard him, which was probably his intention. I said to him, "what did you say?". His response was, "I didn't say anything". At that point the bell rang, and Mr. Gray started the class lecture. However, I knew he said he would take me to the Inaugural Ball, I was not hearing things. I thought I would just connect with him later to further the discussion.

Later that day, I ran into him on the long pathway between buildings at our school. He was leaning against the rail trash talking with some of the folks he knew, as he always did. I went up to him and softly asked him, since I knew he wanted this to be just between the two of us, did he mean what he said, that he would take me to the Inaugural Ball. His response was "yes". That was a relief to me. At the time, I had never been on a date. My mother would not allow it. However, since I was the Vice-President-Elect of Wildcat Nation, I had to go to the Inaugural Ball to be inaugurated. So, I needed a date. How is that for getting MaMe to say yes for going out on a date?

I didn't know that much about this classmate. I knew he had the gift of gab because he demonstrated it every day in Algebra II class. I also sensed that he was not a loose cannon or a bad person. He was handsome and had a beautiful smile. He was a 17-year-old senior. He would be graduating in May 1977. Also, an important item for me, he had a car. I didn't have to worry about how we would get to the ball. I had no idea what kind of driver he was. I was 16, I was not thinking about that. I did know that he had to meet my mother and get her approval before we went to the Inaugural Ball together. I mentioned to him that I would go with him, but only after my mother approved, and he had to meet her. He agreed, and we arranged the meeting date.

When he came to the house for the meeting, all my siblings, who usually were very busy, including my older sister who was not even living with us and was in college in Baton Rouge, found a way to be home *right* during this afternoon event. My brother, who was a sophomore at Lake Charles High School, knew my date and vouched for him. This guy was a charmer. His gift for gab came through in a positive way. The whole family really liked him. I believe that was the beginning of my family, in some way, treating him like he was a member of the family. My mother gave her approval, and it was a done deal. I was going to the Wildcat Nation Inaugural Ball with a date.

Next, we had to plan our presence at the ball. This included coordinating our outfits, pickup time, etc. My mother bought me this green floral print gown that I could wear. I discussed this with my date who rented a formal black tuxedo for the affair. This was going to be an actual inauguration and ball. Lake Charles High School had publicized the event throughout the city. The local newspaper printed a story on Wildcat Nation and the Inaugural Ball. It included a large picture of Jimmy Plauche and me. We were holding the emblem of Wildcat Nation, and our high school mascot. (Taking this picture became the first of many professional photo shoots I would do to publicize all sorts of things over the years.) The word was getting out about this event.

I would take the oath of office first. It would be the actual oath taken by the Vice-President of the United States. Jimmy Plauche would also take the actual presidential oath after me. My date would hold the Bible for me. I would raise my right hand while putting my left hand on the Bible to take the oath of office. We discussed all this beforehand so he would know what to expect and to ensure he was ok with it. (Yes, I know, who wouldn't be.) He was required to come to rehearsals with me so we could go over this together to ensure everything would go smoothly on the big night. He was very accommodating about all of this.

I must say that I did not view going to the Inaugural Ball with this person as a date in the purest sense. I was the Wildcat Nation Vice-President-Elect. I was going to be inaugurated at the beginning of the Inaugural Ball. I needed a date. He asked me in a unique way, but he did ask. So now I had a date and transportation. I viewed this as a business relationship. I had not discussed this with him, so I didn't know what he was thinking about all of this at the time. Every conversation we had about the event focused on logistics. How's that for a date? I would soon discover something a little different on the evening of the Inaugural Ball.

At some point during our planning, I asked my date if he was a Nationalist or a Federalist. It turned out, he was a Nationalist. After several weeks of planning, the day of my inauguration, and the Wildcat Nation Inaugural Ball, finally arrived. My gown had been chosen, and I was ready to wear it. I did my own hair and makeup for the event. The evening was to begin with the inauguration of the President and Vice-President and end with the ball. My date arrived early to pick me up. He had a corsage for me, and my mother helped me put it on. We took a few pictures and off we went. He was a perfect gentleman, walking around the car to open the door for me, and checking to ensure my dress was in the car before he closed the door. I noticed.

On the drive to the Lake Charles Civic Center, I noticed he was a little nervous. I had never seen him nervous, just always clowning. I began to look at him in a strange manner; thinking, *is this the person from Algebra II class*? I guess he was thinking about the events to come that evening. Then the car started acting up. It began to sputter. He said, "don't worry about this, it happens every now and then". He pulled over and took a gallon of water out of the back of the car. It was on the floor on the driver's side. He brought the water to the front of the car, opened the hood, and poured it somewhere in the car. He then shut the hood, placed the empty gallon back on the floor of the driver's side in the back, and got back in the car. That did the trick, and we were on our way.

We arrived at the event in the middle of excitement. Many of our fellow Wildcat Nation participants were there looking great in their evening attire. There were reporters there, including a TV crew from the local television station. They filmed this event and took pictures. At the appointed time, Jimmy Plauche and our dates lined up to take the oath of office. I went first. My date was given the Bible to hold for me. Our Assistant Principal, Mr. Ieyoub, delivered the oath of office. He asked me to place my left hand on the Bible and raise my right hand and repeat after him, and I obliged. Within a couple of minutes, I took the oath of office in front of many bright lights, a TV camera, and many other flashing cameras. I was now Vice-President of Wildcat Nation. Next, Jimmy Plauche and his date were up. Jimmy took the oath, and he became President of Wildcat Nation.

Next, it was time to party. I traversed the room, along with my date, to receive congratulations and greet everyone. This was new territory for me as an extremely shy introvert. On the other hand, my date was an extrovert and he thrived in this environment. I believe we connected with everyone there, shaking hands, receiving hugs, and taking pictures. We also chatted with President Plauche and his date before working our way to the dance floor. Throughout the evening I saw a different side of my date. He was well mannered, kind, and considerate. He was also very sensitive. He was really caught up in the moment. He was in the middle of the action, also appearing on television and other media outlets. I think he knew just about every classmate attending the event. I found myself being drawn to him. The attraction became stronger as the evening progressed. I didn't quite know what was happening, as there were so many things going on that evening.

We both loved to dance and were great dancers. There were times when we owned the floor. As the evening progressed, I looked forward to slow-dance songs so I could dance close to him. This was also when I learned he had a beautiful, soft tenor voice. It was a mutual attraction, but again he was a perfect gentleman. We stayed until the end of the scheduled event, dancing and greeting Wildcat Nation constituents. After saying our final goodbyes to President Plauche and others lingering, we left. We didn't say much on the way home, just a few words about our amazing evening and how we thoroughly enjoyed it.

We arrived at my house. My mother had left the porch light on for us. He helped me out of the car and joined me on the walkway to the porch and up the steps to the door. I reached into my purse for the key and then turned to look at my date. He flashed his beautiful smile and extended his hand to shake mine. I responded and we shook hands. Then he pulled my hand closer to him, and my body followed. We had a long, passionate kiss. I was excited, my heart was racing, and I did not want to stop. But we did. We both smiled at each other as I unlocked and opened the door to the house and walked in. It was an exciting and unforgettable evening.

I slept well that night, even though I was on a high. However, I had to get up early Sunday morning to prepare for Sunday School and church service. It was the third Sunday, and the youth oversaw service. I played the organ as usual as the Junior and Youth choirs sang hymns and special selections during the service. I found myself having difficulty concentrating as I was thinking about the previous night and smiling. After service, many of the church members came to me happy and smiling. They had seen me on the news the previous evening and were overjoyed by the event. I had a lot going on in my head, with the excitement of the event, but more importantly to me at the time, my thoughts of my date. This was something new for me, and I was trying to process all of this.

Monday morning was another school day but not a typical one for me. I saw my former date in our Algebra II class, and we were smiling at each other from ear to ear. I don't remember much about the class that day, and he appeared to be more subdued than normal. We spoke between classes, and I struggled to keep myself from getting too close to him. Over the next few weeks, we talked off and on. He also visited me and my family a few times. By the end of January, he asked me to be his girlfriend, and I accepted. We spent the next several months, before he graduated in May, in a whirlwind romance.

Off and on, I vacillated among several professions to consider for a future career. However, all of them were related to Science, Technology, Engineering, and Math (STEM). My targeted profession did not become clear to me until late in high school. In my sophomore year, my counselor encouraged me to take the Preliminary Scholastic Aptitude Test (PSAT). I did not know what it was, and she did not do a good job explaining it to me when asked. However, I took it due to her strong recommendation. I was so ignorant about this that I did not know how taking the exam, and my subsequent score, would impact my future. However, beginning the later part of my junior year, I began to receive mail from schools around the country and from some professional societies. For example, I consistently received mail from Massachusetts Institute of Technology

(MIT) and the professional actuarial society. I ignored this mail initially; I was just intrigued. Since the mail kept coming, especially MIT, I decided to investigate this. I learned a little about MIT being an engineering school. I was not interested in learning how to drive a train, so I continued to ignore the details.

One day as a junior, I received mail from Southern University in Baton Rouge, Louisiana, describing its Engineering Summer Institute for High School Students (ESI). While I was still uninterested in learning how to drive a train, I was attracted to getting away from home—and chores—and staying in a college dormitory. In addition, growing up, I was always encouraged to go to a black college in general, and Southern University specifically. It was like a mantra from my family. This mail from Southern about the ESI program got my attention. I applied and was accepted. I was excited about the opportunity to live on campus as a rising high school senior.

There was a romance to foster in the interim. My new boyfriend's best friend dated my best friend, Trudy. We spent months double dating, going to the movies and other events. Also, from time to time, we would ride our bikes together all over the city, exploring new and different parts of the city as well as some of our favorite locations. This included the beach and the steps behind the civic center. It was a great place to go and watch the sunset and think about the future. My boyfriend and I also went on a few dates alone. We got to know each other better. He would sing to me in his sultry tenor voice and write me beautiful love poems. I was in heaven.

I soon thought of him from a different perspective. He was a beautiful person behind the facade of a jokester. He was also a talented, intelligent person and was hiding this behind the jokes. I recall the love–hate relationship he had with his English teacher, Miss Finnegan. She was amazed at his vocabulary and literary skills but very upset with him when he pulled pranks and didn't take himself seriously. It was interesting to watch. I tried to discreetly encourage him to focus more on class and less on jokes. I came to realize that was his way of keeping a wide set of friends. In my opinion, he didn't want to be known as the bookworm that he was. In fact, he used so many big words during our conversations that I had to carry a pocket dictionary with me to learn what they meant.

We were in love. He became my high school sweetheart. He was graduating in May, so we took advantage of it and enjoyed every moment we had together. Life was so simple and fabulous! He had enlisted in the US Air Force (USAF) in December 1976, before we started dating. At the time no one had encouraged him to pursue college, so he moved forward to plan a future that he knew. We had many conversations about how he wished he would have known more about college. He was certainly capable of succeeding in college; however, he had already signed up to enlist in the USAF.

Every spring, LCHS hosted homecoming. This was held instead of a high school prom but was very similar. We had a homecoming court, which included representatives from each class, as well as the homecoming king and queen. In addition, it included a musical show with a theme that changed from year to year. The Spring 1977 homecoming theme was *A Salute to Broadway*. My high school sweetheart was in the school chorus. He and another classmate, Linda, auditioned and were selected to sing a duet as part of the homecoming program, "What I Did for Love", from *A Chorus Line*. He wanted me to be the accompanist. I initially rejected this idea because I didn't think I was good enough to play for such a large crowd. He convinced me otherwise, and we proceeded to rehearse for the show.

I also had to prepare for the homecoming dance. I did not want to spend a lot of money that I did not have on this, so I decided to make my gown. I found a pattern I really liked and bought the fabric, pattern, and all other materials to make it. I used my mother's sewing machine to make the dress. It was a beautiful powder blue gown with a matching sheer jacket with fake fur in the front. He rented a powder blue tuxedo to match my outfit, although he wore a black suit for the show.

The homecoming show was amazing. It was my first time attending the show, and the dance afterwards. It was modeled after the typical junior–senior prom, so my mother only allowed me to attend since I was a junior. The spectacular show began in the school gymnasium with the announcement and recognition of the homecoming court. The sophomores, as male-female couples, were first introduced, followed by the juniors, then the seniors. They were all dressed up, the ladies in beautiful long white dresses and tiaras, the gentlemen in black tuxedos. The lights in the gym were dimmed so the spotlights were on them as they arrived in the gym. The last to arrive were the king and queen, with their crowns and much fanfare.

Next, the show began with many short Broadway musical hits and other productions. When it was time for my high school sweetheart and Linda to sing, I moved to the piano while they approached the microphone. I can still remember the introduction of the song that I played, while they began to sing, he sang the first stanza, followed by Linda with the second. They sang the chorus together. They went back and forth like this for the full song. For that moment, it was beautiful and magical.

After the show, it was time for the dance. We changed into our evening attire and headed for the Lake Charles Civic Center where the dance was held. Once again, we showed off on the dance floor while also getting a little closer every now and then on the slow songs. We danced the night away. It was a wonderful evening spent with my love. Life was good!

He graduated in May 1977. It was the end of my junior year. He spent the summer at home before preparing for the Air Force, traveling to Lackland Air Force Base in San Antonio, Texas, for basic training. I prepared for my time away from home to participate in Southern University's ESI. I was excited about the opportunity but weary of saying goodbye to him. He would depart for San Antonio before I returned home. However, I was full of glee and excitement about the opportunity to go several weeks without having to wash a single dish, even if it meant learning how to drive a train!

Southern University is a historically Black land-grant institution founded in 1880. It is located on the northern edge of Baton Rouge, about five miles north of downtown, which includes Louisiana's state capital building. Southern is on a bluff known as Scott's Bluff overlooking the Mississippi River facing west. It is a beautiful campus that is inviting for walkers, especially the views of the Mississippi from the bluff. This would be my home away from home for the summer.

ESI was a summer program for high school students, which included living in the dorm and taking special introductory classes in electrical, mechanical, and civil engineering. My time at ESI was life-changing. I made new friends with technical interests just like mine who looked like me. In high school, I took all the advanced math and science classes offered, mainly because I enjoyed them. The school's counselors did not advise me to take these courses, although they did not advise against me taking them. While the school was about 40% black, less than a handful of Blacks took these advanced classes. At ESI, it was exciting to meet so many new friends from all over the state. I felt right at home from day one of this summer program.

We moved into the dorms on the weekend, and classes started on Monday. The first day of classes was an eye-opener for me. This was when I learned about the other engineering profession, and it was shocking. How could I have not known about this? I was just grateful for learning about it then, just prior to starting my senior year in high school. I was immediately drawn to electrical engineering. There was something about this discipline that just clicked for me. The more I learned about it over the weeks of ESI, the more I knew this was something I was born to do. Even though I was unaware of this profession and had no counseling from school officials or my family about this, I intrinsically was preparing to be an engineer by my selection of foundational high school courses. Looking back now, I know these were ordered steps.

I also learned that engineers were well paid relative to many other professions. I was told it was very hard and tough to do well in the discipline. This confused me, as it was exciting and easy for me. However, I liked the fact that engineers were paid well. That worked for me.

We went on several field trips that summer. It was basically to refineries and chemical plants in the Baton Rouge area. We also traveled to New Orleans—about 80 miles away—for a trip. Those trips were very educational; I learned that I did not want to pursue a career with chemical or oil companies. They were not that interesting to me. What piqued my interest was digital technologies, digital logic, integrated circuits, and how computers worked. Just the thought of doing that kind of work was exciting to me. We had professionals, including Southern University alumni, who would come and speak to us. Somehow, the name IBM really stood out for me during my tenure at ESI. I made a mental note of it.

The weekend before my high school sweetheart left for San Antonio, he and his best friend came to visit me. They picked me up from my dorm, and I gave them a tour of the campus. We parked the car, and walked for part of the tour. I remember walking to the bluff overlooking the Mississippi River. It was a hot summer day as we sat under the trees and felt a gentle breeze. Our paths were going in different directions, but the love we shared was strong. We did not know what the future would be for us, we just knew we wanted to be together. We embraced and held each other tightly as we said our goodbyes. After a few hours, he went back to the dorm to drop me off. Then he and his friend drove back to Lake Charles.

By the end of ESI, I knew what I wanted to do in life. I also knew I wanted to attend Southern University. I felt like that was a place where we loved and supported each other, including the professors. My competitive spirit shifted into overdrive during this time, as we had friendly competition in our classes. I made lifelong friends that summer. The whole campus felt like family. I didn't want to go anywhere else. I went back home with a plan, finish my senior year with the best grades possible—given my new competitive spirit—and apply and get accepted to Southern University and major in electrical engineering. I didn't even think about applying for scholarships. By that time, I knew that VA and social security benefits would cover my college expenses so financial aid of any kind for college did not concern me.

My high school senior year was great. I did well in school, and I did not have a care in the world. I was working on my plan and applied to Southern University in Baton Rouge. My high school sweetheart and I regularly exchanged letters, and we spoke by phone from time to time. He wrote brilliant, heartwarming love letters that melted my heart. I always needed to have a dictionary nearby when reading them so I could understand some of the words he used. It became a great vehicle for me to improve my vocabulary.

I was busy with extracurricular activities, including student council, honor society, math club, Spanish club, and other entities. I was also actively playing the organ for my church's youth Sunday, funerals, and whatever other activities the church's minister of music requested.

I participated in the Debutante Ball as well. This was a formal event sponsored by the local chapter of Zeta Phi Beta Sorority, Inc. I and my fellow participants spent several months preparing for this event. This included workshops on how to set a table and properly eat, formal dancing, etc. There was also talent show component as part of the process. It was hosted by the sorority shortly before the formal ball, when we would be introduced to society and formally escorted by a male partner. My high school sweetheart, who was then stationed at Ellsworth Air Force Base near Rapid City, South Dakota, planned to be home for the ball. He would be my partner.

We spent weeks practicing our talents for the show. I decided to do something different from what was expected. I used my previously unknown—to others—talent for acting. I was intrigued by a play that I had recently read, *A Raisin in the Sun*. I decided to act out two characters in a couple of scenes from this play. I put together an introduction and then engrossed myself in these two characters who were having a conversation with each other. I switched from one character to the other as part of the scene. I didn't want to just compete in this event, I wanted to win. Each week as we rehearsed for the show, I tried to perfect the scene. There was no other debutante who used acting as their talent. They mostly played the piano or some other musical instrument. My friend, Trudy, played the clarinet, and a fellow classmate, Carla, played the flute. They were both good during the rehearsals, which motivated me to improve my technique.

The day of the talent show arrived, and we were excited about performing. All of us performed well, as good as our best performances during our practice sessions, except Carla. Her performance was significantly better. In the end, I won first place, Carla was second, and Trudy was third. We graciously accepted our awards. A picture of the three of us was displayed in MaMe's house for many years.

The Debutante Ball came next. My high school sweetheart came home from South Dakota for the event. It was a wonderful evening where we were introduced to society and then danced the night away. I was in heaven because he was home, and we took advantage of every minute. After a wonderful weekend of activities, it was time for him to depart again, and the painful separation became more difficult to endure.

I was accepted into Southern University in the Spring 1978 and was looking forward to matriculating there. I also received a letter from ESI announcing a follow-up meeting that spring. Most of us attended that event, and it was great to see everyone again. We learned that all of us were given four-year scholarships to attend Southern. That was an exciting and pleasant surprise. Now, not only was I going to receive benefit checks, but I also had a scholarship.

LCHS's homecoming my senior year was also in the Spring 1978. Since my sweetheart was away in the Air Force and my friend Trudy's boyfriend was away in the Army, we decided to ask a guy to take both of us to the homecoming dance. Donald Johnson —unrelated to me—was elated. He picked both of us up, individually, in his car and off we went. We had a good time, and I think Donald had the best time. We took individual pictures with Donald, a photo that was also on display in MaMe's house for years.

I graduated from high school in May 1978. My sweetheart surprised me by coming home a few days earlier than planned. He was able to catch an earlier military flight from South Dakota. I was a happy camper. In addition, MaMe and her two sisters and brothers-in-law planned a graduation party for me and my two cousins, Schirrell and Theryl, who also graduated in 1978. Schirrell and I were in the same high school class, while Theryl attended a different school, Marion High School. Our party was a few days before Schirrell and I graduated. It was held at the Lake Charles Civic Center. My adult relatives served as chaperones.

I wanted to wear a specific dress for the party, but my mother had other plans. She and her sisters thought it would be great to have the three of us wear the same outfit. I did not want to do that, as we are different people (especially me), and I wanted our party to reflect that. However, I could not find the dress I wanted to wear, as my mother hid it from me. So, I wore the other dress and did not like it one bit. I am grateful for the party, but this outfit was a sore spot for me (especially given I still remember it over 40 years later).

The Senior Class Honors Assembly was held a couple of days before our graduation. It was in the school gymnasium with the girls wearing white. It was an official program where the senior class marched into the assembly. During this program, my classmates and I were presented with several awards and scholarships. Our class had seven valedictorians and a salutatorian. I finished 13th in a class of 231. While I did not graduate at the top of my high school class, I had a plan for rectifying the situation. I had a goal of studying hard to get the best grades and graduate at or near the top of my college class.

During the honors program, most of the awards were presented to the top students. However, to my surprise, I received nearly as many awards. This included the American Legion Award, Mathematics Achievement Award, and the Southern University scholarship. I was most surprised by the American Legion and Mathematics Achievement awards. In fact, as the presenter described the characteristics of the award recipients (one male and one female), he talked about the love of country and demonstrated commitment to democracy, etc. I was thinking, "who could that be?" Then he called my name. *"What?"*

For the Mathematics Achievement Award, I was thinking this is for a math whiz. They called two names. The first name was Cathleen Jones, one of the valedictorians. This was no surprise. They then called my name. That was a surprise. We were the only two. (Cathleen went on to get a Ph.D. in Physics in 1991 from Caltech. She spent two decades working as an experimental nuclear physicist at Argonne National Laboratory and Caltech before joining the Radar Science and Engineering Section at the Jet Propulsion Laboratory.) It was a great day for me.

Our high school graduation was later that week, on a Friday. It was held at the coliseum of the Lake Charles Civic Center in the evening. It was a memorable, relatively short program lasting slightly over an hour. We marched in our cap and gowns, the valedictorians and the salutatorian spoke, and so did a few officials. We then each walked across the stage to receive our diplomas. This was a ritual I participated in three more times as a graduate. At the time I had no idea that would happen. I did not even dream of such a thing.

After graduation, it was time to party. I went home and suddenly saw the dress I wanted to wear for my party earlier hanging on my bedroom door. I changed into that dress, and my sweetheart came shortly thereafter to pick me up. We were out all Friday night long, attending several graduation parties. Next, we went to "The Plantation House", a local restaurant, for breakfast. This was followed by going to the steps in the rear of the Civic Center to watch the sunrise Saturday morning and talk about our future. We still did not know how, but we were going to be together. After this unforgettable night, and morning, he took me home.

I arrived home around 6:00 AM. I had a funeral to play for at 11:00 AM, five hours later. I went to bed and slept for four hours when my mother awakened me at 10:00 AM. I quickly dressed and made it to the church before the funeral started. The dearly departed was an elderly lady who my mother informed me was a distant relative. However, none of my relatives attended the funeral. In fact, Schirrell, my piano partner, was not asked to attend and play. The minister of music only asked me to come and play the organ.

There were few people who attended the funeral. The choir did not sing, they were not in attendance. The only funeral music was me playing the organ. It was a typical type of funeral when it's sparsely attended. This all changed when the minister was delivering the eulogy. Amid his remarks, the front doors of the church opened. Two women dressed in their Sunday best, including hats, stumbled down the long church aisle. When they reached the closed casket with the flowers centered, they moved the flowers to the foot of the casket, opened it, and began to view the body. Everybody there, including me, was startled. For a few seconds, no one did anything. The pastor stopped talking, he was stunned as well. Then a couple of men went to join the ladies at the casket to close it and get them to sit down.

That is when the fight started. Those ladies started swinging and cursing. They said, "leave me alone mother f***** can't you see I'm trying to do this intelligently?". I was facing them about 10 feet away, but I could still smell the strong alcohol in their breath. This woke me up from my sleepiness. These women were strong, and it took several men to pick them up over their heads and carry them out. All the while they were kicking, screaming, and cursing. The women never came back. The service continued where it left off after the interruption and ended shortly thereafter. This is a funeral I will never forget. The image of those ladies fighting and screaming has remained with me through the years.

That was a graduation weekend to be remembered for a lifetime. However, life goes on. My sweetheart soon left to go back to South Dakota. This goodbye was the most painful. We were high school sweethearts; our love was strong. However, I was about to transition to college, and we began to wonder about our future. He left and I started a summer job as a Kelly Girl. I had temporary assignments filling in as a typist for local businesses. It was a wonderful summer as I prepared for my new life as a collegiate. Finally, in August 1978, it was time.

2

The College Years

CHAPTER 4

Early College

I SPENT THE SUMMER OF 1978 working and preparing for college matriculation. I opened a checking account for the first time. I bought college necessities in anticipation of my collegiate experience. This included clothes, shoes, toiletries, sheets, pillows, bedspreads, suitcases, and a trunk. I was excited about the possibilities. I also ensured I had the paperwork needed for a smooth dormitory check-in and registration process. This included the documents needed to ensure my scholarship payments.

Finally, in August 1978, it was time. My two cousins who shared the same birth year with me, Schirrell and Theryl, were also off to Southern University in Baton Rouge. We packed up the cars with suitcases and people and formed a caravan to the city. We arrived on campus over two hours later. Here I was, back on campus after about a year. It was as beautiful as ever, especially the Mississippi River views from the bluff. But enjoying the view would come later, there was work to do.

We pulled into the parking lot of the freshman complex shortly after our arrival on campus. It consisted of Ulysses S. Jones (or Jones) Hall, the dorm for men located in the front, Dunn Cafeteria (located between the two dorms), and Alice Almira Boley (or Boley) Hall, the dorm for women located in the rear. (Boley Hall was named after a Southern University employee who worked as an instructor from 1916 to 1942. In addition, she was the Principal of the Southern University Laboratory School, 1942–1958.) Boley Hall was a six-story residential building that included multiple suites per floor. Each suite contained four rooms, two beds per room. There was also a shared bathroom and a communal living area, including a living room and a study area. Jones Hall was a similar facility for freshman males. Dunn Cafeteria provided the residents of both dorms with three full meals each day.

Upon arrival, there was some confusion about how we should proceed to get a dorm room. We had our paperwork, but those in charge did not seem to have it together. MaMe and her sisters, never the type to sit and wait but instead take charge and make things happen, left to assess the situation more closely. When they came back, they had us checked in. Shortly afterwards, we received our keys and went to check out our rooms. We were on the third floor, suite 301. We were the first three of the eight ladies to arrive at the suite, so we had our pick of rooms. Schirrell and Theryl picked one room, and I picked another. My roommate, Rosemary Jones from Greensburg, Louisiana, was to arrive shortly. We both attended ESI the previous summer and decided to be roommates when we learned we were both attending Southern.

Next, we unloaded the car and got everything to our rooms. Then we unpacked everything and set up our rooms into nice, comfortable (but small) living spaces. Rosemary arrived while we were in the middle of unpacking. We helped her bring up her bags and set things up.

I was so excited and looking forward to life as a college student. The idea of having the freedom to do what I wanted to do and not be constrained by asking permission from a parent or other adult was heaven to me. This would be more freedom than I had ever previously experienced. The thought of meeting new friends, broadening my horizon, embracing, and enjoying life to the utmost was exhilarating. I seized the opportunity to live my own life, make my own decisions, and be a grown-up. It was not my intention to go wild and crazy and lose my mind. That was not going to be me. I would be free but responsible, intentional. I had a mission, a goal to graduate at the top of my class. I could not wait until they left!

I was mentally trying to prepare for a long lecture from my family on what to do and not do. Be careful about this, watch out for that, do not go overboard with this, and on and on. I was trying to have a poker face, making it appear as though I would be listening carefully but in fact trying not to hear anything. MaMe, her sisters, and their husbands all sat down in our communal area and were ready for the lecture. Aunt Rosa Bea, the eldest, was the designated spokesperson. I thought, oh no! This woman is a talker. She speaks vociferously about everything and is long-winded. There were few times in my life when I experienced her conversations as reserved or restrained. I was therefore shocked when she became reticent. She said one word, *think*. And with that, they prepared to leave. I was taken aback. I did not know what to do or think. It was completely unexpected and completely out of character for her. And so, the chains were broken, and I was free, and I began to *think*.

We soon left the suite and went out to explore our new surroundings. Over the course of a few weeks, I met new friends and became reacquainted with some of my fellow ESI alumni. I also learned more details about the yard, as we affectionately called the campus. (I was restrained in my movements on campus while attending ESI, so I did not get a chance to tour the entire campus on foot.) During these social interactions, I learned that engineering was a prominent set of majors on the yard. Engineering majors were considered smart, especially as upperclassmen. My thought was, *"oh really?"*. I did not let such talk go to my head, especially since I only took one engineering orientation class each semester as a freshman.

I soon settled into a routine of attending classes, eating meals, meeting new friends, and hanging out with them. We would go to parties, mostly on campus, as well. For me, not too many. Every now and then I attended a party off campus, mostly in a group as someone always had a car. I was intentional about just attending parties to have fun, dance, and have a drink or two but not get drunk. It was a great way to enjoy life as a college student, an adult. I was a happy, content, and carefree freshman.

That first year, I did not have a car. I walked all over campus for everything, along with my friends. We would cross the bridge to the fast-food restaurants on Scenic Highway, buy food, and walk back to the dorm. Our mascot is the jaguar. We had a live mascot, Lacumba (meaning Heart of Africa), living on campus. For some time, she was the only live mascot living on the campus of an HBCU in the nation. She was the head cat on the yard from 1971 to 1991. We would make sure we made our rounds to see Lacumba as we headed to the bridge for food.

From time to time, I would see my high school classmate, Orlando McDaniel, low riding on campus. He was well loved in high school, having been a star athlete in football and track. In fact, he led our high school Wildcats to state and national track competitions. He was also very affable, having the ability to establish friendships across races and genders. Orlando had a football scholarship to Louisiana State University (LSU), which was also in Baton Rouge on the other side of town. As a freshman, he had time to low ride. He would always see me first, blowing his horn as he drove along. Most of the time, we would just wave to acknowledge each other. However, one day, I was close enough to his car that he stopped to chat. I asked him what he was doing on campus and why he was not at practice with his Tigers. He just looked at me. I asked him what he was majoring in at LSU, and he said "campusology". We had a good laugh with that. I did not see him for the remainder of my tenure at Southern. Orlando went on to be a star wide receiver at LSU. He was eventually drafted into the NFL in the second round by the Denver Broncos.

One of the guys who hung out with us was Alvin Jackson. He was attending Southern on an athletic scholarship. He was a great basketball player, in fact, a star player at my cousin Theryl's high school. I was surprised that he had time to hang out, even in the few times that he did. I later learned it was because school had just started, he was just coming in as a freshman, and basketball had yet to take over his life. As a result, most of the students did not know who he was. However, that changed quickly. By the time he was a sophomore and beyond, he was a star player. We did not see much of him later, but he was always good when we did run into him. (He was drafted by the Utah Jazz in the sixth round in 1982.)

We also learned about the serenading *Human JukeBox*, the Southern University Jaguar band. From time to time, an ensemble of mainly percussionist band members would jam for us right outside Dunn cafeteria in the freshman complex. It was awesome, and we could not help but dance to the beat.

Soon the fraternity and sorority members would have an impromptu step show at the complex. They were members of Black Greek-letter organizations collectively known as the Divine Nine. Most of them were created in the early 20th century. During this time, many Black collegians felt isolated and faced many barriers at their predominately White institutions and in general. Those at Black colleges faced the isolation and barriers they experienced from the general population. These nine organizations were created—separately and at different times—to provide sisterhood and brotherhood. They had the opportunity to pursue lifelong service in the cause of social justice, to break economic barriers, to make a difference in their communities, and to encourage and inspire the generations.

Members of the Divine Nine include Alpha Phi Alpha Fraternity, Inc. (Alphas); Alpha Kappa Alpha Sorority, Inc. (AKAs); Delta Sigma Theta Sorority, Inc. (Deltas); Kappa Alpha Psi Fraternity, Inc. (Kappas); Omega Psi Phi Fraternity, Inc. (Omegas); Phi Beta Sigma Fraternity, Inc. (Sigmas); Zeta Phi Beta Sorority, Inc. (Zetas); Sigma Gamma Rho Sorority, Inc. (S G Rhos); and Iota Phi Theta Fraternity, Inc. (Iotas). All were founded on college campuses and have had an impact—individually and collectively—on campuses and cities around the country and globally.

We eventually saw the Deltas, AKAs, Zetas, Omegas, Kappas, Alphas, and Sigmas put on a show. I loved Southern U! I loved the Jaguars! I loved my new friends, the yard, my professors, the workers in the cafeteria, etc. I felt at home and part of a large family.

The engineering orientation classes enabled me to meet my fellow engineering majors. Some of them later became good friends as we studied and worked together and provided moral support as upperclassmen. I was a fan of soap operas during this time. Most of my classes ended in the early afternoon. I would go to my dorm room, sometimes after lunch, or right after class, to watch my favorite program. This was also the time I used to do my homework. I soon discovered that I was able to do my homework, including calculus, chemistry, and physics, during the television commercials. Every now and then I would encounter a challenging problem, causing me to postpone working on it until my programs ended. At that time, I had completed my homework assignment and was ready for dinner. I was under no illusions. I knew this would become more challenging as I progressed, but for the time being, I was enjoying this.

I tried very much to adjust to the food in Dunn cafeteria. Having grown up eating food cooked by a master Cajun chef, it was a difficult thing to do. In addition, the cafeteria closed early for dinner. While I was able to make it to dinner before closing most evenings, I found myself getting hungry many nights. That's when I got to know one of my engineering classmates better. Mikel Johnson is from Baton Rouge. He lived at home and had a car that he used to attend class. A group of us in the freshman complex, mostly engineering majors, soon learned that Mikel was willing to pick us up later in the evening to do a run to McDonald's a few miles from campus. I would always buy a Big Mac special for $2.37. We eventually had a routine, patronizing McDonald's every night. It got to the point where we would just call Mikel and say hello, and he would be on his way. We were so happy with Mikel; it solved our hunger issues. We also learned about the late-night times that Krispy Kreme would make their doughnuts. Off we would go with Mikel to pick up a dozen of those warm tasty treats; so good!

It was not long after the semester started that I began to look for a church. There were no entities on campus that provided the type of service that interested me. However, I soon learned that a local Baptist church near campus provided buses to pick up students on campus, take them to church to attend Sunday morning service, then bring them back to the dorms after service. I began to attend services at this church as a result. However, sometimes, the service was too long. In such instances, I would miss lunch because Dunn cafeteria would close before we returned to campus. I would then have to scramble to find someone to take me, and others who attended service, off campus to get lunch. Over time, I attended the service every now and then.

Many of the freshman males tried very hard to initiate romantic connections with the women on campus. My male engineering friends would sometimes confide in me their frustrations because the women seemed to be so attached to their high school sweethearts. I did not have a lot of sympathy for them, as I was one of those women. At least until about the middle of the fall semester.

We had wall-mounted rotary telephones in every room in our dorm. One Saturday in late October, I received a call from my sweetheart. He seemed to be more animated than usual, and I soon found out why. He told me he was now a Christian; he was saved now; he had found Jesus! I told him I thought he was already a Christian, and he just laughed. He said the elders in the church where he grew up in Lake Charles were a joke. He said they would pretend to be all holy on Sundays but did ungodly things the remainder of the week.

He also mentioned one of the youth field trips while he was a member of his home church. He said the chaperones were drunk half the time. They were not examples of how Christians should live. I listened to him and thought *what does this have to do with your relationship with Christ?*. However, I did not say anything to him about this, as I was dismayed listening to him. What came next was even more startling.

He was very excited when he told me the world was soon coming to an end. He said as a result, there is no need to be enrolled in college. At the time he was an accounting major at a local college in Rapid City, South Dakota. He informed me he had dropped out of college and had given his books away. He encouraged me to do the same, drop out of college. He then asked me to come to South Dakota so we can be together when the world comes to an end. *What!?!?*

I loved him with all my heart. I loved so many things about him and to me it was a joy for him to be a part of my life. However, something happened that clearly changed him. In fact, he had lost his righteous mind! I may have loved him, but I was not a fool. There was no way I was going to jeopardize my future by running to a faraway place to be with someone who had lost whatever sense he may have had. I told him I did not think the world was coming to an end, and even if it was, I was not going anywhere. That was the end of our relationship. It was extremely painful for me, but I had no doubt it was the only option for me. Slowly but surely, I managed to move forward from this heartbreak.

I was not much of a sports fan during my tenure at Southern. However, from time to time, I loved attending football games—primarily—and a few basketball games. Football games at HBCUs provide a significant nongame entertainment experience. The Battle of the Bands—from both schools—is a half-time show that is not to be missed. In fact, most revelers do not go to the concessions stands until after the show. Each band steps out with their own swag style, (high) stepping, stomping, or marching to the popular music of the day—R&B, pop, hip/hop, etc.—as well as old school and the traditional Sousa. They dance, move, and groove to bring the house down! The band is always accompanied by a dance troupe—typically represented by ladies—that dance to a couple of songs during the show. For Southern University, the troupe is known as the *Dancing Dolls*.

I was absolutely delighted to see the Southern University band—the Human Jukebox—perform during halftime. They were thrillingly entertaining as they stepped and danced to the music. The show always starts with the sole drum major high stepping onto the field with his baton. He turns around to face the home crowd, then bends over backwards until his high-top hat touches the ground. He then pumps his baton up and down a few times and blows his whistle, signaling the beginning of the show. The first time I saw this as a freshman I was amazed. I just knew it was going to be a moving, grooving, memorable sight to behold. From the precision steps and soulful dancing to the *Dancing Dolls*, to displaying the half-time game score and the SU initials in human form, they always rocked you to a plateau of exhilarating and electrifying ecstasy. I could not help but dance to the beat of every song!

I also loved to see Mama Jaguar, an elderly lady who was an avid Southern supporter, at the game. Mama Jag, as she was affectionately called, would be dressed to the hilt in her blue and gold Southern attire. She would always be on the sidelines at the game near the cheerleaders. She would cheer us along, even when the cheerleaders took breaks. We had some great cheerleaders. I loved the cheers they led with soul. In addition, we sang the Southern University fight song, with the help of the band. At the end of every game, we sang the Southern University Alma Mater, again with the help of the band.

There was always a dance after the game, which was held on Saturday nights when hosted by Southern. Sometimes I would go to the dance, sometimes not. I was not a fan of loud music, and you could not have a decent conversation at such events. However, every now and then, when I felt like dancing (especially if we won the game), I would go for a while. In such instances, I would always be back in my dorm room at a decent hour. I had to get a good night's sleep to complete any outstanding homework the next day, in preparation for the new week's classes.

Two major events happened at Southern during football season every year: homecoming and the Bayou Classic. During freshman year homecoming was a dream. It occurred in the week of October 9, 1978, culminating in the football game on Saturday, October 14. To see so many alumni in town for the game, from across the country, was awesome. It was like one big happy family participating in events from the campus panhellenic council members performing in a Greek (Step) Show, band percussion members serenading students during the week, to dances and of course the game—including the Battle of the Bands. It was awesome! Unfortunately, we lost the game to Jackson State University 14–41. However, the *Human Jukebox* won the Battle of the Bands!

The Bayou Classic is a bowl game between Southern and Grambling State University, our archrival. It is held every year in the Louisiana Superdome in New Orleans, Louisiana—now known as Caesars Superdome. It is held on Thanksgiving weekend every year, with festivities and other events held from Friday through Sunday. There is typically a Greek show, the Battle of the Bands— sometimes also the Friday night before the big game—a Miss Bayou Classic contest, and a host of high-profile and other events held in hotels throughout downtown New Orleans. And of course, there are numerous parties, large and small.

My first Bayou Classic experience as a freshman was unbelievable. The Greek show was a major production. There was of course the game, including the Battle of the Bands. Never in my life had I entered a building with over 70,000 overwhelmingly Black people. Whether from Southern, Grambling, or just friends, we were all happy and excited to be there and have a good time. It was the largest family reunion I had ever attended. I thought I was in heaven. There was the game, the half-time show, the cheerleaders, Mama Jag in an unbelievable outfit, celebrities on the sidelines. It was an invigorating weekend that, along with the three others I attended as a student, I will remember while there is breath in me. Unfortunately, Southern fell to Grambling 15–28 on Saturday, November 25, 1978. However, without a doubt, the *Human Jukebox* won the Battle of the Bands, and I partied all night with my school mates.

I also went to a few basketball games. This was especially true for my upperclassman years, as Alvin Jackson became a powerhouse for Southern.

My engineering-related courses commenced my sophomore year. The electrical engineering (EE) curriculum had a balanced focus with courses in communications, power systems, solid state devices, computers, and electronics. As an EE major, I was not required to take any engineering-related courses until my sophomore year. The exception was an engineering orientation course that was more informative than challenging. Some of my freshman courses included freshman English, calculus, chemistry, physics, and volleyball. It was an enjoyable year overall, including my coursework.

However, I had an unexpected challenge with my volleyball class. Rosemary and I both took this class in our first semester. On the first day of class, the instructor gave a high-level overview of the course, including the book we would use. That was the first and only time she mentioned the book or taught directly from it. For the rest of the semester, we played volleyball in each class. She taught us the rules and techniques of the game, including how to serve, hit, spike, etc. We also learned volleyball strategy. It was all in-person processes and techniques.

Then on the very last day of class, she gave us a test based on information in the book. We were stunned. She had never mentioned anything about a test, or that we should study the information contained in the book to learn or understand anything. In fact, I don't remember ever opening that book. My fellow students and I, including Rosemary, panicked. None of us knew the answers to any of the questions, so we guessed. (There was no correlation between the test questions and the volleyball rules, techniques, and processes we learned during the semester.) That was the first and only test I've ever taken—up to that point—where I did not have any idea it was coming, and I did not know a single answer. Since we had not been graded during the semester, we knew it was important to do well. I was in a bind, especially given my ultimate objective. I just guessed and turned in my test. I never saw the test results, but shortly thereafter the grades were posted. I got a "B". Rosemary got an "A". I was so upset, not because Rosemary got an "A" (I was happy for her), but the results were random. It was not a reflection of what we learned in the class. However, it was a lesson learned for me. It also turned up the heat for the fire in me to achieve my end objective. I ended the semester with all "A's" and one "B".

As the end of the year approached, I began to look for a summer job. I inquired about opportunities for summer internships with various companies who came on campus looking for engineers; however, few of them were looking to hire freshmen or rising sophomores. As a result, I decided to look for a summer job at home in

Lake Charles. When the year ended, I packed up all my things in the dorm room and made it back home for the summer.

I used my typing skills to get a job working as a Kelly Girl for Kelly Services. I was sent out from business to business, most of the time for one or two weeks. I did light typing and other secretarial tasks, replacing the permanent help while they were on vacation. I liked going into an office to work and get paid. While I liked to type, conducting such monotonous activity for weeks made the job jading and disheartening. This gave me more inspiration to do well in college so I would not be low on the totem pole once I graduated and started a career. I looked forward to my sophomore year at Southern and I awaited its arrival with great anticipation.

In August 1979, the moment arrived. I went back to Southern with all my things in tow. Rosemary and I were still roommates, but we moved to Progress Hall on campus. It was part of a set of dorms for non-freshmen women on campus. Progress looked more like a motel, with doors opening directly into the rooms in both the front and back of the dorm. There was a bathroom between the two rooms, so four women shared a bathroom. Our room was on the second floor and close to the laundry room. It was also conveniently located close to the stairs, and we enjoyed this location. It was not long before we settled into a routine, going to the cafeteria for meals, going to classes, and participating in social events.

A new family member also started as a freshman in the Fall 1979. My brother, Gregory, began his Southern journey with the intention of majoring in electrical engineering. He later switched his major to electronic engineering technology, also within the College of Engineering on campus.

My technical engineering journey was initiated that fall. I took an initial electrical engineering class and lab, electric network theory (electrical circuits). This class was held in the James B. Moore Hall, the building that housed the College of Engineering's administration, faculty, staff, and classrooms. This would be the first EE class I would take in this building; I was so excited! I also enrolled in calculus, physics, and technical communications classes. I was fascinated by the electrical network class. It was thrilling to learn about how voltage equals current times resistance ($V = I \times R$) and power equals I squared R ($P = I^2 \times R$) or V times I ($P = V \times I$). Other than the ESI summer classes, I had never been introduced to the specifics of this topic. It was invigorating; a natural fit for me. It reaffirmed my belief that this is the field of endeavor I was born to pursue, although I did manage to burn a few resistors in the lab.

I had a laser focus on all my courses, especially the EE ones. It was an inspiring adventure. The first EE-related exam I had was the electrical circuits class. I spent quite some time studying and preparing for this exam, as I had for all my previous exams as a freshman. (This became my modus operandi for my entire college matriculation.) It was taught by Professor Isaac Porche. I remember him interacting with the students during the first few lectures with the new crop of EE students. I discerned that he was trying to determine which student would rise to the top, and this initial exam would give him his first inkling. I had the highest score in the class on this exam. I remember him having a big smile on his face as he handed my exam back to me. From that moment until graduation, Prof. Porche would challenge me ever so slightly to push me beyond what I thought were my limits.

I had an interesting experience during my physics class as a sophomore. We had an exam where the professor, Dr. Rama Mohanty, asked us to use a pencil. There were several math-related questions, and he knew we would need to use the eraser a few times before settling on an answer for some of them. I was one of the first students in the class to finish the exam. I signed my name on the front page, in pencil, gave the exam to Dr. Mohanty, then left. A few days later we got the results. Dr. Mohanty called out the names of my classmates at the end of the lecture, and one by one they received their test results. He never called my name, and I became concerned. I went up to his desk in the front of the classroom and got in line to inquire about my test once class ended.

After a few minutes, I reached the point where one of my classmates was having a conversation with Dr. Mohanty, and I was the next in line. I was right in front of his desk so I could see the stack of test results from those who had not attended class that day. I saw my test at the very top of the stack. I was flabbergasted that my name was not on the test. I looked a little closer and saw that a fellow classmate had erased my name and replaced it with hers. I began to freak out. Without waiting for Dr. Mohanty to finish his conversation with my classmate, I raised my voice and told him that someone else got access to my test and replaced my name with theirs! Of course, this was a serious allegation, that happened to be true, and Dr. Mohanty suggested that I be careful about what I was saying. I was unperturbed. I said to him, "look at it. This is my handwriting. Look very closely. She erased my name and wrote in hers. She didn't do a good job erasing my name because you could still see my name on the paper!" You could also see that my erased signature was very similar to the handwriting on the rest of the exam. My classmates still in the room were stunned.

Dr. Mohanty took my exam, brought it close to his face and examined it thoroughly. He removed his eyeglasses and reviewed the results again. He was convinced that my accusation was credible, and in fact true. I asked him what he was going to do about it. He asked me not to worry about it, that he was going to take care of it. I asked him again, "what are you going to do about it?". He asked me to calm down and not to worry. I would get credit for taking the exam and getting my score, I got an A$^+$, recorded as such. He asked me not to worry about anything else, he would take care of it. I unsuccessfully tried to press him a bit more to ensure this woman's nefarious behavior would not go unpunished. I eventually calmed down a little and left the classroom, as he convinced me he would do right by me.

It took some time for me to process what had just happened as I left. I had to walk on campus for a few minutes before going to my next class (and I was late but that was alright). I could not believe someone would have the unmitigated gall to do such a thing! What if she attended class that day and took my exam results? What if my exam had not been at the top of the stack of remaining exams on Dr. Mohanty's desk where it was clearly visible to me? Had I not seen the exam, he most likely would have gone through those exams and not found mine, as my erased signature was visible but only when closely examining the page. What would have happened to me then? How could she do such a thing!! I became angrier but ultimately calmed down and focused on the blessing of her not being in the class that day and me seeing the exam at the top of the pile. Ultimately, I received the A$^+$ I earned. I never saw this woman again, not in the physics class (or other classes I took with her), not on campus, nowhere. This was the first of several similar situations I experienced during my education years.

My remaining courses for the year were challenging but enjoyable and immensely satisfying. My brain was working overtime for the most part, but it was an exercise that was preparing me for the academic challenges to come. For the rest of the year, my academic experiences did not rival the drama of my physics course that semester. In the end, I earned all A's for the entire year. I was halfway to my goal set during my high school graduation and pleased with my record.

I participated in a plethora of activities as a sophomore as I broadened my horizons. I became active in some student organizations and later in the year started to think about increasing my activities as an upperclassman. I was happy with my academic performance and felt I could further participate in campus life without adversely impacting my academics. I became a member of the local student chapters of the Institute of Electrical and Electronics Engineers (IEEE) and the Society of Women Engineers (SWE). I started to look at the Greek-letter organizations and their public service-related on-campus activities. My first choice was always Delta Sigma Theta. I thought they were the leaders, the movers, and shakers on campus and in the country. They did not sit around and wait for things to happen; they made things happen; they made a difference. However, I wanted to peruse the yard to determine what was happening.

Homecoming in Fall 1979 was amazing. It was held in the week of October 1, 1979, culminating in the football game on Saturday, October 6. I remember the mid-term examinations (mid-terms) were that week, so I spent quite some time studying and preparing for the exams early in the week. However, I attended a pep rally at our stadium later in the week. This was right after I took my last mid-term exam. I recall walking to the stadium with friends, including my boyfriend, Charlie McLaughlin, and others in our engineering circle. There were these huge speakers set up for the event. When the music started, the sound emanating from them was deafeningly loud. Michael Jackson's *Off the Wall* album was recently released, and we danced and sang to his music and cheers from the cheerleaders. *Don't Stop 'Til You Get Enough* is still ringing in my ears as I recall this event. In fact, from that point on, every time I hear that song, I must get up and dance and not stop until I get enough! There was also *Workin' Day and Night* and *Rock with You*. We were celebrating the end of mid-terms as well as the pending homecoming weekend. I cannot remember the actual football game—although I know we played Alabama State University and won 28–0—but I do remember the pregame party and the Battle of the Bands. Of course, the Human Jukebox won the show, again!

Throughout the fall, and the entire academic year, I attended several talks and seminars that focused on life as an engineering professional after graduation or going to graduate school. I attended as many as my schedule allowed, as I wanted to learn as much as I could about life after Southern before I graduated. At the time, there were no family members working as engineering professionals or in graduate school. I was therefore like a sponge, soaking in all the information and attempting to intellectualize what I was hearing to develop my own plan.

Recruiters from a diverse set of companies, many of them Southern alumni, came to talk about their experiences with life after Southern and encouraged us to consider their companies. Some came to talk about going to graduate school. It was during this year that I started thinking about the possibility of graduate school. It was not a high priority for me at the time, because I was more interested in graduating, going to work, and earning some money.

However, I listened to the passionate presentations from Dr. Howard Adams, the Executive Director of the National Consortium for Graduate Degrees for Minorities in Engineering and Science, Inc. (GEM). He strongly encouraged us to consider graduate school. At the time, GEM only provided fellowships for obtaining a master's degree. He encouraged us to consider an extra one or two years in graduate school before going to work. When you consider the longevity of life, a couple of years may not make a difference in terms of education years, but it could make a big difference in stature, influence, and compensation as a professional. Dr. Adams also addressed those who may have been thinking about marriage. He said if it's real love, one or two years will not make a difference; they are not going anywhere.

The seeds for me attending graduate school were planted; however, they had not yet germinated. A representative from Bell Laboratories came to discuss their Cooperative Research Fellowship Program (CRFP) and Graduate Research Program for Women (GRPW). Both were Ph.D. fellowship programs that covered all costs for obtaining a STEM-related Ph.D. as a graduate student. This includes earning a master's degree first. They also provided a living stipend for participants. I took the information handed out from these events and put it in a box and placed it high up on a closet shelf in my bedroom at home in Lake Charles. I was keeping this as an option, although my focus was to start working upon graduation.

I do not recall anyone coming on campus, any professors, or anyone else I met ever suggesting entrepreneurship as an option. This is something that I did not consider. It was never on any of my lists for consideration.

On October 29, 1979, Charlie, and I, along with other friends, attended an Earth, Wind, & Fire concert at the LSU Assembly Center. That is my favorite group, and they did not disappoint. Their unique, melodious harmony has an intoxicating effect on me, and I was the epitome of a fan that night. Maurice White, the leader, was exceptional. Philip Bailey, with his four-octave vocal range has the voice of an angel. Verdine White, Maurice's brother, made his bass guitar sing! It was awesome.

The Bayou Classic that year was held on December 1, 1979, again at the Louisiana Superdome in New Orleans. Southern won this game against Grambling 14–7. Prior to this game, for five consecutive years the Grambling Tigers had dominated the Bayou Classic, winning every year. In fact, we had never beaten Grambling in the Classic while Doug Williams, a former Grambling player and NFL quarterback who had won the Super Bowl while quarterbacking for the Washington Redskins years earlier, was head coach at that time. This all changed, because in 1979, we won the Bayou Classic.

Back on campus, I remember one day as I was walking toward the student union after a class, seeing a table set up with nice drinking glasses. It was a promotion to get students to sign up for a credit card. The glasses were a gift to those who signed up. While I was not interested in getting a card, I liked the glasses, so I signed up. I was ignorant about how credit cards worked. I remember MaMe instilling in us to always pay our bills on time. It was like a mantra that we heard from time to time. She shared with us that early in her marriage to our father, they decided he would pay the car note on their new car. One day while they were visiting MaMa, the car disappeared. It turned out he had not been paying the car note, and it was repossessed. My mother was very angry with him. They eventually got the car back, but my mother's cherished mementos that were in the trunk were lost forever. She learned her lesson at that point to always pay bills when due.

While the paying-bills-on-time mantra was a seed deeply rooted in me, I also learned about layaways. From time-to-time MaMe would buy us nice things and put them on layaway. She would make regular payments until the balance was paid, then we got the goods. It was so exciting when that happened. As I got older, she would have me go to the store and make the regular payment every now and then. I saw the details and knew of no interest charges added for layaways. Given this limited experience, I thought credit cards operated in a manner like layaways.

When I first got my credit card, I was so excited I went to the mall to shop for a new dress. I found one I liked on sale, so I bought it. I decided I would pay it off in three separate billing cycles, as I was diligent in maintaining my budget. When the first bill came, I paid one-third of the balance when due. When I received the next bill, I was perplexed. I saw an additional charge that I did not make. I telephoned the customer service and explained the situation. The representative asked me to explain the charge. I said it was a finance charge that I did not make. He laughed at me. I was not amused and asked him to explain. His response was my education on how credit cards worked. I said to him that I bought the dress on sale thinking I was getting a bargain. You're telling me that since I did not pay the full balance within 30 days, I was charged interest? And would continue to be charged interest every billing cycle until the balance is paid off? His response was in the affirmative. "Then why would anyone want to use such a card and end up paying more for the dress? In fact, you could end up paying more than the original price for that matter. Why would anyone want to do that?" This guy kept laughing at me.

Well, I paid the balance, and from that day forward, I made a concerted effort not to pay interest on credit cards if possible. That experience led me to diligently create a monthly budget, updating it when needed. It also enabled me to know what I could and could not buy. I was a stickler for living within my means. That became a lifelong practice for me, one that paid off long term.

At the end of the Fall 1979 semester, I became tired of depending on others to take me places or using public transportation or riding the Greyhound bus if I wanted to go home to Lake Charles for the weekend. Based on my living expenses and budget, I believed I could buy a car. I grossly underestimated the expense of a car note, insurance, gas, etc., but I was living well below my means thanks to my scholarship. As a result, I had saved what I thought was quite a bit of money. During the Christmas break, I decided to go find and buy a car, a new car. My mother was excited about the idea; however, her sisters tried to talk her out of it. In their minds I was just a sophomore, I was not an upperclassman. Why would she allow me to buy a car? Do you really think she's mature enough to have a car? My thinking was I was going to be the one paying for this so how does your opinion matter (no disrespect of course). In addition, I was insulted. I was mature for my age and would be responsible with a car; however, they did not know that because they did not know me. I was determined to get a car and be responsible for it.

There was an issue with a college sophomore getting a car with no credit history. My income (veteran's benefits and social security benefits) was solid and enough to buy a car. I had no bad credit, but I had no credit. I was unable to get a car in my name. However, MaMe strongly supported this purchase. The car salesman, and me, convinced her to get the car loan in her name. We had an agreement, I would pay the note directly, and the insurance. I would just let her know when the payment was made monthly. I bought a brand-new white 1980 Chevrolet Chevette, with red interior, in December 1979. I was so excited, I had wheels. Like clockwork, I paid the car note and insurance on time every month for the entire three-year duration of the loan. This initiated a level of freedom and independence in me that has endured all my life. I was keenly aware that one of the factors enabling me to get a new car was my persistence in doing well in school. I was reaping some incredible rewards and had no idea this was small compared to future benefits.

I went back on campus as a new woman! My newfound independence agreed with me. I started taking more EE-related courses. They were more challenging, but I met the challenge with enjoyment. I was doing very well on two fronts. First, I was enjoying my coursework so much that I began to think about Dr. Howard Adams' words about graduate school. As part of the germination process, I began to think about graduate school as a remote possibility. It all depended on my future coursework as an upperclassman. Second, I felt I had time to be more involved in student activities. I started thinking about pledging Delta (there was no other choice for me but Delta) and started asking about it and looking into it.

Around this time, one of my professors, Dr. James Anderson, encouraged me to consider joining IEEE and being active in the organization. I didn't know him well, as I had not taken a course taught by him. I suspected that Prof. Porche talked to him about this. He convinced me and I joined the local student chapter. Shortly thereafter, the chapter held their election of officers for the next school year. My fellow chapter members suggested I run for Secretary as this was not my idea.

In the Spring 1980, I was elected to the position of Secretary of the local IEEE student chapter. I assumed this position at the beginning of the next academic year. As a result, I became one of the students attending SoutheastCon 1980, a regional IEEE conference held in Nashville, Tennessee. The IEEE student chapter at Southern, as well as other similar student chapters of engineering-focused professional organizations on campus, had money. Many companies donated to these chapters to assist them in supporting their programs. Approximately 10–12 students were able to attend SoutheastCon 1980 with these funds, flying there and staying in hotels for the duration of the conference.

I had a limited memory of flying on an airplane. This came from the memory of becoming fearful while looking out the window on my grandmother's lap as we flew to Virginia for my father's funeral. I had dreamed of flying as a teenager and thought that it would happen one day. Well, the time had come. From Baton Rouge, we had one stop in Atlanta on our way to Nashville, flying on Delta Airlines. Unfortunately, the weather was bad in Baton Rouge, and our departure was delayed. We missed our connecting flight in Atlanta, and the airline put us all up in a hotel for the night and gave us vouchers for dinner. I was beginning to like this traveling with all its perks. We made it safely to Atlanta and had a great dinner and a good night's sleep at an airport hotel. We had an early morning flight to Nashville and made it there safely.

It was a wonderful conference. It was a whole new world for me. I learned about the various subareas of EE and learned about the great work done by those in my chosen profession. We also met a few fellow students from student chapters in other parts of our region. Our chapter received an award for having the most participants attending from a student chapter. Our chapter president accepted the award on our behalf. In general, it was a great conference, an opportunity for me to grow as a leader, and a milestone experience for me in understanding my profession.

I was so amazed at the idea of getting on an airplane, flying in the air, and going to a distant destination in a short period of time. I also observed how flying was a component of a major industry. From the airports to the hotels, restaurants, ground transportation, etc., I was taking it all in; learning, observing, and enjoying the experience. What was unbelievable to me was all of this was free for me because I had done so well academically, which resulted in my classmates taking an interest in getting to know me. They thought I was more than capable of assuming this position, and they elected me. (This was on top of the fact that my hard work in high school availed me with scholarships to attend Southern at a significantly reduced cost for me. So much so that I was able to buy a car.) It was mind-boggling to me that with hard work, that I enjoyed, this could happen. It was a new world; a different world and my horizons were expanding.

At the beginning of my sophomore year, my Aunt Mae Ruth handed me a copy of an IBM employment application. She had picked it up at a Delta convention she attended that summer. She spoke to the recruiter as she walked through the exhibit hall, informing him that both her daughter and niece were EE majors in college. He was very passionate about summer internship opportunities for EE majors and encouraged her to give us the application and apply. Moving forward, during the spring semester, I began to think about what I would do during the summer. I looked at several summer internship opportunities through our campus placement center. I also remembered the IBM application and applied. Subsequently, I was offered a job with IBM at their Burlington, Vermont facility. I accepted the offer.

I completed my second year of college a few weeks after our return from attending SoutheastCon 1980 in Nashville. I was confident I had chosen the right major, I was growing as a person and a leader, and I was so enthusiastic about my schoolwork. The more I learned, the more excited I became. After a summer working as a Summer Pre-Professional at the IBM site in Burlington, Vermont, I was looking forward to my junior year and life as an upperclassman.

CHAPTER 5

The Upperclassman

M Y TENURE AS A SUMMER INTERN with IBM began in May 1980 with an early Saturday morning flight from my hometown to Burlington, Vermont. I decided to leave my car at home with my brother. I just did not feel like taking the long drive to Vermont from Louisiana. There were three legs to this trip: 1) Lake Charles to New Orleans; 2) New Orleans to Boston; and 3) Boston to Burlington. This was only my second trip flying as a collegiate. I was still in awe of the travel industry and how we flew above the clouds and bad weather to see a blue sky and shining sun. I made it safely to Burlington.

IBM arranged with St. Michael's College in Winooski, Vermont, to house their summer interns on campus. I had my own personal dorm room for the summer. There was no television in the room, but I did bring a clock radio. I was able to settle in and rest after a long trip. The next day, I met with a few of my neighbors, my fellow interns for the summer. They represented a variety of schools, technical disciplines, and geographic locations. We were excited to be there and ready to work.

I arrived at my new place of employment on Monday morning. IBM's facility is in Essex Junction, Vermont. This was a huge facility that manufactures semiconductors and tests computer memory chips and logic devices. It was the largest employer in the area. There was a fellow intern from Purdue University, Raju Rankin, who worked in our department. My manager, Harlin Hill, was very kind and considerate in welcoming us both for the summer. Raju had interned in the same department the previous summer, so he knew the ropes and was helpful in getting me acclimated to the environment.

My initial assignment was to review the electrical and physical fundamentals of making chips, also known as integrated circuits (ICs). This ranged from the sand used to make a wafer, the base of the chips, to the deposition of various chemicals through a clean, sophisticated process, creating several layers on the wafer. These various layers formed the electrical foundation for creating the electrical circuit, including transistors acting as gates to enable or disable the flow of electrical current. I then worked with the chip designers who taught me how to find potential flaws in the design before they went to the manufacturing facility. While I had just two years of college, and no experience in developing ICs, I did have the physical and electrical foundation. With that background, I was able to learn a lot, all the while making a substantive contribution to the department that summer.

During one of my first weekends in Burlington, I went out to explore the area. I could see a busy intersection from my dorm room window. I saw public buses riding through this intersection at regular time intervals. I therefore walked to this area, based on the frequency of the bus arrivals. As I stood by this busy intersection waiting for the bus, I looked around the area and the people in the cars. I stood there for at least 15 minutes and did not see a single Black person. I became concerned, not knowing the culture in which I was now immersed. When the bus arrived, I asked the driver about the bus route, including specific destinations like the mall. I went to the mall to look around, and again, I did not see a Black person. I began to wonder how I was going to get my hair done and other similar activities. I eventually arrived back at my room in amazement, having not seen a Black person all day. I ended up fixing my own hair. For the entire summer, I only saw a handful of Blacks in the area, not counting the three Black IBM summer interns. This was a very different culture for me. I was a Camp Fire Girl in my younger years. I thought about the song we learned years earlier. Part of the words were: "Make new friends but keep the old. . . . One is silver and the other gold". I used it as an opportunity to learn new things and meet new friends.

I also noticed that most of the radio stations played only country music. I enjoyed all types of music, but country was not on the list of genres I liked. However, given I only had access to the radio, I listened to country songs. It was a struggle for me, but I grew to like the popular songs by Rogers. By the end of the summer, I knew the words to all his songs played on the radio and enjoyed singing along. I could not say that for any other artist.

I had many friends that summer, including two fellow HBCU engineering students. We took advantage of our location to travel to interesting places, all new to me. We took day trips to Lake Placid, New York, and Montreal, Quebec in Canada. Lake Placid is about 60 miles west of Burlington; however, it takes about two hours to travel there by car. It was a beautiful drive, and we stopped along the way to visit various towns and sites. While in Lake Placid, we visited the site of the 1980 Winter Olympics. It was an exciting trip with my new friends.

Montreal is about 100 miles north of Burlington and a two-hour drive. There were many people speaking French, and many of the public signs were in that language. I fell in love with this city, as it reminded me so much of one of my favorite cities, New Orleans. While I knew some of the history of Louisiana and Canada, this visit made it come alive. The French-speaking Cajuns of Louisiana are descendants of French Canadians in Arcadia (now Nova Scotia) who were deported by the British in the 18th century. They found their way to Southern Louisiana. So, the language, the food, and other parts of the Cajun culture were like that of Montreal. In fact, parts of Montreal, the Old City, looked very similar to New Orleans.

We went to Boston for the July 4 weekend. I stayed with my cousin, Theryl, who was interning at the MIT Lincoln Laboratory for the summer. The lab is in Lexington, Massachusetts; however, Theryl and her fellow interns lived in an MIT dormitory in Cambridge—Burton Corner—for the summer. We had a wonderful time exploring Boston and Cambridge, including touring Harvard's campus—walking across Harvard Yard—and riding the T throughout the city. My most memorable recollection is hanging out with Theryl and others on the roof of her dormitory, watching the Boston fireworks across the Charles River while listening to the Boston Pops on the radio. It was magical.

The Burlington area had tremendous natural and unspoiled beauty. It is on the eastern shore of Lake Champlain. It is a large lake about 120 miles long, 12 miles at its widest point, and an average of 64 feet deep. It is also the drinking water source for many in its surrounding communities. Early in the summer I was introduced to an IBM employee who was also a Tuskegee alumnus. Two of my fellow interns were Tuskegee students. He invited them, as well as me, to go sailing with him one Saturday. It was a beautiful day to go sailing on the lake. He taught us how to sail, and it was interesting to learn. I was astonished at how crystal clear the water was, even in the deepest parts. I had never seen such a thing. This was very different from the dark waters in Louisiana that had been polluted for decades.

During that summer, there was one phone call from MaMe that was very traumatic for me. It was a Saturday evening when my mother called to inform me that my high school sweetheart got married that day. *"What?!?"* I asked her how she knew he was getting married. She informed me his grandmother called her and told her, inviting her to the wedding. Then she gave me the details. He married a woman who had a little girl, a toddler, and a baby girl. The oldest girl was from the mother's previous relationship. I asked MaMe if he was the father of the baby, and she did not know. She just knew the baby was a few months old. I concluded that more likely than not; he was the baby's father. It had been about 20 months since we had that interesting conversation and broke up. He had clearly moved on, and so did I.

However, I was surprised by my reaction to this news. He was my first love. While it had been some time since our breakup, I did not realize the extent to which he was still in my heart. So many feelings and emotions just came flooding back to me, and I was surprised by this. I had moved on; I had a boyfriend. Now that I learned he was married, at the age of 20, with two children, my next thought was it appears as though he has not yet come to his senses, he has lost his mind, and yes, he has really gone off the deep end. It did not matter whether he found his mind in the future. We were on different paths, I wished him well.

That same day my fellow HBCU interns from Tuskegee came to my room to invite me to go out with them that evening. They had invited me several times previously, but I always declined. This time I was happy to join them, as I needed a distraction. We walked to a popular club in the area. We found a place to sit—a booth—then the guys left to go buy drinks. While they were gone, a waitress stopped by to take my drink order. I ordered rum and coke, my drink of choice at the time. It tasted like Kool-Aid after one sip. I had a few that night, then took a taxi to my room, and slept it off. The next day one of the guys stopped by to see how I was doing. I appreciated him coming to check on me—I was fine. I have never had rum and coke since that night.

By the end of the summer, in early August 1980, I completed my internship and returned home to Lake Charles. It was three plane rides from Burlington to Boston to New Orleans to Lake Chares. After a long trip, I was finally home. Gregory picked me up at the airport in my car. He took good care of it during the summer, and I was grateful, so was he! As I prepared to start my junior year at Southern, I was amazed by the new songs on the radio, the new hairdos by the ladies, and the new slang of my family and friends. I was back in my familiar culture and felt as though I had left the planet for the summer in this regard. However, I enjoyed my summer experience. It broadened my perspective in many ways. I have continued to seek such educational experiences throughout my life.

Soon, I packed my car and drove to Baton Rouge for another college year. I was back on the yard, moving back into Progress Hall, my dormitory, in fact the same room, for the year. I also shared this room with Rosemary again, and we prepared for the coming year as upperclassmen.

My EE courses, which were all the courses I took the first semester, were more challenging and enjoyable. I took engineering electronics, electromagnetic theory, engineering economics, and digital logic design. The more of these courses I took, the more I knew this was something I was born to do. I really enjoyed the electronics and logic design classes. My logic design professor was a visiting professor from Bell Labs. He brought a different perspective to his teaching, having been working for decades as an engineer.

At the beginning of every semester while I matriculated at Southern, MaMe always asked me what courses I was taking. At this point, my response to her was if I told you the names you would not understand what they were. She was unperturbed. She didn't care if she did not know what the courses were or what they meant, she was just excited to hear their names. I therefore shared the course names with her, and she was excited. She was happy I was in college and doing well. This was just one of the ways she chose to support me. We continued this ritual until I graduated.

This semester also welcomed another family member to the yard. In addition to Schirrell, Theryl, and Gregory, another cousin—Arnold—started his Southern University journey. Arnold, starting as a freshman, also majored in electrical engineering. At this point, there were five family members on campus. We all had our distinct personalities and social network so there were few times when we hung out together as a family. From time to time, we would see each other around the yard, acknowledge one another, and keep on strutting. In addition, Gregory purchased a motorcycle to use as his mode of transportation in Baton Rouge, to travel home, and in general. It was exciting to me. In fact, sometimes I would hear him driving around campus but did not see him. However, this was very stressful for MaMe.

While the courses were more challenging, I continued to do well and get top grades. It was during this time that I realized I had more time to spend on community-focused activities. I was already active in the IEEE student chapter on campus, now having the position of Secretary. I decided to become a Delta and kept my eyes and ears open for their Rush—an activity designed to present to prospects an overview of Delta, the chapter's activities, and the process of seeking and securing membership.

I continued to date Charlie, and I was enjoying reconnecting with my fellow EE majors and other campus friends. We enjoyed campus life and attending social events on and off campus. This was great since I had a car and was not transportation-challenged when planning off-campus activities. The highlights for me were homecoming and of course the Bayou Classic. Homecoming was held in the week of November 3, 1980, culminating in the game on Saturday, November 8. After a full week of festivities, we tied the game, 3–3, against Howard University, but the *Human Jukebox* won the Battle of the Bands!

I remember my digital logic design professor, the engineer from Bell Labs, gave us a really challenging assignment over the Thanksgiving holiday break. I attempted to complete this assignment during the break but before traveling to New Orleans the day after Thanksgiving. I looked at it a couple of times and was unable to finish the work. It was too hard. I decided to table my efforts and get back to it after the Bayou Classic. My plan was to go to the game, enjoy myself, then leave New Orleans early on Sunday morning, get a nice lunch, then spend Sunday afternoon completing this work.

I enjoyed the step show, Battle of the Bands, and other activities leading up to the game. Unfortunately, we lost the game 16–43, but we suffered through having a nice meal and partying on Bourbon Street afterwards. Next, just as planned, I got up early Sunday morning, had a nice breakfast of beignets, then drove to Baton Rouge. I started on the homework and was still at a loss. I then went out for lunch, came back, and tried again. I was not going to let this get the best of me. I spent about four excruciating hours racking my brain, slowly but surely making progress until I finally finished. I was exhausted after this endeavor. It also happened to be around the time my fellow Jaguars were making it back on campus. I connected with Charlie, and we went out to dinner.

I turned in my assignment the next day, and we received the results back a couple of days later. The professor was astonished that I completed the assignment, in addition to correctly solving all problems. The last problem was extremely challenging. I spent about two-and-a-half of my four hours on it. The professor told the entire class that he deliberately included a difficult problem as part of the assignment to challenge us. He did not expect any of us to solve that problem, much less solve it correctly. No one else completed the problem. In fact, no one else even tried. He could not believe me, pleasantly shaking his head in utter amazement. I was astounded. My initial thought was, well that explains why it was so difficult for me to get this done. It took me a couple of days to process this.

I realized that since I was enjoying my coursework, I was not quite done with my formal education. While being excited about the prospect of going out into the world to work and make a lot of money, I was just as excited about going on to graduate school and going deeper, learning more. I knew I was not done. Around the same time, Howard Adams from GEM was back on campus, using his passion to encourage minority students to become a part of GEM. He convinced me to apply for the program. I prepared the application during my Christmas break and mailed it by the end of December.

I enjoyed connecting with some of my high school friends during the Christmas break, as well as spending time with Charlie. The break seemed too short, but that January, I was driving back to Baton Rouge to commence my second semester, Spring 1981, as a junior. I took Part II of the electronics course, electrical machines, digital signal processing, and a microprocessor-related course. I earned top grades in all of them and started to become passionate about graduate school.

The Deltas on campus, the Alpha Tau Chapter of the sorority, held their Rush early in the semester. I attended and applied for membership. After a few days, I was notified that I was accepted onto the chapter's Spring '81 line. Shortly thereafter, I and 35 of my pyramid sisters started our pledge period. It was several weeks of learning about Delta's history, their years of public service on the local, regional, and national levels, and sisterhood. It was a grueling and time-consuming experience in which I bonded with my line sisters for life.

We learned the history and how to step; we were preparing for the campus Greek show where we would participate. We were also actively engaged in the chapter's public service activities. We planned and implemented our own public service activity. We walked in a line from the shortest to the tallest, 36 of us. At one point during this pledge period, we were given ducks and paddles to carry with us wherever we went. After several weeks, on April 5, 1981, I was initiated into Delta Sigma Theta Sorority, Incorporated with a lifetime commitment to sisterhood and public service. I was number 13 in line. My official individual line name was Mae West 2, and my unofficial name was 3.9, my GPA. Why Mae West 2? Well, my big sisters somehow learned I could act. Every now and then, they would ask me to quote a line by Mae West. Most of the time I would say "why don't you come up and see me sometime big boy?".

I thought Professor Porche became concerned when he learned I was pledging Delta. I believe he thought the time I spent pledging Delta would distract me from performing at my best in class. I recall that one of the most important tests he gave in our Electrical Machines class was during my Delta pledge period. I arrived at my room very late the night before the exam and was very tired. However, I still had a goal to achieve, to earn the best grades possible in college. I spent hours studying for the exam. I think I learned more about the subject matter that night than any other time that semester. I did get enough sleep to stay awake (mostly) and walk around the next day; however, it took me a couple days to fully recover. I was prepared for the exam and received a perfect score. Professor Porche smiled as he handed me my exam a couple days later. I do not believe he was ever concerned about my potential performance after that.

I was not able to attend SoutheastCon '81, which was held in Huntsville, Alabama. This is because I was pledging Delta. Outside of that I was able to actively participate in a leadership capacity as IEEE Student Chapter Secretary that semester. I was also inducted into the Zeta Psi Chapter of Eta Kappa Nu, the EE Honor Society, on March 13, 1981. It was an extremely busy semester for me. I enjoyed most of it, valued my experiences to this day, and ended another semester with all As.

I was accepted into the GEM program and was sponsored by the Johns Hopkins University Applied Physics Laboratory (APL). While the GEM fellowship was for master's degree programs, it also provided summer internships for accepted students after their junior and senior years in college. I sought other internship programs for the Summer '81, including again at IBM; however, accepting the GEM fellowship meant accepting a summer internship at APL. I spent the summer working there in Laurel, Maryland. Many of my relatives, my father's siblings and their families, lived in the Washington, DC area. I therefore stayed with an aunt and her husband in Capital Heights, Maryland, that summer. This time, I drove my car to Maryland. My cousin, Arnold, drove with me, as he had an internship in the area. It was great driving through Mississippi, Alabama, Tennessee, and Virginia before reaching Maryland. I enjoyed driving through the Smoky Mountains of Tennessee with their picturesque scenery.

My job at APL was US defense-related work. I was not very excited about working in a defense-focused environment. I could not see myself making a career out of working on such projects. While I know it is important work that must be done to assist in securing our nation's security, it was not for me. I was more interested in working on innovative projects that would directly assist in improving the quality of our lives, how we live and work in our global society.

It was a good experience for me to have, as I learned about the type of work that I could not consciously do and enjoy.

On the other hand, one of the mid-level managers was a Delta. She took it upon herself to meet all the summer interns. Once she learned I was a Delta, in fact a newly initiated Delta, she became very excited. In fact, she informed me that the Washington, DC Alumnae Chapter, where she was an active member, was to have a chapter meeting shortly after we first met. She invited me to attend the meeting and came and picked me up from my aunt and uncle's home to take me there. This was a very large chapter, and it was so overwhelming. However, my sorors were very welcoming and I enjoyed the meeting, it was very educational.

Delta's National Convention was held that summer in Washington, DC. I was able to attend my first National Convention only a couple of months after my initiation. My chapter had elected two sorors to attend the convention as the voting and alternate voting delegates. Unfortunately, the voting delegate did not come, and the alternate delegate, who was a summer intern in New Jersey, had to go back to work. She left me with her credentials, and I sat in the voting delegate's chair for most of the convention, representing my chapter.

It was an experience that has remained with me. Seeing thousands of Deltas from across the country in Washington DC for the convention was amazing. Then to be a voting delegate and experience firsthand the specific business of the Grand Chapter of the sorority as a neophyte were overwhelming. It was very moving and memorable. I learned so much, and it took months to process everything. I was also educated in parliamentary procedure. I determined that if I was ever in that seat again as a voting delegate, I would learn as much as I could about parliamentary procedure and be ready.

That summer was also the first time I spent a considerable amount of time with my father's family. Getting to know all my aunts, uncles, and cousins was a sheer delight. My aunt and uncle had a beautiful home in the DC suburbs, and from time to time they hosted backyard barbeques for the whole family and their friends. They lived just a few miles from Andrews Air Force Base, now known as Joint Base Andrews. I remember during one of their backyard barbeques standing in the yard and hearing a plane flying low overhead. It was very loud. I looked up and saw this big blue and white 747 with the "United States of America" on its side and an American flag on the tail. I thought, oh my that's Air Force One. Then I remembered that President George H.W. Bush, the US President at the time, was to arrive back from Europe on that day.

I was so excited as I thought this was the closest I would get to seeing Air Force One in person. It was really flying low. Then I thought, wait a minute. This plane is so low, what's to stop someone with a surface to air missile from shooting it down. My uncle's neighbor, who worked for the US secret service, responded by informing me there is a decoy, more than one plane. They take off, but only one, the one with the President, is Air Force One. He said most of the time even the pilot is not sure if he will fly Air Force One until he, the pilot, arrives. My response was oh, that was interesting. I did not know that.

It was wonderful getting to know all my family in the area better while I worked at APL in Maryland. I stayed in touch with my aunt and uncle for decades after that, communicating regularly with my aunt even now. I visited them numerous times over the years.

Charlie came to visit me in Maryland during the summer. We had a good time, but our relationship was failing. I ended the relationship shortly after we returned to campus for our senior year.

As my internship and summer in Maryland came to an end, Gregory joined me to help me drive back to Louisiana. In fact, he arrived a few days before our planned departure. My aunt and uncle took him around the area as well. He got a chance to meet our extended family. In addition, we took a weekend trip to Atlantic City and had a great time. However, as all good things must come to an end, we started our journey to Louisiana as planned.

While we were still in Maryland, Gregory started to feel ill. I wondered whether he should see a doctor before we hit the road. He said he could still drive so we started early in the morning. As time moved forward, he got worse, although he could not quite say what the problem was. I became concerned, but he was adamant that we should keep going. I monitored him closely, and his pain did not seem to impact his driving abilities. We stopped for the night at the end of the first day, checking into a hotel to get a good night's sleep. He said he felt better in the morning, so we continued our journey. We made it safely home to Lake Charles; however,

Gregory's condition was much worse when we arrived. He finally went to see a doctor the next day. This became one of a series of doctor's visits, as no one could figure out what was wrong. He was eventually diagnosed with Systemic Lupus Erythematosus (SLE or Lupus). This delayed his matriculation at Southern for the year.

Once I was back in Lake Charles, I began to focus on my senior year at Southern and beyond. I was looking forward to my last year in college and future possibilities. I started the year with great anticipation in obtaining a deeper understanding of my chosen field, as well as my responsibilities in various capacities. I was now the President of the IEEE Student Chapter; an appointed officer, Parliamentarian, of my Delta Chapter; a member of Eta Kappa Nu (EE Honor Society); and an engineering tutor. I was also inducted into the Alpha Kappa Mu and Alpha Chi honor societies. A subset of my classes included communications engineering and control systems.

Fall '81 was one of the best semesters of my Southern tenure. I was excited about the final months on campus as an upperclassman, with all its responsibilities. I was also hopeful about my future, which I thought was very promising.

My Delta Chapter, Alpha Tau, was very active in the community regarding social action. We led letter-writing campaigns, encouraging students and the campus community to write to their US Senators to support the continuation of Special Services, Talent Search, and Upward Bound programs. We also encouraged the community to write to their elected officials asking them to support divesting from companies doing business in South Africa and to support a national Matin Luther King holiday. We had letter-writing tables set up during registration so the students could write their letters while waiting in registration lines.

Moreover, we participated in lobbying Louisiana legislators to support more funds for Black universities. We held our annual Sickle Cell Anemia Walk-a-thon in Spring 1982. We donated the proceeds from our previous Walk-a-thon to the Sickle Cell Anemia Foundation during its annual telethon in the Fall 1981. We planned and hosted several additional public service events and dances, particularly during home football weekends, to raise funds for them.

We planned for our annual May Week activity, a Delta program established in 1920 to highlight the academic and professional achievements and emphasize the importance of higher education in the community. During Fall 1981, we invited Delta's National President, Mona H. Bailey, to speak for our May Week 1982 event, and she accepted. We were so excited and worked tirelessly to prepare for the momentous occasion. In general, we were a passionate, forward-thinking group of young ladies driven to work in our community, to move forward as we lifted others.

My communications engineering class was challenging. I focused on learning as much as I could about this subject. I was not only naturally drawn toward anything technical, especially anything related to EE, but I was also keenly aware that I was close to reaching one of my objectives, and I was not about to waver now. I took extra time to learn more than was required of us by our Professor, Dr. Ajit Singh. I recall one day, after receiving the results from a test, I spoke to him about my less-than-perfect outcome. He had marked my only incorrect answer wrong, and I was certain my answer was correct. I spent quite a few minutes going back and forth with him on this, passionately attempting to explain to him why my result was correct. He eventually came around to seeing what I did, informed me I was correct, noted so on my test, and changed my grade to an A+. By the end of the semester, as I checked the final grades on his door, along with George F. Smith, III, a classmate, I saw I got the only "A" in the class. George mumbled under his breath that I messed him up again. I did not respond.

My cousin, Theryl, reminded me of this episode when I approached her about our Southern experiences when writing this book. She was one of the students waiting in line while I went toe to toe with Dr. Singh. She said she had another class and had to leave before she had a chance to speak to him because we took so long. She also informed me of something to which I was unaware. She said she only took a limited number of classes with me, about two or three, during her Southern tenure because I had a reputation for bursting the curve. She said many of our classmates, including Theryl, felt they did not have a chance to get a top grade in a class if I was in it. She was surprised I did not know this. No, I did not know, no one told me, not even Theryl. One thing I do know is I did not feel as though my classmates held this against me. Life was good.

Homecoming was held in the week of October 26, 1981, culminating with the game on Saturday, October 31. It was bittersweet participating in the activities, as I knew this was my last homecoming as a student. This was my first opportunity to participate in a stepping event as a member of Delta Sigma Theta Sorority, Inc. In fact, I led one of the steps during an outside, noncompetitive stepping event on campus. It was such a joy to participate. We unfortunately lost the game to Tennessee State 18–28, but the *Human Jukebox* won the Battle of the Bands! In addition, the Deltas hosted a homecoming dance after the game, and we raised quite a bit of money for scholarships.

The Bayou Classic was held on Saturday, November 21, 1981, at the Louisiana Superdome, as always. My classmates and I went all out celebrating our last Bayou Classic as students. Many of us sat together at the game, and we nearly brought the house down after the Battle of the Bands show, it was unforgettable! In addition, we whipped Grambling 50–20. This time we partied for two days.

During Fall 1981, I contacted Dr. Howard Adams to see if I could change my sponsored organization in GEM. I learned from our conversation that while this was possible, it was a sensitive subject because the sponsors took pride in their selected students after a rigorous selection process. However, given my sentiments about working in the US defense industry, he could work with me on obtaining a new sponsor. In the meantime, I initiated the process for applying to graduate school. I selected a group of targeted schools to apply, some of which included Stanford University, MIT, and Georgia Tech. I also decided to apply for jobs just in case graduate school did not come to fruition. I interviewed on campus with several companies, based on my interests. A few of them invited me to onsite interviews, including Proctor & Gamble in Cincinnati and Hughes Aircraft Company in the Los Angeles metropolitan area.

I vividly recall my trip to Los Angeles for the Hughes Aircraft interview. I flew to Los Angeles, and they provided me with a rental car. They included a map as part of my pre-trip package. I got up early on the morning of my interview to allow ample time to get ready, have breakfast, and drive to the facility. It was about 15 minutes from my hotel; however, I left an hour before my scheduled arrival.

I am happy I left early. I do not have problems with directions. If I have a map, I will closely follow the map and arrive at my destination. I would only be late if the map was wrong. In this case, the map was wrong. North was south on the map, and east was west. I knew I had to go east, based on the map; however, after about five minutes of driving "east", I found myself headed straight to the Pacific Ocean. Of course, I knew the Pacific Ocean was west. I was confused. I pulled over and studied the map very carefully. That's when I figured out the map directions were wrong. So, I just traveled in the opposite direction, based on this incorrect map, and I arrived 15 minutes ahead of schedule. While it was stressful, it was exhilarating to see this mighty ocean named for peace. It was so awesome to see. This was my first introduction to the Los Angeles area. There would be many more to come, but here I was again, living a fulfilled dream.

My interview with Hughes was good. I had a great time, and the people were friendly and welcoming. I just could not see myself living in Los Angeles at that time. After all my morning drama, I forgot to mention to them that the map was incorrect. However, I always wondered if they deliberately gave me an incorrect map.

My visit to Proctor & Gamble in Cincinnati was also a good one. I was not provided with a rental car, and my trip was in the middle of winter. That is not a good time for this Southern girl who had no recollection of experiencing snow to go on an interview trip there. It was cold, and there was snow everywhere. I thought I was open minded during that time in my life, but I just could not see myself living in such an environment at the time. My heart was someplace warm and sunny, and maybe graduate school. I did not know this with certainty until that winter trip to Cincinnati.

By the time the holiday break arrived, I prepared my applications for graduate school. I thought seriously about the monthly stipend I would be getting as part of the GEM program. I did not think it would be enough for me to live comfortably. I was keenly aware of the various types of funds available to me in graduate school and made a mental note to start looking for additional stipend opportunities.

One day when I was cleaning out my closet at home, I found the box on a top shelf containing applications for graduate fellowship programs sponsored by Bell Laboratories. I placed them there years earlier and had forgotten about them. At the time, I was not interested in earning a Ph.D. However, I noticed the stipend for both programs was larger than the one for GEM. I also thanked God I found the applications before the deadline. I decided to apply for CRFP due to the larger stipend. My goal was to drop out of the program after earning a master's degree in EE because I was not interested in committing the time needed to stay in school to earn a Ph.D. I was more interested in earning a master's degree and then starting a career and making a lot of money. I applied just before the deadline.

I enjoyed the holiday celebrations with my family at home, including ringing in the new year. I was back on campus in early January 1982 to commence my last semester at Southern. My class load was the lightest of my college tenure. In fact, the only deeply technical class on my schedule that semester was thermodynamics. I took this time to reflect on my time in college, to celebrate my final months as an undergraduate collegian, and to plan an exciting future.

For seven semesters, I was laser focused on learning, studying, and getting the best grades possible. This final semester, I relaxed just a little. I took every opportunity that presented itself to celebrate. For example, I spent a day in New Orleans during Mardi Gras celebrations. While being there, I ran into Gregory. He had been drinking a little too much as he was hanging out on a corner. I chatted with him for a while, and we celebrated together. He appeared to be well enough to take care of himself, so I moved on to walk the streets in celebration on my own. It was so exciting to be free, to not have a care in the world, to think about my future, and walk the streets in sheer joy! Laissez les bon temps rouler! I also spent more time going out to dinner and the movies and attending other social events.

As the President of the IEEE Chapter on campus, I worked very closely with contacts at the Warner Robbins Air Force Base in Georgia. They were very interested in hosting a busload of engineering students at their facility. After months of deliberation and planning, we traveled from Baton Rouge to Warner Robbins, Georgia, to visit their facility by buses provided by them. We spent a couple of days there learning about the various types of career opportunities and speaking to many employees on site. They told us they had been attempting to do this for some time, and they were happy to finally have it come to fruition. They rolled out the red carpet for us, and we appreciated their hospitality.

My IEEE colleagues and I also attended SoutheastCon 1982 in April in Destin, Florida. We had a caravan of cars that drove from Baton Rouge to Sandestin, a resort in Destin. It was a beautiful place with white sandy beaches. We stayed in a townhouse near the conference center. There were an odd number of ladies and gentlemen, and we needed an even number of each for townhouse assignments. Based on our advisor's recommendation, the ladies and I got together to select the most trusted of our male colleagues to stay with us. All our male colleagues were not happy with us for a moment, except the chosen one.

We attended various informative technical conference sessions. We submitted a robot entry for the student competition. We also found time to socialize on the beach and go out for dinner. In fact, for us seniors, this turned out to be a great pre-graduation vacation. Once again, our student chapter won an award for having the most students attending the conference. It was a wonderful experience whose memories have stood the test of time.

My Delta chapter initiated new members into the sorority that spring. There were 31 ladies who spent several weeks learning about Delta before their initiation into the sisterhood. It was a rewarding experience to help them go through this process. Once completed, I had new sorors, and I was no longer a neophyte.

I was accepted into all the graduate school programs in which I applied. I narrowed my choice down to either Stanford or MIT. I also learned that I was a finalist in the Bell Labs CRFP program. The program connected each CRFP Fellow with a mentor who was an expert in the Fellow's area of interest. The mentor would provide guidance and direction throughout their graduate school experience. Bell Labs sponsored my travel to the New York Metro area—New Jersey—to be interviewed by several potential mentors and to speak with the program administrators and others. They informed me that I was the last of several finalists, and they would make their decision shortly.

Less than a month later, they informed me I had been selected as a Fellow in their CRFP program. They would pay for all graduate student expenses, a monthly cost of living stipend, books, and any potential travel to attend conferences. I was required to work for them in the summer after college graduation. I had the option to work for them any summer after that while I was in school. In addition, I was not required to work for them when I received my graduate degree. I accepted their offer and informed them that I had made the decision to attend Stanford University. From that point until the time I graduated, I never had to pay anything for my graduate school education and living expenses. I was utterly surprised, grateful, and humbled by this opportunity.

With my future graduate school plans secure and the semester winding down, I began to celebrate with each passing day. I eventually reached the period where parties were planned and attended. I was happy for the future but reserved about leaving many of my friends behind. During the final weeks, I took and passed all my exams. My thermodynamics exam was very hard, and I ended up with only my third "B" of my Southern tenure. While I wished I had earned an "A", it was not to be. It was not a traumatic experience for me. I was so happy that I achieved my objectives, this did not rain on my parade.

After attending all the parties, programs, and celebrations in anticipation of graduation, the day finally arrived—Friday, May 21, 1982. I made plans to have breakfast with my sorors, some fellow graduates, and others, before going to the Felton G Clark Activity Center one last time for graduation. We were having so much fun at breakfast that we, the graduating sorors, barely made it to the center in time to line up for graduation. When I arrived, I went looking for my fellow EE graduates. When I found them to get in line, they informed me that some of the faculty and administrators had been looking for me. I found one of the faculty members who quickly escorted me to the front of the line. I asked them what was going on, and they initially did not respond—they were in a hurry. They eventually told me that I was the top graduate. I therefore would be the student marshal to lead the entire class into the center as part of the graduation program.

I, as well as two other ladies, was a *summa cum laude* graduate, which I already knew. My GPA was the highest of the three of us, thus I was the top graduate. I later learned there were extensive discussions between my College of Engineering Dean and the College of Sciences Dean. Since I had the final "B" in thermodynamics, the Sciences Dean thought I would not be the top graduate. My dean was not having it. They sat down with several people in an office to calculate my GPA and that of the number two graduate, a Physics major. (They had already told her she was the top candidate.) I was still on top. They had been trying to reach me for a couple of days—this was before cell or smart phones and voicemail. I was so busy celebrating my pending graduation that I was not home most of the time, which is why they could not connect with me. I did not find out I was the top graduate until that moment, about 30 minutes before the commencement program started. I was shocked.

I spoke to several Southern administrators while awaiting the start of the program, including the President and the graduation speaker who were also lined up to march in. They asked me several questions. One of the administrators asked about my high school in Lake Charles. While I conversed with them, others gave me my *summa cum laude* stole to wear with my graduation robe and a staff of the university to carry into the facility. They all congratulated me. The speaker, the President of Texas Southern University in Houston, Texas, was impressed that I was going to Stanford University to start a Ph.D. program in electrical engineering.

It was all happening so fast I could not believe it. I did not have time to process this or tell my family and friends. They did not know about me being the top graduate until they saw me walking into the facility with a staff stretched forward in my hand, leading the entire student body of graduates to their respective seats. At least, this was true for the ones who recognized it was me from a distance. Most of them, including MaMe, did not know it was me until later.

It was a great program. The speaker even mentioned that as the top graduate, I was going to Stanford University to pursue a Ph.D. When the time came to award the degrees, my name was called first. However, I didn't just walk across the stage, get a handshake and my degree, and walk off. They asked me to come and stand between the University President and the speaker. By that time, my entire family and all my friends knew. They informed everyone that I was the top graduate, then proceeded to read a summary of my tenure at Southern, including my record and all my activities, recognition, and awards. (This was not prepared by me, but they got it right.) They mentioned again that I would be pursuing a Ph.D. at Stanford University on a fully funded fellowship.

They invited my mother to stand and be recognized, and then asked her to join them on stage. She then proceeded to try to go onstage. Unfortunately, a security guard, who did not hear them invite MaMe onstage, prevented her from getting onstage. She went back to her seat where she was the reigning queen in her seating area. That was probably a better outcome for her. Everyone in the audience stood to give me a standing ovation during this part of the program. It was a very moving, emotional moment for me. I thought about all the four long years of unrelenting focus on my studies, except the last semester. I thought about all the struggles my mother went through to get to the point where she too was recognized. It was one of my life's happiest and highest moments.

After the conferring of all degrees, the administrators and faculty proceeded to march out of the facility, and for one final time, I led the students out. I wanted to quickly get to my fellow EE and other engineering graduates for one final goodbye before we went our separate ways. I found most of them. Then I found my family. They were overjoyed about the day's events, especially MaMe. I was still on a high but thought this was my 15 minutes of fame to remember forever. Little did I know this was only the beginning.

The family of one of my sorors and fellow graduate from Baton Rouge invited my family and me to their home for a graduation party. My entire family went, including MaMe, siblings, aunts, uncles, and cousins. We had a great time. LaVerne's family was very happy for me and my future. MaMe told them stories of me as a child. We all laughed and celebrated over some great food.

I had already packed up everything from my dorm room. I said my final farewell to my roommate, Rosemary, who also attended the party, before hitting the road to drive back to Lake Charles. My younger sister, Kimberly, graduated from high school on the evening of the next day. We made it safely home as we prepared for Kimberly's graduation. It was a wonderful program for her.

When we attended church services two days later, we learned there were members of our church congregation, who also attended my college graduation service. They told everyone about the program, and I was a celebrity for two hot minutes. I was a bit uncomfortable with this because it was unexpected. I am one to try to be behind the scenes getting things done, but these church members would have no part of that. A few days later this news made it to my local newspaper.

It took a few days for me to process all these unexpected events. When I was finally able to relax and really think about it, I just could not imagine the emotions MaMe experienced. Can you imagine a single mother who struggled to raise four children after the tragic death of her husband by a drunk driver 19 years earlier? Can you imagine her being proud just to be in the arena attending the college graduation of one of her daughters—the first of her children to graduate from college? She was just happy to be there, that I made it to that point. But then to be shocked by her being recognized as the top graduate? To have my profile read to all in the arena, and then see her receive a standing ovation. Then, for MaMe herself to be recognized and invited onstage. It must have been pure, unadulterated joy! I was so happy for her!

I also attended the high school graduation of a former neighbor, Cathleen Pete. She attended a different high school, graduating as her class's valedictorian. To my surprise, the speaker for this graduation program was the same administrator who asked about my high school on the day of my college graduation. In fact, he mentioned me during his commencement address, encouraging Cathleen to pursue heights like Sandra K. Johnson. I could not believe it. I did not say or do anything but clap like everyone else in the audience. Only Cathleen, her family, and my family knew I was there, and I asked both families to be quiet, as this was Cathleen's moment. The speaker had no idea I was there. It was surreal. Cathleen went on to pursue a degree in EE at Southern. She and Kimberly were roommates. She graduated and then went on to have a successful career at IBM.

I was home just a few weeks before I had to travel to New Jersey to work for Bell Labs that summer. This time, I took my car and made it safely to the New York Metro area. The summer interns stayed in dorms on the campus of Rutgers University, and we were bussed to the various Bell Labs locations throughout the area. I worked at the Lab's Crawford Hill location. My boss started the design of a single board computer (SBC). He handed the task to me when I arrived. I therefore completed the SBC design and then built it with all its parts available to me. I used a soldering iron for the first time as I built the electrical connections between the various components. It was so exciting for me to put it all together.

Some of my contacts were surprised at how I managed to learn how to use a soldering iron with no trepidation. It was not a problem for me because I had used a glue gun for years when crocheting and making other crafts. There was little difference to me between using a soldering iron and a glue gun.

I connected with several interns that summer, especially my Delta sorors. In fact, the Greeks working that summer got together and organized a step show in the parking lot of the dorm. I connected with my sorors in learning new steps and teaching some I learned from my Alpha Tau chapter. We had a wonderful time putting on a show, along with the AKAs, Kappas, Alphas, and Omegas.

The summer soon came to an end, and I packed up my car and headed back to Louisiana for a couple of weeks. I knew I would be leaving for California and Stanford University soon. I wanted to get some rest before heading out and entering a whole new world. It was game on, and I was ready.

3

Graduate School

CHAPTER 6

Stanford University

I REMAINED IN CONTACT with many of our Southern classmates and line sisters after graduation. I remember telling one of them I was looking for someone to help me drive to the San Francisco Bay Area to start graduate school. My brother, my usual driving partner, was not feeling well. Corlette, my line sister and fellow EE major, was more than happy to assist. She was still a student at Southern, graduating in the Fall 1982. I had my car serviced for the trip, and we agreed to collaborate on this long drive. In early September 1982, I started my journey to a new life.

Corlette lived in Houston, so my first leg of the trip was the two-hour drive to Houston on I-10. I said my goodbyes to MaMe and my siblings and headed West. I met Corlette's family and spent the night with them before continuing early the next morning. Next, we traveled completely through Texas on I-10 West, stopping in El Paso for the night. It was a noneventful day. We just drove and stopped for food and gas.

The next morning, we got up early and had a nice breakfast. Our plan was to drive West on I-10 to Los Angeles and connect with a Southern classmate, Cassy Kinsey. Cassy graduated with me, also in EE in May. She had already started her job at the Los Angeles Department of Water and Power. She invited us to come visit her and spend the night before our drive to the San Francisco Bay Area and Palo Alto the next day. Cassy was temporarily living with an older lady who was taking good care of her. This woman would not accept us staying any other place than with her for the night.

DOI: 10.1201/9781032724270-9

Corlette and I had a good visit with Cassy, catching up on our respective lives. We were fascinated by her work and her ability to meet all kinds of people in the LA area in such a short time frame. She already had an agent who was sending her out on modeling assignments. We had a wonderful evening and a great dinner. After a good night's sleep, and a fantastic breakfast, we said our goodbyes to Cassy as she prepared for work. We then set out on the final leg of our journey—traveling to Palo Alto via I-5 North and US 101 North. It was a beautiful drive through the predominantly agricultural areas of California. We arrived in Palo Alto in the late afternoon.

Stanford University, officially denoted Leland Stanford Junior University, is a private institution established by Leland and Jane Stanford in memory of their son and only child, Leland Stanford, Jr., in 1885. The beautiful campus covers nearly 8,200 acres near Palo Alto, California. The early September day of my arrival was my first visit to the campus, The Farm. With its numerous buildings with Spanish-tiled roofs, its awe-inspiring Palm Drive with palm trees adorned on both sides of the road leading to the Quad, now denoted the Main Quad, to Memorial Church, MemChu, in the Quad's center, to Lake Lagunita, Lake Lag, a man-made lake on campus, to the view of The Dish, a large radio antenna on a Stanford foothill, one can draw inspiration from its many aesthetically pleasing landmarks.

I was excited to be there, to commence my graduate school journey in one of the top departments globally in my chosen field of endeavor, and to learn more and have a deeper level of knowledge and understanding of this area. I chose one of the best and was eager to hit the ground running in my academic pursuits. I soon learned that it would be the most challenging experience of my nearly 22 years. However, upon my arrival, I was full of joy in thinking about my possibilities. Unlike my lofty undergraduate objective, my Stanford goal was to graduate with a master's degree, then get a job, and become a successful career professional in corporate America.

I connected with graduate student housing and obtained my housing for the year. It was a three-bedroom townhouse, 44D, in Escondido Village, the graduate student housing development on campus. The townhouse consisted of three bedrooms of unequal size upstairs and one bathroom. The living room and kitchen were downstairs. It was sufficient and functional for my purposes. I was the first to arrive, so I chose the largest bedroom. My roommates arrived in subsequent days.

Corlette and I soon connected with our fellow Southern alumnus, Joanne. She was the top Southern graduate the previous year and had completed one year of graduate study at Stanford in the same EE department. Corlette had to quickly go back to Baton Rouge and finish her last semester at Southern. I took her to the SFO airport, and she later arrived safely back on campus.

Joanne lived in Blackwelder, a high-rise apartment complex, also in Escondido Village and not far from my townhouse. It was a one-bedroom apartment that housed two students. Joanne had the bedroom, arriving first to claim it. She shared this apartment with another graduate student whose bedroom was the living room, although she concocted a temporary wall that sealed it off from the rest of the apartment. This made her "bedroom" larger.

Joanne quickly introduced me to her social network on campus, which became my social network. They were primarily Black STEM graduate students in various technical disciplines—EE, physics, applied physics, geophysics, physical chemistry, etc. I met most of them at a social event organized to welcome the new STEM-focused graduate students to our cultural community. We were all either Bell Labs CRFP Fellows or had other similar fellowships. I formed friendships with most of them and maintained lifelong friendships with many of them—especially the EEs. This group became a strong support structure for me as I lived the Stanford experience.

I also attended a reception welcoming all Black graduate students to The Farm. There I made other connections. However, my graduate school experience was so rigorous and intense that I did not see most of them again after that event.

Joanne was a good friend and supporter, showing me the ropes around campus. We were in different areas, but she was able to advise on courses in general and on graduate school resources available to me. She was the one person on campus who had similar Southern University experiences, so I took her advice seriously. She was also a social butterfly, organizing many events attended by our fellow Black STEM graduate students. The overwhelming majority of the social events I attended that first year were with this group.

Stanford conferred a master's degree in electrical engineering after students completed an extensive one-year nonthesis program. Joanne, who was also a Bell Labs CRFP Fellow, advised me not to take the full load required to graduate in one year since the work was going to be very challenging. She said that if I was a full-time student, the CRFP program would pay all expenses. She advised me to register for the minimum number of courses required to be full time. While this would mean it would take me up to two years to finish, I would better manage my coursework with the lighter load. Even that was going to be extremely challenging. She said graduate school is much more challenging and time consuming than our undergraduate experience. Not only was Joanne the top graduate in her class at Southern in May 1981, but she was also a *summa cum laude* graduate with a perfect 4.0 GPA. I therefore respected her input, listened, and followed her advice. Even though I was not staying for the Ph.D., I still wanted to do well in graduate school.

I was encouraged to take the Ph.D.-qualifying exam that first year. There were criteria for taking the exam, and an advisor informed me that I would probably have the best record possible for applying that first year. While it was not my intention to stay in this program past the master's degree, I did not share this with the advisor. Out of curiosity, I did some due diligence on my own in examining the requirements for the exam. I focused on the prerequisite courses needed to prepare for the exam and concluded that I did not meet all of them. I would need a year of graduate school to meet them. There was a limited number of times a student could take this exam, if one didn't pass, before they were asked to leave. Given that I did not feel I was ready to take it, and I did not want to stay anyway, I decided not to take the Ph.D.-qualifying exam my first year.

It was challenging to get around campus with a car, primarily due to the small number of convenient parking spaces. Most students had bicycles. I went shopping for a bicycle to get around campus. I later bought a backpack once I knew the coursebooks required—at the Stanford University Bookstore in White Plaza on campus. White Plaza was a dense student activity space centered by a beautiful waterfall. Many cyclists and pedestrians traveled through the plaza on their way to class or other activities. The US Post Office was also in White Plaza, adjacent to the bookstore.

I rented a post office box at this post office and spent many days traveling the plaza. I had a routine each day. The student union was a short distance from the plaza. Some days, I would park my bike, stop by the bookstore, and buy a Mrs. Field's Deborah special (oatmeal raisin cookie). I would then go and check my mailbox for mail and ride to my townhouse for lunch. On other days, I would skip the cookie and go to the student union for the Tuesday special—Mexican enchiladas or burritos. Then I would sit outside and have lunch. Afterwards I would stay and study if the weather was nice. If not, I would ride home and study.

Once all the preliminary preparations and social events ended, it was time to focus on classes. My interests and focus were on computers. At that time, Stanford offered the option of focusing on computer hardware or software. Since I decided to take the minimum load, and I was going to stay for two years, I was able to do both hardware and software. A couple of my courses in the first quarter were computer architecture and operating systems.

The rigorous graduate courses included a voluminous amount of work that required students to work together on problem sets in groups. At the end of the lecture for my first class, my fellow students and I got together to form our groups. I quickly noticed that many of my classmates already knew each other from their undergraduate schools. Most were quickly able to form groups. I asked a few times to be a part of these groups. Every single person, including the women, would look at me from head to toe and say no to me, some with the look of disdain on their faces toward me.

At first, I was not sure if I was just imagining this. However, after this happened a few times, I became concerned because I needed to be a part of a group. Then one of the students approached me and suggested we form a group. This was a foreign student. He was experiencing the same type of rejection and assumed I was too, based upon my perplexing look. So, we formed our group and found another foreign student to round it out. It turned out these students were the smartest in the class. I was in the best group, and we did well with our problem sets.

Throughout my Stanford tenure, this scenario played out with each class I took that required us to work on problem sets in groups. None of the people in my social network were in my area of expertise.

I was the only Black woman in most of my classes, and one of just a handful of women. I felt I was on my own, but looked up to the foreign students, sometimes approaching them to form my group.

I recall another class that first quarter; I had a conversation with one of my fellow classmates, Mitri Halabi, before our class started. He looked very tired, and I asked if he was alright. He responded, indicating he was tired because he had just arrived on campus a few hours earlier after a nearly 30-hour trip from Beirut, Lebanon. Given my love for travel, I was intrigued by this and asked about his stops along the way. It was a very friendly and educational conversation prior to the start of the lecture.

Each of my classes were extremely challenging. It was a struggle to fully understand the lectures. In addition, the environment was very different. For example, during the lectures, and at times before or after them, my fellow classmates would speak with such confidence and authority as if they knew all the material. This was something I did not experience at Southern, as we were all there to learn material that we did not know. I became concerned about how well I would do in these graduate classes, because I was there to learn and not pontificate on what I already knew. I just focused on learning as much as I could during the lectures.

Most of my classes were in lecture halls with cameras for broadcasting. This is because many of my fellow classmates were working in technology companies throughout the Silicon Valley area. Stanford would broadcast the lectures to them while they sat in a classroom in their respective work environments. These lectures were videotaped, and they were available for review at the Terman Engineering Library on campus. To prepare for an exam, I made a habit of reviewing every page of every chapter in my textbooks and exhaustively reviewing my class notes. In addition, I checked out every VHS tape of every lecture in the library, found a VCR with earphones in the library, and reviewed every lecture. I was relentless in leaving no stone unturned as I studied and prepared for exams.

Soon it was time for my very first exam at Stanford. I had done everything humanly possible to prepare and I was ready. It was a ten-question essay exam. I read the first question, thought about it a little, and determined I would go back to it, I did not know the answer. I went to the second question, same thing. The third and the fourth questions, same thing. I began to panic because I had done everything to prepare, or so I thought, and could not answer a single question. I just sat up for a second and began to take a couple of deep breaths as I tried to determine my next move. Then I realized there was one thing I did not do, pray.

I prayed silently and desperately to God for help! I calmed down and started over. I read the first question and proceeded to write something down to answer, not quite knowing what I was writing. I did this for all ten questions. I completed the exam before anyone, turned it in, and left the classroom. I felt defeated as I left because I had no idea if the answers I provided were correct, and I assumed they were not. I went over and over in my mind to see if there was anything else I could do to prepare, but I felt I covered all the bases. As a result, if I failed this exam, after trying everything, including praying at the last minute, what else could I do?

This time I skipped the bookstore, post office, and student union and went straight home. I went inside and sat on the living room sofa and just stared at the walls in utter disbelief. I don't recall how long I was there, but at some point, I became so distressed that I decided it was time to go. After all, what do you do when you believe you've done all you can and still cannot answer a single question on a test? I called my mother, during my hysteria, and told her I was coming home. I told her what happened, and I wasn't going to stay. I had done my best, and I was coming home. I then ran upstairs to start packing. I was going to check on flights after that, forgetting that I had a car to drive home.

When I was halfway up the stairs, I heard a knock on the door. It was Joanne and another friend, Edith. She was also a second-year graduate student, and both apparently experienced something similar during their first exam at Stanford, Joanne in EE, Edith in geophysics. They had previously asked me when my first exam was scheduled and together decided to visit me once I returned home after the exam. They came to support me, lift me up, and take me out to dinner.

I was not in the mood to go anywhere, and they were not having it. They literally dragged me out of the townhouse and took me to Tony Romas on El Camino Real, one of the main thoroughfares that traverses through Palo Alto and Silicon Valley. The restaurant was just south of the city, and it served some delicious St. Louis-styled barbeque. It was Halloween, and the restaurant staff were fully adorned in their costumes. I slowly but surely began to relax and enjoy the company and food. They advised that I should at least wait until I get the results of the test before I do anything drastic, which made sense to me. By the end of dinner, I was laughing and joking and enjoying myself immensely. Joanne and Edith were a godsend for me that evening, and I am eternally grateful.

Unfortunately, while I was out to dinner my mother, who was very upset too, called her sisters to ask them to talk to me. They were unable to reach me, and their stress levels elevated. When I arrived home later that evening, I spoke to most of them and MaMe. I was able to calm them down and let them know I would get back to them once I got my test results. I had yet to rule out that I would leave, I just chose to wait until I had results before making a definitive decision.

During the next lecture of this class, and before we received our exam results, I noticed the teaching assistant (TA) was very friendly toward me. He knew my name and initiated an engaging technical conversation. I was very uncomfortable with this because up until that point, we were not introduced. At the time, I was trying to figure out how he knew my name. Even though I stood out as the only Black woman, the only Black person in the class, that did not mean that he knew my name.

Prior to this, the TA would not give me the time of day. The few times I looked at him, he would see right through me as though I was not there. It felt as though I was invisible to him. So yes, with no prior introduction and absolutely no communication, it was unsettling to experience this dramatic turnaround in his behavior toward me. I only engaged in a short, friendly conversation. I did not know what was happening, and I found the exit and left.

A few days later, we received the results of our exam. All my responses to the questions were correct. I studied the questions and answers closely. I clearly had answered the questions, but still did not fully understand my answers. I spoke to a couple of classmates on my way out, just to gauge their results. These same people who were so boastful prior to the exam were now silent or had very little to say. That piqued my interest. I was trying to understand what was happening. Eventually I realized, and later learned, that I did well on this exam. My score was one of the highest in the class.

This was an eye-opener for me. My classmates had projected and spoken with a strong sense of confidence in their voices and body language, while at the same time attempting to draw some shade on me. I realized they were no more knowledgeable or smarter than me. They were just playing mind games with me. I also realized in the classes prior to receiving my test results, the TA must have already graded my exam. He must have realized I was someone who was not to be minimized or ignored. I was someone he could learn something from; hence, he initiated a conversation with me.

I subsequently spoke to my mother and aunts about my test results. They were happy and relieved at my outcome, and my decision to stay. This was the first and last time I was so dramatic and emotional about what was a unique and unpleasant experience for me. I learned to be calmer when facing what may appear to be outright failure, to let time and a cooler mind prevail in such seasons, and to think critically about what is really happening.

I was grateful to God that I came to these conclusions before it had an adverse impact on me. Once I understood what was happening, I knew that to some of my classmates, and others, I was expendable unless I had something valuable they could leverage. Now, I could be an asset to them, I was worth their time to be seen and communicated with. It was a dramatic turnaround and very educational. I approached the situation and the environment in a different manner. Moving forward, their mind games and sometimes shade were not going to have a negative impact on me. In addition, I was not going to be used. I experienced this behavior in all my classes, and some interactions, on campus. This is when I fully realized that I was in a different environment and had to mentally approach it using a different methodology compared to my undergraduate experience. I was no longer in Kansas.

For the most part, for the classes that did not require me to work as part of a group, I worked on my own. There were a couple of my colleagues who took the time to provide guidance. For example, one day during the winter quarter, Joanne invited me to a study break at another graduate student dorm. I was struggling with how to start on my homework assignment. I needed a break, so I welcomed the opportunity. When we arrived, I saw my classmate, Mitri, the one who had traveled to school from Beirut. We struck up a conversation, and he asked how things were going. I told him I needed some help with my homework for one of my classes.

Mitri was very smart. He was also knowledgeable about the subject and wanted to help. We went off to find a cubby hole to review my class material. He walked me through the basic concepts in a manner I was able to understand. He did not do my homework for me; he just gave me the tools I needed to do the work myself. I was so grateful for his assistance. I asked him why he was willing to leave a study break with refreshments to help me. He responded by reminding me of the first day we met in class, when I inquired about his long trip to San Francisco. He said most of our classmates were not friendly to him. On the other hand, I took an interest and initiated a conversation with him. This was endearing to him and helping me with my homework was his way of thanking me.

In general, most of my classes were challenging, and that was to be expected. It was very intense and stressful. While I fully enjoyed learning the information, concepts, subjects, etc., my new environment tested my limits for learning amid adversity. Stanford University's campus is so beautiful, especially during the spring. However, being on the receiving end of comments that were condescending, minimizing, disrespectful, or mocking, or feeling invisible or alone in an unfriendly environment, even in a crowd, takes its toll. I did not fully enjoy the beauty of the campus until I left after graduation and came back later for visits.

It took every ounce of inner strength I had to counter that environment. Many times, revisiting the positive mantras I heard as a child, from my mother and other family members and friends, was medicinal. Also, remembering the love and support I received from my classmates and professors during my HBCU days would make me smile and help me make it through the day or the week. While the coursework did not get any easier, adjusting to my new, undesirable environment was more difficult than my classes. However, by God's grace, I was able to adjust with the right mindset. I did very well in some courses and well in others.

On many occasions, I would take breaks to allow my mind to rest. For example, I would jump into my Chevy Chevette and take drives on I-280 just west of Palo Alto. This highway was much less crowded than US 101 which ran parallel to I-280 to the east of the city. I would always go north, heading toward San Francisco. There were three vista points along the way. I liked the second of the three best. On a clear, beautiful day, one could see the entire Bay Area looking toward San Francisco. It was so stunning and peaceful to see. Sometimes I would drive up to the visa point, sit outside, and just enjoy this beauty of nature for hours. During that time, I could just feel the stress being lifted from my body. I always left that place lighter and refreshed.

My social network of good friends was a lifesaver while matriculating at Stanford. We were all in different fields or subfields of endeavor, so for the most part we were unable to help each other academically. Sometimes we laughed and joked about this fact, suggesting that maybe it was intentionally architected by the powers that be. However, we would get together from time to time for social events. Joanne or another friend, Peter, a physics Ph.D. student, would plan them. Many times, I was asked if I would be interested in some type of event. I would respond in the affirmative. Sometime later, I would get a time, date, place, cost estimate, etc., and I obliged.

We went horseback riding on the beach in Half Moon Bay, a beautiful coastal town just south of San Francisco. We also went on a weekend camping trip to the California Redwoods in Marin County north of San Francisco. We pitched our tents, roasted marshmallows by fire at night, and slept in sleeping bags on the ground. This was the first time I went on a camping trip. I discovered that sleeping on the ground was not for me. I have yet to do that again. We also went canoeing down the Russian River. I recall Peter turning over my canoe, and I was not happy with him. We also had many potluck dinners, movies out, and an outdoor concert here and there that we attended. This was all a welcome relief to my life on The Farm. The support from my friends who were also going through was invaluable. I never underestimated its power.

I flew home to Lake Charles for the Christmas holidays while I was a Stanford student. I stayed in the Bay Area for all the other holidays. Joanne invited me to the home of her family friends, Earl and Leola Washington, for Thanksgiving during my first year. They lived in San Francisco. On the morning of the holiday, Joanne and I drove up to their home on the scenic US 101 highway. They lived on Ocean Avenue in the southern part of the city in a wonderful row house. Earl was a native San Franciscan, and Leola was from Crowley, Louisiana, also Joanne's roots. They were a childless couple a generation older and treated us like their long lost and beloved children. They were also good cooks, both great at preparing authentic Cajun, Creole, and a variety of other dishes. It was wonderful, delightful! I was home. I was in heaven. I made new friends that day that lasted their lifetimes.

From that day, until the day they each left this world, I stayed in contact with them. I started with visiting them every now and then while I was still at Stanford, many times without Joanne. However, throughout the decades I stayed in touch, especially with Leola. I visited them every time I had a trip to San Francisco. They became more like dear friends who provided me with much-needed support while being a student, and a couple of my biggest cheerleaders as I graduated and left to focus on my life pursuits.

One day, I was in the EE department's office copying some papers. There was an elderly man using the copier while one of my friends and I waited until he finished. Once I started using the copier, my friend asked me if I knew who was using the copier previously. I said no. He enlightened me. The elderly man was Dr. William Shockley. He was an emeritus professor in our department. Also, he was a 1956 Nobel Prize winner in physics for coinventing the transistor. In his later years, he conducted scientific experiments which he claimed to quantify that Blacks were inferior to Whites. My immediate thought was, *really? You don't say?* That incident initiated a thought process in me. I went from being angry at the thought of a highly accomplished scientist being so blatantly racist, to me thinking, *well I'll show you Dr. Shockley.* At the end of this process, I decided to pursue a Ph.D. in electrical engineering. I already had the fellowship, now I had a strong motivation.

I continued with my classes for the remainder of the academic year. I was doing well and thought of taking a break during the summer and going to work at Bell Labs in New Jersey. I discussed this with my mentor and decided to do just that but only after taking a couple of classes in the summer just for fun. One of the classes I took was tennis. I had played off and on recreationally in high school and was interested in the sport. I also thought it would be a great way to channel some of the negative energy I had toward some of my professors. I remember going to the tennis court one time with a friend. I never quite got the hang of serving, but I mastered the volley. I remember my friend making a comment about how good I was at volleying. I told her I pretended the ball was my professor. Then she completely understood. I kept playing recreationally, often volleying against a wall on the tennis courts for the duration of my Stanford experience.

I spent a few weeks working for Bell Labs before starting my second year on The Farm. My experiences that year were roughly the same as my first year. At that point, I had adjusted and was used to the routine. I found it amazing at what the human being could adjust to. I had challenging classes, a more challenging environment, and several social events with friends interspersed among the events.

Graduation with a master's degree was approaching, and I thought about my next steps in the Ph.D. process. I talked to my fellow Ph.D. graduate school friends in STEM, especially those in EE. They shared with me the details of the process. With that knowledge, I started to think about a targeted area of expertise. I loved my computer-related courses, especially the hardware-related ones. I thought that was a natural and exciting fit for me. After some due diligence, I narrowed my area to computer architecture. I reached out to a couple of professors on campus, those that could potentially be my Ph.D. thesis advisor. I spoke to them about research possibilities in computer architecture.

Based on my experience with these professors, I also thought about pursuing this degree at another school. I reached out to my Bell Labs mentor to discuss possibilities. He thought it was a good idea for me to seriously think about another school, even suggesting Rice University in Houston, Texas, his alma mater. I listened, evaluated all my options, considering their advantages and disadvantages, and eventually took my mentor's advice and chose to apply to Rice.

Shortly after I submitted my Ph.D. application to Rice, I received a call from a professor there, Dr. Fayè A. Briggs. He was a tenured professor in Rice's electrical and computer engineering (ECE) department with a research focus that included computer architecture. Dr. Briggs is a native Nigerian who is highly intelligent and accomplished. He mentioned to me that for years, he had been unsuccessfully trying to encourage Blacks to pursue advanced degrees in ECE. When my application arrived, he was excited. It turned out that Dr. Briggs and one of his mentors, Dr. Kai Wang, had just published a book on computer architecture. This book became widely used by graduate students across the nation for a few years. He advised me to go and buy it at Stanford's bookstore and start reading it before I arrived on campus.

He never mentioned whether I would be accepted into the program, and I did not ask. However, his reaction to my application was certainly favorable so I was hopeful. I did not want to be big-headed into thinking sure, they would accept me, I was soon to be a Stanford alumnus. Shortly after my call with Dr. Briggs, I received a letter from the department informing me I was accepted into their Ph.D. program. With my next step on this journey secured, I proceeded to complete my Stanford tenure and prepare for graduation.

MaMe and other relatives were excited about my pending graduation at Stanford in June 1984. I learned that four aunts, two maternal and two paternal, were planning to attend, along with a cousin. I advised them on the best accommodation during their stay, as well as other logistics.

During the spring quarter, the Stanford campus went through a metamorphosis. This included, for example, the planting of new flowers and an overall grooming of the grounds that reflected the new birth of the season. It was exciting to witness, especially near the end of my second and final year on campus. I was finally reaching the point when I could exhale and breathe. I was also excited about hosting my family during their trip to my graduation. The day finally arrived on Sunday, June 17, 1984.

My relatives arrived a couple days earlier and had settled into their hotel rooms. Before graduation, I took them on a walking tour of the campus. They were excited and impressed with the surroundings. We stopped for a snack break in the middle of the day. I suggested that we get some frozen yogurt at the student union and go sit outside and eat it, as the weather was beautiful. MaMe was adamantly against getting yogurt; she did not like it and refused. I did not force her. She didn't want anything, so she held our chairs while we went in for the snack. All of us came out with various flavors. We were enjoying it thoroughly, making pleasant faces and noises as we ate. Then MaMe, not wanting to miss anything, asked me to get her some yogurt. She enjoyed the yogurt too, it was good.

It turned out that my mother never had frozen yogurt. She thought I was talking about the regular, plain yogurt with no flavor when

I suggested it. Once she realized this was like ice cream, she joined the party. In fact, she enjoyed it so much that when they arrived back home in Lake Charles, she regularly asked Aunt Roy Lee to take her to get some frozen yogurt. It became a summer routine for her. This was one of the many experiences I had in helping my mother broaden her horizons in understanding and appreciating this big world in which we live. There are so many possibilities, so many options to explore. I was happy to be a vessel for her exploration that summer.

Stanford's commencement service was held for the first time in the Sunken Diamond baseball field, with approximately 20,000 attending. It was moved there from the Frost Amphitheater where it was held for half a century. First, it had a capacity of about 10,000, and 17,000 had jammed into the facility in 1983, hence the move. This was my first time attending a Stanford Commencement service, and it was an eye-opener. There were two services, one for all graduates and one for the specific majors.

The main ceremony was like a big party. Some of the graduates were dressed in shorts, jeans, T-shirts, sandals, etc. Many of them had their graduation gowns wide open. Everyone was laughing and joking and not really paying attention to the program. Throughout the program, the graduates were popping champaign and spraying it about the raucous crowd. This was in direct contrast to previous commencement ceremonies in which I was a graduate, or just attended.

During my Southern commencement program, the ladies were mostly dressed in white dresses under their caps and gowns and wore dark shoes. For the men, it was dark dress pants and a white shirt with a tie and dark shoes. Everyone marched in a dignified manner, and the program was solemn, enriching, and inspiring. The Stanford program was very different. All my family members were also shocked. We have never seen such a thing. One of my aunts was perplexed when she asked the question, are these the future leaders of our country? We all concluded, me after some due diligence, that this was a cultural difference in how Blacks and the majority population view a commencement program at that time.

The speaker for the program was Dr. Richard Lyman. He was a former president of the university, and at the time the President of the Rockefeller Foundation. I do not remember most of the program, including Dr. Lyman's remarks. They were overshadowed by the party.

The second program, where our degrees were conferred, was less rowdy but still not as dignified as what I was used to culturally. There was still the casual attire for the graduates, especially sandals. The EE program was held at Roble Field, which was close to the location of the department's office on campus. The program was short and efficient. There were a few remarks by the department chair and others, and then the conferring of the degrees. I walked across the stage, just like my classmates, and received my degree. It was a wonderful experience, another milestone under my belt. I had gone from *summa cum laude* to *thank you laude*! I was grateful for the growth of both experiences.

My relatives stayed a few extra days. We used this time to tour the Bay Area, including San Francisco, visiting my friends Earl and Leola Washington, the 17-mile drive along the coast, and other sites. The 17-mile drive routes through Pebble Beach and Pacific Grove on the Monterrey Peninsula south of San Francisco. It was a beautiful day for a scenic, awe-inspiring drive. We stopped and had lunch at the clubhouse on the golf course in Pebble Beach. In fact, from our table, we watched golfers play at the 18th hole. It was a sheer delight.

The time came for my relatives to leave and go back to Lake Charles, Washington, DC, and Maryland. I enjoyed hosting them, but we said our goodbyes, and they left with memories that we talked about for decades.

I spent the next few weeks slowly preparing for my move to Houston. I socialized with my friends—the ones still on campus. It was so good to be able to do this with no stress. I had not done that in a couple of years, and it was great. One day, just a few days prior to my departure, I received a call from one of my friends, Thurmon Deloney. He had made a cassette tape of my favorite songs for me to listen to during my drive to Houston. He suggested that I stop by his apartment later in the day to pick it up, and I was happy to do so. As the time approached, I was not feeling well. I called Thurmon and relayed this to him. I said I would take a nap, then stop by later to pick up the tape.

When I woke up, I got ready and headed south to Sunnyvale where he lived. Once I reached his apartment complex, I noticed the bright red Porsche that looked very similar to one owned by another mutual friend. Marc Hannah had left Stanford, while still a Ph.D. student in EE, to be a cofounder of Silicon Graphics with his advisor and other students. Every now and then I would run into him on campus and catch up. I recalled the last time I had seen him; he was driving a Porsche. I was walking on campus with a girl-friend who he also knew. He pulled over and asked us if we wanted a ride. Of course, we did! It was a wonderful, thrilling ride. I wasn't sure if the car I saw in the parking lot of Thurmon's apartment com-plex was Marc's, after all this was sunny California, Silicon Valley.

I made it to Thurmon's apartment and knocked on the door. I could hear loud music playing, which was unusual for him. He opened the door, then I immediately heard "surprise!!". Wow, I was really surprised. So surprised that I almost missed my own surprise bon voyage party. They were having the party without me, includ-ing Marc, and it turned out it was his Porsche. Anyway, I came in the middle of the party, no one had left. This was the first time I ever had a surprise party, and they got me good. I was happy to meet everyone. For many, I have not seen them since that day. It did my heart good to feel the love and know they were still my support!

Gregory arrived a few days later. I picked him up from San Francisco's airport and then took him on a tour of Stanford when we arrived on campus. Earl and Leola wanted to meet him, so we spent a couple of days with them in San Francisco. Earl took us all over the city. It was wonderful. Gregory had never been to the city, so he was all eyes and ears. He thoroughly enjoyed himself. Also, both Earl and Leola left no stone unturned when cooking authentic Louisiana meals for us. They treated Gregory like a king, and he started acting like one.

We went out to breakfast one morning as we prepared for our drive to Houston. We were enjoying our breakfast and our conver-sation when I saw Gregory take out quite a few different medica-tions that he slowly but surely took while he ate. I had not been around him much since his Lupus diagnosis, so seeing him do that was a jolt to my system. I became very concerned looking at my 20-year-old brother taking all this medication. He was heavier than I had previously seen him. He informed me that one of the medi-cations he was taking was prednisone, which had a side effect of weight gain. He clearly was used to taking all those pills. It made me realize that this was a very serious ailment. I knew there was no known cause or cure for Lupus. It wasn't until a few years later that I realized just how life-threatening it could be.

The evening before our scheduled departure, a friend of mine, Faye Marks, invited us over to dinner. She fixed us a wonderful meal, along with some fried chicken for us to eat while we traveled. It was a great gesture that we appreciated. After the meal, we went back to my graduate student townhouse for one last night before our departure. That evening, I thought about my two-year stay on The Farm. It was a significant learning experience for me academically, intellectually, emotionally, spiritually, and socially. I made new friends, many of them for life. I achieved one of my original objectives, graduating. I was a Stanford alumnus. I also evolved in my thinking and approach to my future. I now had a new goal, that of earning a Ph.D. in electrical engineering.

However, of all my learning experiences on The Farm, my greatest was encountering how people who are different than you, particularly from a race or gender perspective, can be so cruel, cold, and calculating. Their level of prejudice was amazing. My greatest lesson was how I learned to deal with it, tapping into an inner strength I didn't know I had. As I awakened the next morning to commence my journey to the next chapter, I did not know this would be the strong foundation I would use and build upon to thrive amid adversity and mountaintop adventures in future seasons.

CHAPTER 7

Rice University

G REGORY AND I AWAKENED EARLY in the morning and headed out sometime thereafter. We had packed the car the previous evening, so we were ready to go. We got a quick breakfast at a local drive-thru restaurant then headed south. We traveled on US 101 and eventually connected with I-5 South. The plan for our first leg was to arrive in the Los Angeles metro area just before dinner time. Gregory had a college friend he wanted to connect with while we were there. It was a great drive through the heart of California's agricultural region before arriving in the LA metro area. We stopped just on the east side of downtown, traveling now on I-10 East, and checked into a hotel for the evening.

Gregory was looking forward to meeting his friend after a long hiatus. He called the friend who said he was on his way. I got comfortable and relaxed in bed and watched TV. Gregory went outside to the balcony and waited for his friend to arrive. He never did. Gregory was very disappointed and did not say anything as he finally came in and discussed our dinner options. We decided to have a quick dinner at a local restaurant. Gregory did not say much, as he was still disappointed with his friend's no-show. We went back to the room and prepared for bed. I let him be.

We awakened early the next morning and prepared for the second of three legs for our trip. After a quick breakfast, we headed east to El Paso. This was a full day's drive through California, Arizona, New Mexico, and finally Texas, all on I-10 East. We had quick stops for gas and food in Phoenix, Tucson, Las Cruces, New Mexico, and other towns along the way before arriving in El Paso. The ride was scenic but uneventful. We had interesting conversations as I thought about my future in Houston. We finished eating the chicken Faye cooked for us at some point during the day. After checking into a hotel in El Paso, we had a nice dinner at a local restaurant. We then went to the hotel, relaxed a bit, then rested for the night. I was beginning to get excited about our arrival in Houston the next day.

After a good night's sleep, we prepared for the final leg of our drive, heading east on I-10 to Houston. It was a long drive and day, but we arrived safely in the city just before sundown. My plan was to share the apartment that Schirrell and Darlene were already living in. Another cousin, Dottie, had just left the apartment to attend graduate school in the state of Washington, so it worked out well for us. Gregory and I went straight to this apartment when we arrived. After greeting everyone, we proceeded to unload my car after a nice meal. I was finally in my new home in Houston and was ready for the possibilities.

The next morning, I went to the apartment complex's leasing office to sign the necessary paperwork and get my keys. It was a smooth process, and I was in and out in a few minutes. My next stop was the campus of Rice University. Prior to my arrival I carefully reviewed the backgrounds of the professors in the ECE department to determine if there were others with a better match for me regarding research interests. There were none, so Dr. Briggs would be my thesis advisor. He suggested that I arrange meetings with other professors to create my Ph.D. committee. Following his advice, I planned to meet a couple of professors during my first day on campus.

When I arrived, I went straight to the parking lot of the Abercrombie Engineering Laboratory building. I visited the ECE department office, which was located on the building's second floor, and introduced myself. My advisor informed me that he would be out of town attending a conference but suggested that I introduce myself to the department upon arrival. I met and chatted with the office administration team before heading to my meeting with an ECE professor who was a potential member of my Ph.D. committee. We exchanged greetings as I walked into his office. He asked me to be seated as he closed the door.

After some initial chit chat, he proceeded to tell me about his views of my arrival to the department. He proudly and boldly articulated that "I don't think you are going to make it here at Rice, but since you came with an outside fellowship, we'll take the money". My mental reaction was *What?! Did he just say what I thought he said?*. While I was thinking this, he sat quietly at his desk while he smiled. In my mind I was thinking, *Well wait a minute sir, you clearly do not know who I am. I am a child of God and Gloria Dean Johnson's daughter, and I don't take too kindly to you speaking to me in that manner. I will certainly make a believer out of you before I leave this place, with a Ph.D. degree.* While I was thinking this, I never articulated it to him. I just confidently smiled at him.

I did not have much to say to him after that remark and the meeting ended. I felt I dodged a bullet with him because he had similar research interests and, technically, would have been a good fit for my committee. I was just grateful that he proudly exuded his true nature to me, letting me know that I should not and did not ask him to be a member of my committee. This was my welcome to the campus. I did not share this with my advisor, or anyone else, for 38 years.

I had not yet taken a tour of the campus, so after my infelicitous introduction to the department, and the *confidence man*, I conducted my own personal tour. It was an opportunity for me to process what had just happened while I walked the grounds of the beautiful campus.

Rice University, founded in 1912, is adorned with thousands of trees, predominately live oaks, on its 300-acre campus. The trees, with their long winding branches, added a touch of grandeur to the campus that provides a soothing impact to the soul. Many of the campus buildings are developed in the Mediterranean Revival style, including the light brick facades, archways, and columns of the central quadrangle. This main quad also until recently hosts a statue of the school's founder and benefactor. William Marsh Rice directed in his will that the university be created to provide tuition-free education to White students only. I walked the campus, including the main quad where I viewed Rice's statue, not knowing the founder's directive. I thoroughly enjoyed my initial walk on campus. It was a calming and comforting experience. I did not go back to Abercrombie to meet other professors that day; it was not time. I went home.

I soon met Dr. Briggs after his return to campus and settled into a routine. As a Ph.D. student I was not required to take any classes; however, Dr. Briggs suggested I take a few courses to prepare me for my research. I thought about other professors to approach as potential members of my committee. I focused on completing the process of establishing my thesis committee, preparing for the Ph.D.- qualifying exam, and initiating my thesis research. I spent time discussing my interests with my advisor, as well as many open questions in my chosen area of focus. I discussed my thoughts about potential thesis committee members, including those in the mathematical sciences department. I spent countless hours reviewing research papers in journals, conference proceedings, etc. Within a couple of months, I had a thesis committee and a research focus area.

Soon after I arrived on campus, I entered a computing lab in the computer science department to do some work. This lab was only available to graduate students. The lab assistant, the only other person in the lab at the time, came to me and initiated a conversation. He told me, with confidence, that I was in the wrong place. Of course, I knew I was in the right place, and I responded that I was. After a few rounds of this, he became frustrated and began to ask me questions. This master's degree student soon realized that I was a Ph.D. student with an influential advisor. He began to get nervous and eventually apologized. My response to him was "that's ok this time, but the next time someone who looks like me walks into this lab, don't be so sure of yourself".

The Ph.D.-qualifying exam in the department consisted of written and oral components. I received information on the nature of the exams from the department and my advisor. I also spoke to fellow graduate students about the exam. It was scheduled for later that fall. I spent the first several weeks on campus in the courses I signed up for, as well as studying for the qualifying exam. When the time came, I took both the written and oral exams. I did not think I did well on the written exam, and I know I did not master the oral exam. There were questions on the exam I had never seen before. One subject area of the written exam had questions based on an orthodoxically different approach. Another set of questions focused on an area I had minimum knowledge about, quantum mechanics. For the oral exam, my mind just went blank, I could not remember my name.

I failed the exam. It was the first time I had ever failed an exam. For the written exam, I am not attempting to blame the questions for my failure. However, I subsequently learned the questions behind the unorthodox approach were submitted by a professor who for years had unsuccessfully tried to publish a book on his method. This professor also happened to be the *confidence man*. Also, while I had studied some of the quantum mechanics questions previously submitted for the exam, and had learned from them, I did not know quantum mechanics. I do not know why my mind went blank for the oral exam. I did, however, learn from this experience and made some adjustments.

For example, I obtained a copy of the professor's unpublished book to learn his method. I obtained a broader set of quantum mechanics questions previously submitted for exams and learned what I thought I needed to know to avoid failure. My research focus was computer engineering, a subset of the broader electrical engineering field at the time. The Ph.D.-qualifying exam included questions from many areas of electrical and computer engineering, including electrical and power systems, solid state devices, communications, electromagnetic theory, quantum mechanics, etc. I discerned that outside of the exam, it was highly unlikely that I would use the knowledge of quantum mechanics in the future. I chose to review previous exam questions versus taking a quantum mechanics class as a calculated risk mitigation action. I also did not spend an overwhelming amount of my time studying for the exam. I spent more time enjoying life, relaxing, preparing mentally and spiritually for the exam. When I took it the second time—the last opportunity I had to take it and pass before I would have to leave the university—I not only passed but also came out on top versus other students who took the exam.

Once I passed the Ph.D.-qualifying exam and established my committee, I proceeded to conduct preliminary research. The next milestone was to present a research proposal to my committee. During my first few months on campus, I narrowed my focus from computer architecture and performance evaluation to the performance of cache coherence protocols in high-end multiprocessors. I focused on computer systems with several processors or engines. Each process has its own cache memory, a subset of a global shared memory that is accessible by all processors. The issue to address is what happens when a processor modifies data in its private cache, and this same data is accessed by another processor. Each processor should access the most recently updated copy of the data. If not, there is a data or cache coherence issue among the data in the various caches.

At the time, there were several protocols for addressing the cache coherence issue. My proposed research focused on evaluating the performance of a handful of cache coherence protocols when executing computationally intensive numerical algorithms on such high-performance machines. My proposal to the committee was to leverage a software program that simulates the execution of these algorithms on the high-end systems using various cache coherence protocols. I proposed using not only a few cache coherence protocols but also several computer architecture design alternatives—cache size, cache replacement methodologies, etc. I would quantify when protocols performed best for certain cache strategies and computationally intensive algorithms. I presented the proposal to my committee, and it was accepted. I spent the next several years conducting this research, learning and making contributions to knowledge in the process.

Years later while reading the book *Hidden Figures*, I learned that Dr. Christine Darden, one of the four women profiled in the book, invented the computational fluid dynamics (CFD) algorithm. It is one of the computationally intensive algorithms I used in my Ph.D. research. I was ecstatic to learn that I stood on her shoulders and wanted to meet her. The opportunity came when she came to town for a dinner talk in Raleigh to discuss her life as a hidden figure. I contacted the host, who graciously seated me next to Dr. Darden during this dinner. We shared our career experiences and learned about a few surprises. I was grateful for her work and her time.

I spent about a year conducting this research, conversing with my advisor regularly on my progress. This was an area of research where I was to be an expert on this topic. I had a deep technical focus on the subject matter, understanding the state of the art, its limitations, and how my research addressed some of them. I had to think about all potential approaches to the issue, and the advantages and disadvantages of each approach. As part of the research process, I also had to think about defending my work, including its thesis, methodology, results, and analysis. I was required to explain why my approach and results made a significant contribution to knowledge in the field. This was the essence of my work and research in general. It required me to think critically about all aspects of this and similar issues. Studying, reading, learning, and contributing to the body of knowledge became my life's *modus operandi*.

It was through this process that I developed a love for reading. It was not technical papers alone but any type of reading. Over a short period of time, I began to read nontechnical books as a recreational activity. I dreamed of reading such books on a warm sunny beach someplace far away. It was my refuge from a technically demanding work environment and a way to keep my ideas and creativity flowing.

My Ph.D. process was technically challenging and mentally, emotionally, and physically draining. This was exacerbated by the fact that I could not see the end process. I did not know exactly—or even have a hint at—when I would finish. For months, in fact years, my discussions with my advisor ended with recommendations for additional areas to pursue, options to consider, or digging deeper to understand the results. While I believed my advisor was more supportive than the other professors in the department would have been, he was my advisor. I did not have a support system of peer graduate students like I did at Stanford. I felt as though I was on my own regarding these technical pursuits, and it took every ounce of inner strength I had to keep moving forward.

My support came from family and friends. I lived with Darlene and Schirrell in a two-bedroom apartment in the Astrodome area in Houston. It was about five miles from campus and on a good day about 11 minutes away, straight down Main Street. While we got along, we had very different personalities, and many times we did our own thing when socializing. From time to time, I would attend social events with them or my friends, usually on weekends. For example, I connected with one of my friends who grew up with me in the same church in Lake Charles. We also attended the same church in Houston. We would usually go to the 7:45 AM service on Sunday mornings, then get together with a larger group of church members for Sunday brunch after the service. In addition, I regularly attended my Delta sorority meetings and events; I was a member of the Houston-Suburban Ft. Bend Alumnae Chapter. I would go out with one of my Delta line sisters on a Friday or Saturday night just to relax and unwind after a long hard week. It was during one of these social outings that I met my future husband.

At some point over a year after I started at Rice, I hit a wall. After spending months focusing on my work, enhancing the performance simulator I developed, obtaining and analyzing results, making adjustments, and running the simulator again, repeating this several times, it became clear that I was not making any progress. In fact, I reached a point where I could not understand what I was doing. I had burned out. I recalled that my advisor noticed this in me. He told me of his Ph.D. journey, and how he reached a wall and burned out. He took some time off from his work and went fishing for several weeks. He did not think about any of his research during this time. He shared that he came back refreshed and ready to continue. He suggested that I consider taking a break. At the time, I ruled this out because I was not sure I would come back if I left.

However, I had put so much time and effort into this, and I was enjoying the work as it was exciting and intellectually stimulating. I eventually realized that I had burned out, I needed a break, and I would come back and finish. I discussed my options with my Bell Labs mentor assigned to me as part of my fellowship. He suggested I spend all or part of a semester at Bell Labs in New Jersey. He would work with me to find a small, contained project I could work on, that could take my mind off my current academic pursuits. He convinced me that I should do this.

Next, I went to my ECE department chair, Prof. Sidney Burrus, to explain my situation. He was very helpful and empathetic to my plight. First, he questioned me to ensure I would be willing to return after a couple of months. He described to me the process of withdrawing from the university and returning a short time later. He showed me kindness at a time when I really needed it, and I am forever grateful to him. (Prof. Burrus later became Dean of the Engineering School at Rice. I had a few intellectually stimulating conversations with him during subsequent visits to Rice after I graduated. He passed away in April 2021.) The department staff were also very helpful in this process. I left Houston in the Fall 1985 to work for Bell Labs for the remainder of the year.

The time away from Rice was very relaxing and educational. I basically spent my time going to work, then coming home to relax and enjoy my time away, primarily in solitude reading books. I came back to Rice in January 1986, and I was amazed at the change in my ability to make progress. It was just as my advisor described to me about his journey. I was refreshed, I had significantly more energy, and my mind was clear. As I continued my research, I prepared to present my research proposal to my committee, another milestone in the Ph.D. process in this department.

Also, while I loved sharing an apartment with my family, I had longed to have my own private space. My family would from time to time engage me in long social conversations when I felt I should be spending more time thinking and focusing on my research. When I returned from my break, I moved out of our shared apartment into my own one-bedroom apartment that was literally down the street, still in the Astrodome area of Houston. This gave me the freedom not only to focus more on my work but also to stop by and visit the family from time to time. It also enabled me to have some privacy as my relationship with my future husband became more serious.

I immediately began making progress on my research, including my formal Ph.D. dissertation proposal. I presented it to my committee in February 1986, and it was approved. I spent the next 18 months or so focused on my research. It was still technically challenging and stressful; however, the break enabled me to move forward in a methodical and progressive manner. My circular research process enabled me to learn from the analysis of a simulation execution, make changes, and learn more. As a result, I was able to write my dissertation in parallel with conducting the research.

I began writing my draft dissertation soon after my proposal was approved. I had been using the Internet since 1982, primarily for email. This was decades before the prevalence of web browsers, word processors, and the like. I used some of the software that comes with the operating system we used, UNIX, to write my dissertation. Specifically, I used LaTeX, document preparation software, and vi and emacs as editors. I became an expert in creating and using the various macros in the editor and competed with my office mates on speed and expertise. As a result, I made progress not only on my research but also in writing my dissertation.

In my view, the technical research environment can be unpleasant at best, hostile at worst. Part of this process requires that you present your work to the broader research community, including your peers. In my observations and experience, there is a tendency to be combative, and in some instances, to attack one's work. It is accepted by some as part of the overall research process. It is a rite of passage for Ph.D. aspirants to ensure they have fully evaluated all options of pursuit and evaluation. If an audience senses a weakness in someone presenting their work, they go into attack mode, flooding the presenter with questions. To elaborate further, the audience expects reasonable, well-thought-out responses. I noticed this not just in my department at Rice but also in the broader research community. This was also the case at Stanford and at deeply technical conferences. As a result, the best way to prepare for a presentation or conversation is to thoroughly research your subject matter, anticipate any type of question and prepare substantive responses. Otherwise, in many instances, audiences were not friendly with those who fell short. It could be brutal if you are unprepared.

I absolutely loved my work, my research. It was not a problem for me to go deep and explore possibilities, to brainstorm with Dr. Briggs who advised on options I may have missed or did not seriously consider. I thoroughly prepared for my presentations and discussions with others. Even though I was really in a hostile environment, I ignored the negative attitudes. I loved it! I thrived; this is what I was born to do. I felt I was in my element, I was home. I also took opportunities to show how one can challenge a person's work in a nonhostile manner.

In the Fall 1986, Dr. Briggs informed me that he was leaving Rice University and moving to California to work in industry. He said he would remain an adjunct professor at Rice, which enabled him to continue advising me in my research. With two additional committee members still on campus and his willingness to avail himself when I needed an advisory consultation, he assured me this would not disrupt my ability to continue and finish my research and subsequently graduate. So off he goes to Santa Clara, California, to work for Sun Microsystems.

It turned out it was not as easy to connect with my advisor for research discussions. In fact, when my research reached a critical stage that required some brainstorming with him, he was not as responsive to my requests to meet. I eventually decided it would be prudent to fly out to California to meet with him. I discussed this with the administrator of my fellowship at Bell Labs, and she agreed to finance my air travel for the visit. Faye was still a graduate student at Stanford, so I flew to San Francisco, stayed with her, and borrowed transportation. I was able to connect with my advisor, and we had very good, substantive conversations that provided oversight for him and insight for me. It enabled me to go back to Houston and make progress on my research.

During the next several months, I continued to focus on advancements in my research and my relationship with my boyfriend. By the end of 1987, during a regular conversation with Dr. Briggs, he informed me that I had just about enough to complete my research. I could not believe it! Over the next couple of months, I conducted a final set of simulations and analysis, completed the initial draft and review of my dissertation, and started interviewing for jobs. At the same time, my boyfriend and I were seriously discussing marriage.

During my last semester at Rice, I took an introduction to personal finance course through its continuing education program. Ever since I learned about how credit cards really worked back in college, I had a passion and focus on personal finance. Now that I was about to start working in the real world—and earning what I anticipated to be an above average and above median salary, I wanted to be more knowledgeable about how best to manage my personal finances. It was an enlightening course that sparked a lifelong passion for personal finance. Through the years, I focused on personal finance, including reading the latest books on the subject and subscribing to personal finance magazines. I managed my personal finances and investments for decades, based on this continuous knowledge until I became too busy to effectively manage them.

During the years I pursued my Ph.D., I thought about what I would do next. I was not interested in teaching; I felt I did not have the patience needed to work with students. However, I loved research, so I focused on opportunities in industrial research organizations. I also considered large companies, primarily in development, to broaden my opportunities. I signed up for interviews through Rice's Career Development department and leveraged my network for opportunities. At the time Bell Labs was in the middle of a hiring freeze, so even though they sponsored my graduate school education, they were unable to offer me a job.

When I discussed IBM employment opportunities at a career fair on campus, the IBM employee informed me that I was overqualified. She said she did not have opportunities for me. Of course, I knew IBM employed Ph.D.'s so I knew she was ill informed. I made a mental note to try other options to inquire about IBM Research opportunities. I spoke to other companies and even went on interviews to their sites, including Hughes Aircraft Company in the Los Angeles area, and development organizations at IBM in Research Triangle Park, North Carolina (NC).

One day, as I walked into my office later than I typically arrive, there was a man there talking to one of my office mates. He was very friendly, even introducing himself to me as I walked into the office. He mentioned he wanted to speak to me after his conversation with my office mate, which he did. He informed me that he was a Rice alumnus who worked for IBM Research. He was there to recruit Rice Ph.D. students for IBM. He asked me about my research and when I was graduating. It turned out my research was the type that interested him, and IBM, and he was thrilled that I would be graduating in a couple of months. He said he would follow up with me to arrange an interview trip soon.

In the meantime, he asked if anyone from the department informed me of his pending visit to campus. He said he reached out to the ECE department weeks prior to his visit, informed them he would be coming to recruit graduating Ph.D. students in specific areas he mentioned. He asked them to schedule meetings for him to talk to these students during his visit. I informed him that no one had told me about his pending visit. In fact, I would not have met him had I not walked into my office while he was there. He was perplexed about why no one told me about him, and so was I. Now I can have an educated guess about why I was not told, but I do not have any facts to substantiate such a claim. I therefore just choose to share the facts with you. He informed the office that he was coming to look for students like me, and I was not told.

He went back to IBM, and within a couple of weeks I scheduled an interview trip, not only with IBM Research in Yorktown Heights, New York but also with one of IBM's development sites in Poughkeepsie, New York. The IBM Research interview required that I present my work at a Ph.D. applicant seminar, which is like presenting at a technical conference. I had been immersed in the hostile research community for years at that point. I had presented my work several times prior to this interview, primarily at internal department seminars at Rice. Since I had spent years working and presenting on this in a research environment, including anticipating the types of questions to be asked, I was ready.

I flew into New York City the night before and arrived at IBM Research early on Thursday morning, January 28, 1988. I was greeted by Fran, a highly regarded computer science researcher at IBM and globally. Fran eventually became the first woman to become an IBM Fellow, the highest technical position at IBM. One of her actions in helping women succeed at that level at IBM, and in the field in general, was to host women who came to interview at IBM Research. I did not know of Fran at the time. I just knew she was warm and friendly, which started my day off on the right foot. As my host, Fran was responsible for putting together my interview schedule, ensuring I moved efficiently from one interview to the next and scheduling lunch and dinner with IBMers.

The seminar went very well. There were a few challenging questions but nothing too difficult to handle. Most of the attendees were not experts in the field. I spent time educating them on some technical specifics. It was a very engaging presentation. Fran ensured my full day of interviews went well. I only had one day at IBM Research, then another day at IBM's Poughkeepsie site. Fran recommended that I drive to Poughkeepsie after my research interviews, recommending a restaurant for me to have dinner that evening in Poughkeepsie. I thought the day went very well, and there were a couple of people very interested in my work. In addition, I was excited about the work done there and could see myself joining the research team.

I made it safely to Poughkeepsie and had a nice dinner. I had a half-day of interviews scheduled the next day, then I would drive back to NYC for a flight back to Houston. My interview in Poughkeepsie was different. I was with a team of solution architects, many of whom were nearing retirement. I understood they were looking for specific types of candidates with the type of background that would fit this highly regarded area. I gave a presentation on my work in the morning, then met with several people from the team for interviews. All of them except the manager were amazingly surprised at my background, my command of my area of expertise, and my broader knowledge and understanding of the field. From the looks of their faces, they could not believe what they were seeing and hearing. I had lunch with the manager before I left for the airport. He was very friendly and supportive. However, there was no way I was going to come to Poughkeepsie and work in this department. I was not paranoid, I was not imagining things, I knew what I heard and saw. It was not going to happen.

On my drive back to the airport and my flight back to Houston, I focused on the possibilities of working at the IBM T.J. Watson Research Center in Yorktown Heights, New York. Arguably one of the world's premier industrial research organizations for my field, this was my first choice. I was excited.

I made it back to Houston and made plans to complete the writing of my dissertation and scheduled my thesis defense. After coordinating the availability for my committee members, including my advisor still living in the San Francisco Bay Area, I scheduled my Ph.D. Public Oral Examination for Friday, April 8, 1988, at 3:00 PM. I provided my committee with a copy of my dissertation. They had ample time to review it, in preparation for my defense, and provide me with feedback to enhance my final copy. Members of my family from Lake Charles planned to be there for my defense. This included MaMa, MaMe, Aunt Rosa Bea, Aunt Mae Ruth, Aunt Roy Lee, and Uncle Noah. In addition, Darlene, Kimberly, and Schirrell—all living in Houston—attended, as did my boyfriend.

MaMe arrived several days before the event, she was so excited. She watched quietly as I rehearsed my presentation, repeatedly until I was satisfied with the flow. It reminded me of the days years earlier when I practiced songs on the piano repeatedly. On the day of the event all my family arrived early and sat in the back of the room to give me support. Several professors and fellow students arrived, and finally my committee; then I began.

I spent about an hour presenting my work, something I had done many times before. My committee asked a few challenging questions which I sufficiently answered. Others asked questions as well. I was able to answer all of them to their satisfaction. After about 90 minutes, I was finished. I passed! At that point, I was a doctor. I was overjoyed and relieved at the same time. My family could not understand anything I said, but they were happy I passed. My committee thanked me, discussed the final processes for completing my dissertation and getting their signatures, then went on their way. It was Friday, I was done, and I took my family for a tour of the campus. We all went to the quadrangle, surrounded the statue of William Marsh Rice, and took pictures with big smiles.

As my tour with my family was completing, I ran into the professor I met during my first day on campus, the *confidence man*. He attended my defense and had this big smile on his face. He came to me excited and told me I had done an outstanding job. He told me "I don't have to ask you if you passed, I know you passed. The committee would be crazy if they did not pass you". I told him thank you, but mentally I thought, *mission accomplished*. I made a believer out of him!

I received a job offer from the IBM T.J. Watson Research Center in Yorktown Heights, New York. It was the one I wanted so I was so excited. I accepted. I would start work on June 27, 1988. In the interim, I was given the opportunity to travel to Westchester County, New York, to look for a place to stay. I took advantage of this and found an apartment in Mount Kisco, New York. As a result, the next chapter in my life was in place. Now I focused on getting new transportation and graduation.

Throughout my college and graduate school experience, I had my same Chevy Chevette. It was barely hanging on, so it was time for a new car. I did a little research on the type of cars I liked and settled on a Volkswagen Jetta. I bought a car with manual transmission, it was cheaper. I had spent time years earlier learning how to drive one from Dave, MaMe's boyfriend. However, I did not quite get the hang of it. I had established good credit based on my Chevette car payments—even though it was not in my name. I and my mother convinced the dealership that I made every car note payment. In addition, I had an offer letter from IBM that established my income, so I did not have any issues getting the car, which I bought right before graduation. After a few days of jumping around as I learned how to use the manual transmission, I got the hang of it and was good to go.

The 75th commencement exercise for Rice University was scheduled for Saturday, May 7, 1988, at 9 AM in the Academic Quadrangle. My family was so excited about this event. In fact, three of my father's siblings Dora, Phyllis, and William Louis, and his wife, Mary, and cousins Jammie and Victoria, all from the Washington, DC area, planned to attend. I was the first doctor in my father's family, and the second in my mother's family. My cousin, Bryan A. Lewis, earned a Ph.D. in microbiology years earlier from the University of Southern Mississippi in Hattiesburg. In fact, for some in my father's family, this was their first time flying; they were thrilled.

On the graduation day, both my family from the DC area and from Lake Charles were there to support me, along with some friends. As I waited in line in my cap and gown for the procession to begin, I thought about the journey that got me to this place. Through ten years of highs and lows, I always had strong support from my family. I was grateful. I also received support from friends, acquaintances, and professors, most especially my advisor, Dr. Fayè A. Briggs, in this journey. My appreciation of their love and support will remain with me for a lifetime.

However, the strongest emotion I felt that day was relief. After ten long years of study, focus, and sometimes sheer exhaustion, I was done. I thought there would be no more education for me. I was completely wrong about this, as I have become passionate about lifetime learning. However, at that point, I was ending a chapter that, mentally, was one of the most challenging in my life. I was just happy it was over.

The commencement was very nice. My fellow graduates and I were happy about the end of this chapter and the beginning of a new one. It was a cause for celebration. I took many pictures with my family that I have cherished over the years. At the time, I did not know I was the first Black woman to earn a Ph.D. in electrical and computer engineering. That would come later. I and my family just cherished the moment of a significant milestone achieved.

In the next few weeks before my move to New York, I attended a few events. First, my family planned and hosted a reception in my honor in the family center at my home church in Lake Charles. I was also the guest speaker during the annual honors day for graduates at this same church. Finally, I attended my ten-year high school reunion in June 1988. It was great to see my fellow Lake Charles High School Class of '78 graduates and catch up on our lives. It turned out I was the first to earn a Ph.D. from this class.

There were two other classmates who subsequently earned Ph.D.'s. Cathleen Jones earned her Ph.D. in Physics as I have previously mentioned. Cassandra Simon earned her Ph.D. in Social Work from the University of Texas at Arlington in 1992. She is an Assistant Professor in the Department of Social Work at the University of Alabama at Tuscaloosa. Both were part of the group of six valedictorians in our class. What is so interesting about our small Ph.D. group is all three of us are women, and two of the three are Black women, including Cassandra. This is from an integrated public high school in the deep south that was approximately 60% White at the time.

Once all the festivities and celebrations ended, I was back in Houston to prepare for my move to Westchester County, New York, and to commence what would be a historic career in a profession I loved and was born to make global contributions. At the time, I was just thrilled to prepare to finally join the work force!

4

Blazing the Trail

CHAPTER 8

A New Life in Westchester

I WAS EXCITED AS I PREPARED to move to the New York City Metropolitan Area. I assisted the movers who came to pack up my furniture and other things for the long trip. I also thought about the opportunities and prospects as I commenced this next chapter in my life. My boyfriend came with me, as we were planning a life and future together. Once the movers completed their tasks and the truck left, we completed packing up my new car and headed west. We picked up MaMe along the way, as she was going to help us get settled in our new home. In a short time, we were on the road. After a couple of days and stops along the way, we arrived at Mt. Kisco, New York and unpacked the car. The movers arrived shortly after we did. It took a couple of days after everything was unloaded to get everything unpacked and put away. We were then able to relax and explore our new home. MaMe left to go back home shortly after my first day of work.

I arrived at work on June 27, 1988, starting as a Research Staff Member (RSM). This is a position unique to IBM Research. In fact, one can have the position of RSM for their entire IBM career. I therefore did not think about promotions. My office was at a satellite location in Hawthorne, New York, and not the main research facility in Yorktown Heights, New York. This location contained the computer-focused and other similar researchers. It was a great day as I was onboarding with all the human resources-related paper-work, followed by moving to my department. I met my new coworkers, including Caroline Benveniste who I would work closely with for several years and who became a lifelong friend.

My graduate school research, as well as my initial IBM research, focused on parallel processing, a relatively new concept at the time. Parallel processing potentially enables a reduction in the time needed to execute computer programs and an increase in a computer's computational capability. An instance of a computer program is broken into several computational units, with each unit executing on a separate processor simultaneously, hence executing in parallel. All these multiple processors, or multiprocessors, are part of the same computer.

For an analogous example, consider a large field, *e.g.*, one acre, with high grass that needs to be cut. One may have a lawn mower that can cut the field in about an hour, or four lawn mowers can be used to cut the same field. Furthermore, one could divide the field into four sub-acres, each a quarter of an acre in size. Each lawn mower would cut each quarter of an acre at the same time, in parallel, with the entire field completed in 15 minutes, reducing the single lawn mower time by four. This significantly improves the time needed to cut the field. Likewise, parallel processing can reduce computer algorithmic execution times and increase computer computational capability.

My IBM Research group was working on the Research Parallel Processing Prototype (RP3). This was an early-stage multiprocessor system designed to analyze, support, and compare several parallel computational models for computationally intensive and other applications. Many applications such as numerical weather forecasting, structural simulation, computational drug discovery, and aircraft simulation used such high-performance machines. The RP3 was designed to accommodate up to 512 processors using a less complex computer instruction set architecture than was traditional at the time.

When I joined the RP3 team, the machine was not a shared memory machine; all processors did not share the same computer memory. Since shared memory multiprocessors were the focus of my Ph.D. dissertation, my job was to conduct research to explore design alternatives for enhancing the RP3 architecture for shared memory. I used as a foundation for this work a simulator that Caroline developed. I enhanced it to accommodate the performance evaluation of various shared memory cache coherence protocols. It was a trace-driven simulator, and I obtained traces of computationally intensive applications from some of my fellow RSMs at the research center. This was an extension of my Ph.D. research, so I was excited about the opportunity to make a significant contribution to a bleeding-edge research project that was widely known and regarded globally. I started right away.

One of the measures of technical research success in my field of endeavor, computer architecture, high-performance computing (supercomputers), and performance evaluation, was determined by the number of a researcher's peer-reviewed technical papers accepted and presented at competitive conferences. This evaluation of work was like that of an academic professor developing their portfolio of work for tenure. The more work presented at highly respected conferences, and cited by others in their publications, the better. In IBM Research, part of my work performance evaluation was based on papers presented at highly regarded conferences, on whether other IBM researchers and those in development leveraged the work as a valuable contribution, and, to some extent, on patent applications.

Within several months of starting work at IBM, I obtained results that assisted other RSMs in their related projects. For example, I conducted a study of the workload characteristics of parallel applications to assist in focusing on the design alternatives for a shared memory RP3. The work was also used by those designing other parts of the machine or in optimizing parallel applications in general. Shortly thereafter, I submitted papers to be published on this work. A few of them were accepted. For example, two papers were accepted to the International Conference on Parallel Processing, held in University Park, Pennsylvania, in August 1989. One of these two was a portion of my Ph.D. thesis from Rice University, and the other focused on my memory reference behavior work. Subsequent papers were submitted, accepted, and presented at the International Symposium on Shared Memory Multiprocessing in Tokyo, Japan (April 1991) and the International Conference on Parallel Processing in Austin, Texas (August 1991).

I was able to learn about the advantages and disadvantages of several design alternatives for cache coherence protocols, as part of my shared memory focus. As I discussed the preliminary results with my manager, he became excited and informed me that this work could result in obtaining a patent. I asked him how this could be, as I had yet to build anything. That's when I learned that a working prototype is not required to file a patent application. One must only describe the invention in such a manner that someone with an ordinary level of expertise in the area can build the invention. I learned that since I was contributing to knowledge, I was an expert in this area and no one (globally) had produced such results based on the design alternatives and I had performance numbers to quantify its advantages, as my ideas were good candidates for potential patents.

I was not completely convinced because I thought one had to design and build an invention that was a game changer. Something that completely revolutionized the way our global society lives or functions. An example was the personal computer, which had been invented for commercial use more than a decade earlier. However, I agreed to move forward with the process because this would be a learning experience, and I just might get a patent. Discussions with my manager, and my next manager, resulted in a handful of ideas to improve my design. As a result, we initiated the internal IBM review process for potential patent applications. This resulted in my first patent application. *Optimum Write-back Strategy for Directory-Based Cache Coherence Protocols* was filed on May 23, 1991, at the US Patent and Trademark Office (USPTO). Subsequent patent applications on this invention were filed in Canada and Japan. The patent was issued by USPTO on May 17, 1994.

There were two additional types of outcomes for ideas submitted for internal review. They included: 1) publishing the idea in the public domain and 2) closure. The objective of the public disclosure is to prohibit others from seeking intellectual property (IP) protection for the idea. It is typically published via an IBM Technical Disclosure Bulletin, and later IP.com. Closure resulted in no further consideration of the idea. One of our ideas was published in the technical disclosure bulletin in 1990 and was later published on IP.com in March 2016. The remaining ideas were closed.

While I was getting acclimated to my new job and surroundings, my boyfriend and I decided to get married. He secured a job in Manhattan shortly after we arrived, and we subsequently set our wedding date for February 11, 1989. The wedding was held in Lake

Charles, and I spent several months planning it from New York. I also worked with Aunt Mae Ruth and Aunt Roy Lee, who were our wedding planners. MaMe came back to Mt. Kisco to help plan the wedding, including helping me shop for my wedding gown. I settled on one I found in the garment district in Manhattan. It was an exciting and stressful time, as I was planning a wedding, adjusting to living in a new region of the country, and making an impact with my new job. However, my fiancé and I were about to do it with minimal drama and confusion.

We had a beautiful wedding weekend. The wedding rehearsal and dinner were right before the big day, and it went off without a hitch. My aunts were methodical and efficient in ensuring everyone knew their roles and positions for the ceremony.

It was cloudy on the Saturday morning of our big day; however, by the time our wedding started, it was a beautiful and sunny winter day. I had my nails done a few days earlier. I was not used to long nails and broke a couple of them within hours of leaving the nail shop. I went back to get them repaired. On that Saturday morning, I went to get my hair done, while my aunts and MaMe were busy with the final wedding logistics. Also, I visited MaMa, at her request, to fix her hair. I was her first granddaughter to be married at a wedding in town, and she wanted to look great as part of the festivities.

We had two bridesmaids and groomsmen, as well as the maid of honor and best man as part of the bridal party. Our colors were red and ivory for this pre-Valentine's Day event. Everyone arrived on time, and we started at the appointed time. It was a beautiful religious ceremony, followed by a memorable reception.

We honeymooned in Maui, Hawaii. After years of dreaming of traveling to this place, I was ecstatic and happy that we arrived and had a fabulous time.

When we arrived home, we joined the Antioch Baptist Church in Bedford Hills, New York. I sang in the choir and became a Sunday School teacher. I also became active in the local chapter of Delta Sigma Theta Sorority, Inc., the Westchester Alumnae Chapter. I worked on various committees in the chapter and worked tirelessly in many of the chapter's community activities. In general, I was happy and productive in my career and making a difference in my church and community. We created an exciting, fulfilling, and meaningful life in Westchester County.

Early in my tenure at IBM Research, I learned that RSMs were required to give a first-year review sometime after their first-year anniversary. My first-year review was scheduled for November 1989, which turned out to be a 17-month review. As previously mentioned, RSMs were evaluated according to their substantive contributions to other IBM business units, contributions to knowledge in their area of expertise, IP contributions, and other similar activities. I presented the results of my memory reference behavior for computationally intensive engineering and scientific applications in parallel processors and my research on the design and simulation of cache coherence protocols. I presented the IBM impact of this work, as well as its global impact.

In addition to the published papers and inventions, my work was leveraged by teams within IBM Research and other parts of the company, including development divisions working on the design of specific mid-range and mainframe systems. I was also a technical session chair of an international technical conference on parallel processing. My first-year review was a great presentation with positive feedback. In fact, my second-level manager emphasized this is the type of good, solid work he likes to see from our new RSMs. He mentioned he sat in on many first-year reviews that did not meet the standard. It was excellent feedback on my initial work at IBM. I was happy to be making a significant contribution.

I continued to conduct research in this area for a couple of years. The results of my memory reference behavior work were leveraged and embraced early. For example, one of the RSMs had previously conducted seminal work on Single Program Multiple Data (SPMD), an area of parallel computationally intensive applications. Once she saw my results, she invited me to share my work with her team. She later recommended that I write a paper on this work to be included in the *International Journal of High-Speed Computing*, which I did. "An Evaluation of the Memory Reference Behavior of Engineering/Scientific Applications in Parallel Systems" was published in this journal in 1989. In addition, she invited me to present my work at a workshop at the Third International Conference on Supercomputing in Crete, Greece (June 1989) a couple of weeks before the scheduled workshop. This was all one year after I started working at IBM, which was amazing.

I was delighted as I prepared to travel to the Greek Isles for this supercomputing conference. Unfortunately, I did not have a passport, and I subsequently learned that I would not be able to get one and have sufficient time to travel to Crete to present. I was unable to attend. Given my dream of travel as a teenager, I was very disappointed about this. However, I still went through the process of getting a passport and vowed to minimize the likelihood of encountering this type of dilemma in the future. I also thought I would have another opportunity to visit the Greek Isles in the future. By the summer of 2023, I had yet to go but I planned to travel there soon.

However, I was able to present at conferences in University Park, Pennsylvania; Tokyo, Japan; and Austin, Texas. I was really excited about the opportunity to travel to Tokyo. I had not been to the land of the rising sun and the country of my birth, Japan, since I was nine months old when my parents moved back to the United States. (This was also the last time I had a passport.) I thought it was interesting that the first foreign country I visited, outside of North America, since I was a baby, was also the country of my birth.

I had been tapped to help IBM HR with recruiting at the national convention of the National Society of Black Engineers (NSBE). It was held in Los Angeles just prior to traveling to Tokyo. NSBE is the largest student-run organization in the country. Their national conventions are attended by tens of thousands of students. I was looking forward to attending the convention as well.

My husband planned to travel with me to Los Angeles and Tokyo. We planned to extend our stay in Tokyo for a vacation, then on to Hong Kong, with great anticipation. The NSBE conference in Los Angeles was fantastic. While we both had been to the LA area previously, we dedicated some time for sightseeing, visiting sites we had yet to see. We traveled to Hollywood, including the walk of fame and the wax museum, Rodeo Drive and other sites in Beverly Hills, and additional selected areas.

Unfortunately, I caught a cold during this spring trip (April 1991). I tried to take over the counter medication to get better before our flight to Tokyo. I felt a little better and continued to Tokyo. By the time we arrived shortly before dusk at Narita Airport, I was feeling horrible. All I wanted to do was to go to bed and get some rest. It was a long ride to the hotel from the airport, but I managed to find the strength to see the sights along the way. Tokyo is a very large city, and I had an eyeful seeing bright lights. I recall seeing company after company, all that I recognized, in bright lights along the way. This included Sony, Nissan, Mitsubishi, Toyota, and Yamaha. This did not seem to be such a foreign land.

I managed to get more over-the-counter medication from the hotel gift shop. It was a challenge just to buy something, given that I do not speak Japanese. While we stayed at a hotel with English-speaking workers, non were onsite when I went looking for medication. However, I was able to succeed in getting what I needed using nonverbal communication. I went to our hotel room, took the medication, and went to sleep. Over time I felt much better and was able to attend all sessions of the international shared memory conference. I was also able to successfully present my paper and had a very engaging discussion about possibilities at the end of the presentation. I did some networking while there, including engaging with others regarding their presentations. Overall, it was a very enlightening and enjoyable experience.

In the meantime, my husband did some sightseeing as a tourist while I attended the conference. Unfortunately, he caught the cold I had. He took the over-the-counter cold medicine I used, but he did not get better. To make matters worse, he was very uncomfortable with the hotel's short bed that was low to the floor, as he is about 6 feet 5 inches tall and was 220 lbs at the time. Even his ride on the bus from the airport to the hotel was uncomfortable. Japanese are typically not that large or tall. I made plans to take him to the hospital. I had a travel guide that included the closest hospitals to the hotel with English-speaking workers. I had the hotel staff at the front desk write down his symptoms in Japanese to give to the hospital staff, just in case. I also had them write our destination request, to and from the hospital, in Japanese to give to the taxi drivers.

We arrived at the hospital and after initial registration, waited to be served. While waiting, an American student, suspecting we were Americans, came over and introduced himself. We had a good conversation. He spoke Japanese and was able to let us know when they called my husband's name. The doctor did not speak English, but the nurse did. She served as the interpreter for the doctor. I remember her asking how much he weighed, in kilograms. I pulled out my calculator to make the calculation. Before I finished, she looked at him and assumed he weighed about 100 kilograms, she was spot on. I was impressed. We only spent a few minutes with the doctor. He prescribed antibiotics for him, and we went to the hospital pharmacy with the prescription. We waited and waited for them to call my husband's name. After a considerable amount of time, I went to the window to check. The medicine had been ready for quite a while, but they butchered the pronunciation of his name, we did not know.

Once we got his medication and made it back to the hotel, my husband took his initial dose and was finally able to get some rest. He recovered quickly, so we were able to enjoy our remaining days in Tokyo. One thing that I recall that really stood out was his height. Everywhere we went, children would stare at him, and adults would look at him through the corner of their eyes. It was clear that few had encountered seeing someone of his height. It was comical to us. Also, we were able to navigate the streets of Tokyo, including the trains and restaurants, because there were pictures everywhere. The restaurants had pictures of their menu options, the trains had graphical pictures, so it was relatively easy to navigate. One time, a Japanese man was so excited to practice English that he literally got in our faces, our space, and started speaking to us in English. He was thrilled. One of my thoughts was *how did he know we spoke English?* as we were not talking during that time. Then I assumed he was just guessing. In general, we had a wonderful stay, then prepared for our next destination, Hong Kong.

Hong Kong is a densely populated coastal city of approximately 428 square miles in east Asia. It is located along the southeastern coast of China at the mouth of the eastern Pearl River Delta. The city is officially known as the Hong Kong Special Administrative Region of the People's Republic of China. We visited Hong Kong prior to its handover to China by the British in 1997. During our visit, Hong Kong was considered a British Colony.

Hong Kong consists of three basic regions: Hong Kong Island, Kowloon, and the New Territories. It is a city of stunning natural landscapes and urban architectures and environments. Its Central Business District (CBD) on Hong Kong Island is a major global financial and business hub containing many multinational companies. Hong Kong also has many mountains, hills, and peaks, with one of its most famous the Victoria Peak which has a majestic view of the city.

Our entire time in Hong Kong was vacation. We had both recovered from our colds, so we were healthy and energetic for the trip. Our plane approached landing at the airport just after sundown. (This was the old Hong Kong International Airport, Kai Tak Airport. The new Hong Kong International Airport, Chek Lap Kok Airport, opened for commercial operation in 1998.) We flew over Victoria Harbour and Kowloon Bay before landing at the airport, which was on a peninsula and part of Kowloon. Seeing the night lights of the skyscrapers on Hong Kong Island and the mountains of Kowloon to the north and the waters of the harbor and bay was simply magnificent and awe inspiring. It was one of the most beautiful skylines I had ever seen.

We stayed in a hotel in Kowloon that was a short walk from one of its major streets, Nathan Road. We spent most of our time there just walking the streets of Kowloon. We spoke to people from around the world and ran into several Americans who recognized our American accent. We went on tours around Kowloon and Hong Kong Island, including visiting the CBD, numerous parks, Victoria Peak at 1181 feet, and cruising Victoria Harbour. It was during our mornings in Hong Kong, and everywhere we went, that I noticed people practicing Tai Chi. Their slow, intentional, methodical, spiritual movements were something to behold and admire.

My husband wanted to get some tailored suits made for him during this trip. We found a great tailor who was able to make fine, high-quality suits in just a few days. Our visit to Hong Kong lasted only a few days, but they were enjoyable and memorable. However, our visit came to an end, and we embarked on our long trip home. We made it safely back to New York and prepared to go back to work. Shortly thereafter, while I was at the office, I ran into the Computer Science Director at IBM Research. He mentioned that he had recently spoken to the chair of the conference I attended in Tokyo. He was a good friend of the director and told him he was very pleased with my presentation and subsequent discussions at the conference. My director praised me for receiving such excellent feedback on my work and encouraged me to keep up the good work. I was so happy to hear this.

About a week after we returned from our trip to Asia, my husband awakened in the middle of the night and left the apartment. I was trying to determine what was happening. He came back about 45 minutes later, being very upset. He had taken his new tailored suits, as well as one of my older suits, to the dry cleaners. He had seen a large fire from our apartment window in the direction of the cleaners. He could not wait until daylight, he had to see if the business was on fire—and it was. In fact, it had burned to the ground so there was no hope of recovering our clothes. Their insurance paid for the value of our clothes that were destroyed. He was able to call the tailor, who still had all the details of his suits, to have them remade. He received his package containing the suits about a week later.

My first couple of years at IBM were successful. I made an immediate impact and was able to be recognized as such by my peers, other colleagues in supercomputing and computer architecture, and my management. I was happy to be off to a good start.

CHAPTER 9

Moving on Up

M Y LIFE IN WESTCHESTER was balanced, and I was happy. I recall a conversation over a meal I had one day with my sorority sister. Once she learned about my background, and my work, she became very excited. She mentioned there could not be too many people in this country who look like us with your background. She said that I was a role model, and I should be visible to encourage and inspire young people. At the time I was so busy trying to set up a great life that I did not seriously think about this, but she planted the seed.

Shortly after that conversation, I started to get requests for the type of visibility my soror encouraged. I was invited to be the keynote speaker for the 30th Anniversary Celebration for Southern University's College of Engineering. I also appeared in several IBM advertisements or was profiled in a few publications, some of which included *The Black Collegian, Engineering Horizons,* and *Careers and the Engineer,* all in 1991. I appeared a few years later in the 1995 IBM Annual Report, a *Women in Computer Science* careers booklet (1996) and *Science* magazine (March 29, 1006). I was featured in the documentary *Minerva's Machine: Women in Computing,* which appeared on PBS in 1996.

In STEM environments, excellent research happens when people from multifarious backgrounds come together where they are supported, valued, respected, and highly regarded. This is true independent of the type of research organization: academic, industrial, or governmental. Such an environment optimizes a person's ability

DOI: 10.1201/9781032724270-13

to fully energize and leverage their innate abilities, skills, and experiences. This facilitates deep technical exchanges, intellectually stimulating conversations, and potentially constructive criticisms that are important for breakthroughs in innovation and creativity. It enables the greatest innovation for the team, the organization, and our global society.

Research subject matter experts are the best on typically a narrow subject. Such an individual must be able to sufficiently respond to any discussion or challenge on the topic. The expert must be thoroughly knowledgeable on the topic, having studied and examined past and current research efforts. They should have knowledge about the advantages and disadvantages of methodologies used for the state-of-the-art, as well as of potential areas for future research and further advancement. When presenting their work, the expert needs to think about and consider all potential questions that may be asked, including other approaches and whataboutisms. They must have well-thought-out responses to each potential question, or any other material matter that may surface as a part of detailed engagement with others. This is the typical methodology for advancement in the field.

A significant number of people in the STEM research community are pleasant, thorough, and firm when engaging with experts in the field. However, many others, whether reviewers, evaluators, challengers, or audience members, use mean-spirited and nasty methods for asserting their views or asking questions. Some can be passionately hostile in sharing their perspectives. It can be unsettling to the presenter, even when thoroughly prepared. It takes a strong, confident, and competent individual who is made of steel and focused to work, thrive, and succeed in such an environment. This was the environment in which I worked at IBM Research. It enabled me to be at my best every day and to engage in broadening, intellectually stimulating, and challenging conversations. I was tapping into my highest level of brainpower. I was in my element!

In the Spring 1991, the RP3 Research Project was shutting down. My tenure as part of this project was very good. I extended my Ph.D. thesis research during my early IBM Research years. I was the expert and successfully defended my work in the research environment, both internally at IBM and in the broader research community. Now I was looking for other research opportunities within

IBM. While I looked for areas that interested me, unlike my previous research, I would be moving into an area where I was no longer the most knowledgeable.

I joined the research team developing the Vulcan machine. It was designed to be a massively parallel machine with up to 32,000+ processors. This was a unique system with very few in the world that compared to its performance potential. However, there was little focus on the input/output (I/O) performance of the machine. Here, I/O refers to the machine's ability to transfer massive amounts of data from its external data storage to its internal memory. This memory is located close to the processor to enable fast access to data for high performance. There was a critical need to quickly transfer the data into (input) and out of (output) this processor-associated memory. This was an area that interested me and that few people had studied. It was an opportunity to contribute to an important research area and become an expert.

There was no work done on the design and implementation of an associated parallel file system. A component of this file system controls the movement of the data into and out of the machine. Furthermore, no one focused on the potential performance evaluation of algorithms or memory references for such a massive machine. This was bleeding-edge research, and I was galvanized by the opportunities to be a pioneer in the design and development of such massive supercomputers.

I became part of a small team that focused on the I/O subsystem, the parallel file system, and the performance evaluation of Vulcan. As we began initial discussions on this project, one of our first objectives was to name the file system. Vulcan was named after the mythological Roman god of fire, metalworking, and the forge. We wanted to keep the same theme, focusing on Greek gods or goddesses whose name begins with a "V". While we considered Venus, we settled on Vesta because it was lesser known, just like our file system, and it would not be confused with the planet. Vesta is the Roman goddess of hearth, home, and family and is closely associated with fire. Thus became the birth of the Vesta Parallel File System (VPFS).

There were five members of our team. We focused on the design and performance evaluation of VPFS, as well as the performance evaluation of the parallel I/O system. We had many brainstorming sessions focusing on the design of VPFS. We examined this area with precision, thinking about all possible options and areas to pursue. We methodically focused on design alternatives, discussing their pros and cons. We were all Ph.D.'s immersed in the STEM research culture. We knew this was required not only to facilitate breakthrough innovation but to also prepare for challenges to our efforts, some of them brutal and vicious.

We worked well together. We also had similar interests in other areas. For example, we all loved to eat, and we regularly went out to lunch. We would pick a day, say June 15. We knew that somewhere in the world, somebody was born on June 15, so we went out to lunch on that day to celebrate their birthday. Also, from time to time, the main facility of IBM T.J. Watson Research Center would host external conferences. On those days, we would meet just outside of the auditorium where snacks were provided during the breaks. This was an excellent opportunity for us to learn about the technical presentations of the conference while we ate the free snacks and beverages. We especially enjoyed the afternoon snacks. They were typically fresh-baked cookies—I know, we were mischievous. We were a great team that produced outstanding research results.

We ultimately completed an initial design, which was led by two team members. They also worked to implement the initial version of VPFS. I then leveraged the design to develop a simulator of the Vulcan I/O subsystem. It was used to evaluate the machine's I/O performance and potential memory reference behavior. Working together with the small team in various capacities, we wrote and submitted papers to various conferences. The papers I coauthored were presented at workshops and conferences, including, but not limited to, Supercomputing '93, the International Parallel Processing Symposium (1993, 1994, and 1995), and the International Conference on Supercomputing in Barcelona, Spain (1995).

Our work was also published as chapters in books and the *IBM Systems Journal*. I was invited to be a member of the program committee for a conference on parallel and distributed systems and chaired technical sessions at similar conferences. In addition, I was invited to present my work and give technical lectures at universities and workshops. Examples include lectures at the University of California at Berkeley and Rice University, and at a workshop on parallel I/O as part of a conference in Cancun, Mexico (1995).

Furthermore, I obtained four patents as a coinventor for this and similar work. Two of them were in the top 30% of all patents issued to IBM Research in the year of issue.

There were many times where we actively engaged in brainstorming sessions over the years. Some were planned, and some were extemporaneous. For example, we had many discussions with the team and sometimes others during lunch in the cafeteria. We would use the napkins on the table to draw illustrations as we engaged. This is a popular activity for engineers. I recall one time we had a conversation about a typical technical design, then left the cafeteria and went back to work.

Several weeks later, one of my team members came to my office. He reminded me of our previous lunch conversation and informed me that someone at the lunch table, although not one of our five-person team members, had taken the idea, written it up, and submitted it to be reviewed for a potential patent application. We were dumbfounded. We subsequently learned that a member of the patent review board responsible for reviewing such submissions recognized the idea, as he was also sitting at the cafeteria table with us during the discussion. He therefore recommended a close for the submission. It was a wake-up call to me to be more careful and discerning about my technical discussions in the future.

As part of the process, the team encountered a plethora of feedback on our collection of work. It was mostly positive and helpful. Many suggested additional areas to pursue that we had not thought about. In some instances, it was openly hostile; however, we had prepared for such situations during our brainstorming sessions, and we were able to address the substantive issues raised. In some situations, getting together to have our favorite beverage after a grueling session was medicinal.

These presentations enabled me to continue with my love for travel, both throughout the United States and around the world. When I traveled outside of the country, I typically stayed a few days after the event for vacation. My husband traveled with me to Barcelona and Cancun for these vacations. On our way to Barcelona, we had a long layover in Paris, France. We took advantage of this to go on a mini tour of the area. Once in Barcelona, and when my duties with the supercomputing conference were complete, we had a lovely time touring the city. Although we spoke little Spanish, it was easy to get around, primarily using the metro system. We strolled through La Rambla and visited the Sagrada Familia, a large, magnificent, unfinished church designed by Antoni Gaudi. We took siestas during the day and adjusted to the late-night meals. We also toured the site of the Barcelona 1992 Olympics. We sat out on the patio of a local restaurant with a specular view of the Mediterranean Sea. It was a beautiful sunny day, and I recall thinking about the African continent just on the other side of the body of water. At the time it was the closest I had been to Africa, and I felt a slight longing to be on the continent. We had a great trip to Barcelona!

Earlier in 1992, we traveled to Cancun. It was a wonderful vacation after my technical work was done. We spent time on the beach and toured the Cancun community, as well as other surrounding communities. For example, we spent a day on a boat trip visiting Isla Mujeres, an island off the coast of the Yucatan Peninsula. We also spent a day visiting the Tulum Mayan ruins. Tulum was a pre-Columbian Mayan city that was a major port. It was a very educational and informative journey. On another tour of a Mexican city, my husband convinced the driver, tour guide, and all other tourists on the tour bus to ditch the original tour and visit places patronized by the locals. I recall visiting a local taco stand serving Mexican tacos as opposed to the Tex-Mex ones I was used to. It was barely standing on the side of the road, about a block from the beach. They were the best tacos I have ever had. It was a fantastic trip that we enjoyed immensely!

IBM Research's objective was to be famous for science and vital to IBM. We were encouraged to make contacts in development divisions and engage in discussions about our work. The objective was to ultimately transfer the technology to a development division within the company that would then develop a product based on our work. I connected with many people, primarily within IBM's division that develops high-end computers. They were located primarily in Kingston, New York, and Poughkeepsie, New York. I spent many days traveling to these locations to present my results and engage in discussions.

Vulcan was enhanced to develop an IBM product, eventually becoming the IBM RS/6000 Scalable POWERparallel (SP) machine. The results I presented to the SP design teams assisted them in selecting from several design alternatives. In addition, the VPFS development team was able to develop and offer a parallel file system to the market. A notable fact about the IBM SP machine is that it is the base machine for IBM Deep Blue, its world-famous chess machine. The Deep Blue team essentially took the IBM SP machine and customized it, using hardware accelerators for chess among other applications. This machine then played the world chess champion at the time, Gary Kasparov, in 1996 and lost two games to four in a six-game match. They played another six-game match in 1997, and this time Deep Blue won by winning two games and drawing on three. It was incredibly exciting for us, although we realized there were relatively few people worldwide cheering for the machine.

I was very active professionally during this time. Years earlier, I met a woman named Anita Borg in the bathroom of a conference. She informed me the few women attending the conference were getting together to share a table for lunch. She invited me to join them, which I did. That was my introduction to Anita and other women working in similar computing research areas. In the subsequent years, I was invited to participate in several programs designed to increase the number of women in this space.

In addition, I became part of the Systers network. It was initiated as an email distribution of predominantly Ph.D. women conducting computer-systems-related research across North America. The conversations were very helpful and engaging for me. I specifically recall one day reading an email sent out by a Systers member making the explicit comment about not having any Black women, or women of color, participating at this level of research. Without hesitation, I responded to her with facts. In addition to me, I informed her of another African American woman at this level who was also in this elite group. This is how many others in the group knew we existed. In response, many of the women reached out to me to learn more about my experiences. Sometime later, I was invited to participate in a new organization created by the Computing Research Association (CRA).

The CRA membership consisted of the Ph.D. granting institutions, as well as representation from industrial and governmental research labs. All institutions focused on computing research across North America. Membership consisted of electrical and computer engineering, computer science, and other relevant departments. A nonprofit organization, CRA's objective is to unite "industry, academia and government to advance computing research and change the world". Its Board of Directors are elected to provide guidance on CRA policies, based on its vision. CRA's board authorized the creation of a committee to focus on the improvement of women in computing. The CRA Committee on the Status of Women in Computing (CRAW) was organized in 1990. Its initial members were some of the top women in the field. Having connected with me via Systers, they invited me to participate as one of the initial members of CRAW.

We did quite a bit of work during CRAW's initial years. We proposed workshops on academic careers for women in computing, including graduate students. We provided guidance and words of wisdom on the academic process. We wrote and submitted proposals to government funding agencies such as the National Science Foundation in the United States to support some of this work. We received funding for many of our activities. We worked to connect with women who were great candidates for professional recognition at the Fellow level for relevant professional organizations such as the Institute of Electrical and Electronics Engineers (IEEE) and the Association for Computing Machinery (ACM).

I learned a lot, some of which included enlightenment about how to get tenure in academia, how to improve research collaborations between academics and industrial and governmental research labs, and the process for seeking and obtaining recognition at the highest levels in professional associations. I also expanded my professional network to include many highly regarded women in the field. These women made significant contributions to the field. I had their ear and was working closely with them on professional projects. Little did I know then that many of these women would become strong supporters for my journey to become an IEEE Fellow.

As part of CRAW's focus, I actively worked to put together a graduate school information document for women in computing research. It included providing information on graduate fellowship programs. After conducting research on the relevant methodologies and programs available, this work was published broadly in relevant publications such as *Computing Research News* and *Communications of the ACM*. In addition, CRAW published the information as a booklet that it distributed to participants at workshops it sponsored, as well as similar events that focused on women. In addition, I presented at a few of CRAW's workshops for Academic Careers for Women in Computer Science and Engineering, presenting industrial research careers as another option for graduate students to consider as they evaluated academic and other career alternatives.

The CRA published the results of its annual Taulbee Survey in its *Computing Research News* publication. The survey is the "principal source of information on the enrollment, production, and employment of Ph.D.'s in information, computer science and computer engineering" in North America. I learned about the Taulbee Survey during my work on CRAW. As part of my due diligence, I reviewed the results of Ph.D. surveys. I recall examining closely the results showing the number of Black women Ph.D. graduates in these fields over the years. I could not find a single Black woman who graduated before me, in 1988. It was at that point that I realized I was the first, or at least one of the first, to earn this. I was speechless.

My work as a member of the Westchester Alumnae Chapter of DST increased significantly. I love to encourage and inspire people, and I was drawn to committees within the chapter that enabled me to leverage my skills and abilities to do so. After a couple of years of actively working on programs as a chapter member, I was approached to be a candidate for second Vice-President of the chapter in 1992. This was intriguing to me, as with most organizations and leadership, one starts with lower-level leadership positions such as committee chair, secretary, or treasurer, then moves to the more powerful positions. I assumed, without asking, that at least one other person who paid their dues was also a candidate for this role and they needed someone else to run so that members would have a choice. I therefore agreed to be a candidate. To my surprise, when the nominating committee presented the slate to the chapter, I was the only candidate. *What?!?!*

I began to panic. I did not believe I had the time to commit to this role. I am the type of person to be all in regarding a commitment. I try not to half step but to do it to the best of my ability with excellence. I conducted some due diligence on details regarding the role, responsibilities, and time commitment for the position. I realized I should have done this before I agreed to run for the position, but I needed to address the issue, given the situation at the time. After individual discussions with previous sorors in the role, I understood the commitment was not as demanding as

I originally thought. I therefore embraced the possibilities. I was subsequently elected.

I did one term as the second Vice-President, then moved on to one term as first Vice-President, and finally two terms as President of the Chapter, 1996–2000. We instituted a few new programs under my leadership and enhanced others. I thoroughly enjoyed working with my sorors, working on projects vital to our Westchester County community. We focused on projects associated with educational development, economic development, physical and mental health, political awareness and involvement, and international awareness and involvement.

As chapter first Vice-President and President, I was part of the New York Metropolitan Presidents Council, which consisted of the top two leaders of New York Metropolitan area chapters. We met quarterly to discuss programs and projects of common interests. As a result, I traveled throughout the region, from Manhattan to Nassau and Suffolk Counties, Queens, the Bronx, Staten Island, the Mid-Hudson Valley, and Rockland County, in addition to Westchester County.

One project I recall was the rite of passage and final service of a well-known soror, Betty Shabazz. She died in 1997 in a tragic fire started by her grandson. Dr. Shabazz was a member of the New York Alumnae Chapter. The NY Metropolitan Presidents Council was responsible for her Omega Omega service, something available for all deceased Deltas. As part of the council, I participated in this service, held at the Unity Funeral Home in Harlem. It was a very moving experience for this strong woman.

One of my chapter members was a journalist for the *Westchester County Press*, the Black-owned newspaper in the county. As a result, there were numerous articles in the publication about the work of our Delta chapter, as well as my own professional accomplishments over the years. I was visible in the county during that time and received several requests to speak to young people. It was sheer joy to encourage and inspire them to be all they can be during these engagements.

In addition, I attended numerous Delta leadership workshops and other related activities. It was during this time in my life that I focused on learning about leadership and used my Delta roles to perfect my own leadership skills. My time in chapter leadership was a wonderful, enlightening experience. I loved expanding my leadership horizons and networking with high-profile, powerful Deltas. At the same time, I learned critical leadership skills that proved invaluable for my professional career.

In addition to my active professional and community activities, I was active in my church. I continued with my strong faith and Christian life during that time in my life. Every year, on the first Saturday in November, the choir hosted its annual concert at the church. It was always standing room only crowds as we were known for our spiritual performances throughout the local region. In fact, the choir participated in recording two songs with separate artists on two separate occasions during my tenure as a choir member.

Westchester County is an exclusive county just north of New York City. Our church was in the northern part of the county, where there were few Black Baptist churches. Given the choir's stellar reputation, we had several celebrity guests who visited the church from time to time. I recall one Sunday, as I was sitting with the choir in the choir stand overlooking the congregation, I saw Kathleen Battle enter with a guest during the service. I did a double take, as I could not believe it was Kathleen Battle, the gifted soprano opera star. I began to look around to see if anyone else noticed her presence. Most people did not notice; however, one member did and sent a note to the pastor. He acknowledged her presence and asked her to stand and be recognized. That was the highlight of my day.

CHAPTER 10

Rough Waters Ahead

M Y LIFE IN WESTCHESTER was well rounded and full. My husband and I moved from our initial apartment in Mt. Kisco to a rented townhouse in Ossining after a couple of years. It was my goal to buy a house soon thereafter. After several months searching for a house in the Spring 1994, we bought a house in Ossining in June. It was a ranch-style white house with red shutters, 3 bedrooms, and 1.5 bathrooms, and over 1,700 square feet on 0.47 acres. It had a two-car garage with separate garage doors, just like we wanted. It was a 30-year-old house that was well built and maintained. There were literally no issues with the house, and we were excited to be homeowners. It was a dream come true for me.

A couple of months after moving in, we had a housewarming party that included a blessing of the house by our pastor. By this time, we had created a great network of friends, coworkers, and church members whom we invited to the celebration. We tapped one of my coworkers who loved to cook to make us great hor d'oeuvres for the occasion. My husband cooked most of the food we served. We had a large crowd who came to help us celebrate on a beautiful mid-September afternoon. We spent time out on the deck, overlooking our above-ground pool, on this bright and cheery day.

During this time, my husband and I were trying to have a baby. It did not take long before I knew there was a problem. My gynecologist was also a fertility doctor, and I went through several activities under his direction in my quest to have a baby. From numerous tests to fertility medications to outpatient surgery, I went through the

DOI: 10.1201/9781032724270-14

process. After several months, and shortly after the initial scheduled surgery, I conceived. Given my high-risk pregnancy, we decided not to share this good news until we at least reached the middle of the second trimester. In the meantime, my doctor scheduled numerous tests and other actions to ensure a problem-free pregnancy. My husband was so elated about this that he could not keep it to himself. I knew the cat was out of the bag when I started getting congratulatory calls.

One of my first doctor visits after learning of the pregnancy was an ultrasound. It was to ensure there was a heartbeat. This was scheduled at around six weeks and was a standard procedure for high-risk pregnancies. My husband came with me, and we were exhilarated about the possibilities. Shortly after we arrived in the room, the doctor arrived and began the examination. He ensured we saw the screen as he closely examined it. He was silent for quite some time, when he finally said, "this is not a good pregnancy". *What!?!?*. I thought I was hearing things, so I asked him to repeat what he said. His response, "this is not a good pregnancy". I asked him what he meant. He described what we were supposed to see in this sonogram, but there was nothing like that. We did see something, but it was a motionless image that has remained with me for decades.

He informed us that since this was not a good pregnancy, it needed to be terminated. He discussed scheduling a dilation and curettage (D&C) procedure shortly and asked his staff to work with me to help schedule it. This was too much for me to process in such a short time frame. I was silent, speechless during most of this time, and my husband, who is a talker, had stopped talking after hearing "this is not a good pregnancy". I do not recall what I did or said to my husband or others in the days after hearing this news. I still had not told anyone in my family, but I had to face those my husband had informed. Several days later, I had the D&C. It was a horrible experience I shall never forget. Tears were falling down my face during the procedure, as I knew my baby was gone. I just wanted to go home and go to sleep for a while. I recovered by relying on my faith and the hope of trying in the future.

We tried for several months. After more tests, the doctor recommended surgery to remove my fibroid tumors. This was in-patient surgery, and I had some complications. However, I got pregnant several weeks after I recovered from the surgery. I couldn't believe it, and I was very guarded by this time. Once again, the doctor scheduled an ultrasound for around 6 weeks. This time, I went by myself because my husband was unable to join me. The sonogram was different this time.

As I examined the screen closely, I thought I saw two of whatever it was I was seeing. I still did not see any movement and was about to really panic when the doctor said, "twins!". *What!?!?* He said it again, "twins". I was really astounded. I stopped looking at the screen and was really trying to wrap my head around what he said. I was thinking, *my God! Am I going to have twins?* I was into my thoughts and did not initially notice that my doctor was silent for a very long time. I looked back at him and the screen. I was examining what he was seeing very closely when he finally said, "this is not a good pregnancy". *What!?!? Are you kidding me?*

There was a long pause before I said anything. I was dismayed and in disbelief. I had gone from a high state of excitement, euphoria, at the thought of having twins to a low state of darkness in just a few minutes. I was numb, without words. My doctor shared that he knew I did not know what a good pregnancy looks like on a sonogram, but he assured me that mine was not. He began talking about another D&C, and I just shut down. I didn't hear anything else he said. I found enough strength to walk slowly out to the waiting room, and eventually to my car. I just sat there for a long time in a daze before I struggled to make it safely home and call my husband. I went to sleep and pretended, at least for a while, this was not happening again.

Reality slowly reared its ugly head, and leaning on my faith with great intensity I began to address the situation. I wanted a second opinion before making any decisions. I found one of the best fertility doctors in the New York Metro area. He was based in Manhattan. I took the commuter train, Metro North, alone to his office. After a thorough examination, he confirmed the diagnosis from my doctor, as well as the recommended D&C. It was a very sad and low point in my life, but I found the strength to make it back to Grand Central Station and take Metro North back home. During the walk and ride home, I reflected on the situation. I was beyond tears at this point, just struggling to try and understand why, just going through the motions of living.

Slowly, one day at a time, I began to recover mentally, emotionally, and physically, from this jolt to my system. Several weeks went by, then a couple of months. I got pregnant again, but it ended before it reached the stage of a heartbeat. I believed my issues with getting pregnant were resolved; however, there was something greater that prevented me from carrying a baby to term or conceiving in the future. This was certainly a painful life experience for me, something I knew intellectually: we don't always get what we want in life, that life is not always fair or kind, and we may spend a lifetime not understanding why. For that time in my life, the words of Langston Hughes' poem *Mother to Son* rang true: "And life for me ain't been no crystal stair". We must, however, keep on moving, learning to live with the pain and disappointment, seeking professional and spiritual guidance and the support of family and friends while traversing through the healing process.

I continued to actively participate in my church activities, including Sunday School and the choir, and my Delta community activities. Darlene and her husband, Gary, had two children: a son and a daughter, shortly after my experiences. I was able to spend a little time with them while they were babies and as they grew to small children. It was a sheer joy to spend time with them when I could and learn about the amazing things we do while were are young.

Moving forward in time, Gregory began to have more complications with Lupus. When it flared up, he would be in excruciating pain, and had frequent visits to the hospital. It was heartbreaking to know of his painful experiences, but he was a trooper, taking it all in stride. I recall a conversation with him shortly after he had a finger amputated. I was having a tough time dealing with the situation, but he counseled me and lifted my spirits. He informed me that before the amputation, he was in constant, nonstop pain. Afterwards he felt wonderful.

In addition, one year he became gravely ill. My sisters and I worked to get him transferred from one of my hometown hospitals to the Houston Methodist Hospital. A surgeon and his team worked on him for hours to address his issue and save his life. I rushed to Houston to be with him and the family prior to his surgery and was with MaMe, Darlene, and Kimberly during the surgery. During his recovery, he had another complication and was rushed into surgery again. The surgeon was amazing, and Gregory recovered.

My paternal grandfather, and the only grandfather I had ever known, became ill with cancer in the Fall of 1996. My husband and I made it to the Veteran's Hospital in Richmond, Virginia to visit him during his illness. We apparently saw him on his last good day; he passed away a few days later. I was happy that we spent time with him, laughing and joking and having a good time.

Gregory and I represented our siblings at his funeral. My husband and I picked Gregory up from the airport to attend the funeral. It was a somber and happy event. Gregory came with us back to New York and spent a few days with us. He was very quiet and reflective during this time, which was out of the norm for him. I observed him standing and looking out of our sliding glass door to the deck and reflecting on our beautiful backyard. I let him be. He went on to visit other relatives in other parts of the country. Little did I know that it was the last time I would see him alive and well. Looking back at this time, it was like he visited all the relatives to say goodbye.

Slightly more than four months later, Gregory became very ill and was rushed to the hospital. I was not too concerned when MaMe called me with the news because this was a regular occurrence for Gregory. However, when I did not hear from MaMe for over 24 hours, I became concerned. I called the hospital and spoke to Gregory's nurse. She didn't share much with me other than they were working on him. I started calling other relatives at home. I finally reached my uncle who informed me Gregory was fighting for his life, and they did not think he would make it. At this point, I took the first plane home.

I flew into Houston and met Kimberly at the airport in Houston. She had flown in from San Jose, California. We drove home and reached the hospital late that night. Gregory was in a semiconscious state. We began a two-week prayer vigil for his life. During one of my visits to his ICU room, he became very agitated, moving incessantly like he wanted to get out of bed. Darlene was there with me, and I began to panic. I was trying to gather enough strength to leave the room before breaking down, when I began to mentally pray to God for help. Immediately, I heard a voice, a whisper in my ear, instructing me to sing to him. There was no one around me, as Darlene was on the other side of the bed.

I began to sing to him, and slowly but surely Gregory calmed down. He had been agitated the entire time he was in the hospital and was getting worse when I panicked. It was only a couple of minutes after I started singing to him, when he became calm, peaceful, and just rested. I couldn't believe what had happened. I was astounded and in a daze. It took me a while to intellectualize what happened. I believe it was an angel watching over Gregory, Darlene, me, and the entire family. It was soothing for our souls to see him resting peacefully for the first time during this hospital visit.

Gregory had some good and bad days, but I had to go back to New York and work. He had regained consciousness, and I was able to talk to him for a little while from home. However, he was going in and out of a delirious state. He was angry that he was in the hospital in Lake Charles and asked me to help him get to the Houston Methodist Hospital. I informed him that I had already spoken to his doctor in Houston. He had consulted Gregory's home doctors, and they agreed that he needed to get much stronger before they would consider transferring him. That was my last conversation with Gregory. He died shortly after that, in February 1997, at the age of 35.

Gregory was my MaMe's only son, and our only brother. We had a wonderful funeral for him that was well attended, standing room only. He had a beautiful spirit and a heart to help others. As we were cleaning out his room in MaMe's house, we found an incomplete handwritten draft of his autobiography. We were unaware that he was writing this, and we searched everywhere for the rest of it. I even used every tool and trick I could think of to search his computer to see if he had a softcopy. We found nothing. I promised MaMe I would finish it for him and publish it. That made her very happy and somehow tempered her grief.

Completing Gregory's autobiography was an excruciating process for me. I would spend time writing then stop because it was distressing to keep going. Yet I persevered until I just could not do it anymore. After several years, one day MaMe said to me in a sad, somber, and disappointing voice that I was never going to finish the book. At that point, I found the strength to complete it. *Gregory: The Life of a Lupus Warrior* was published in June 2008, 11 years after his death.

The Vulcan project at work was winding down. I transitioned to spend time focusing on a high-performance computing project named Accelerated Strategic Computing Initiative (ASCI) Blue. This was a supercomputer project in collaboration with the Lawrence Livermore National Laboratory (LLNL) in Livermore, California. Its objective was to be a simulator to replace live US nuclear weapons testing. The project was funded by the US Department of Energy and the National Nuclear Security Administration. At the time the machine was installed at LLNL, it was up to 20 times more powerful than any other supercomputer in US government installations.

My time on this project was short. It included actively participating in the architectural design team for this scalable shared memory machine. I made significant contributions to the architectural design and implemented a simulator to evaluate the performance of its cache coherence protocol. The results were presented to the broader team to help optimize the machine's architectural design.

I had several inventions, coinventions, and papers from this and similar work. One coinvention, *Home Node Migration for Distributed Shared Memory Systems*, became a patent. An associated paper won the best paper award at the High-Performance Computing Conference in December 1997. Six additional patent applications were filed, and subsequently issued, for this work.

I worked with a different group of people on this project compared to Vulcan. I did not feel as though all members were mutually respected, including me. I worked harder to ensure I was working at my highest potential, brainstorming, and contributing. It was challenging. I recall one meeting in which we were brainstorming. I made several comments throughout the meeting that were ignored. My manager was in the room initially but left before it ended. During this meeting I took detailed notes, as I do with most meetings I attend. I went directly to my manager's office after the meeting for a discussion with him. I wanted to make sure I was not imagining things, but that I was in fact being ignored. My manager confirmed this was happening. At this point, I was very angry and was about to say a few things I would have regretted later, but I managed to constrain myself.

My background, and that of my manager, is computer hardware and computer architecture. The rest of the team had software and systems backgrounds. I brought a different perspective to the table, one that provided additional value that the team did not recognize or acknowledge. This resulted in ideas that I thought were unique and valuable. This was true not only for the specific designs we discussed for ASCI Blue but also from a broader architectural lens.

I informed my manager that we discussed some things relevant to the ASCI Blue discussion I thought were patentable. I felt we should move forward with writing this up, but I did not trust them. He advised me to go back to my office and immediately write up a description of the discussion from my notes and strongly suggest that we move forward with a patent application and possibly a paper. I followed his advice and suggested that I take the lead in writing both documents. They all agreed to this, and I wrote up the initial drafts of what became our patent application and the paper.

My experience with patents at this point enabled me to have a good idea of concepts that were patentable. This is because the work was leading edge, and I knew about other similar work globally. Given my experience with this group, I would later go to my manager with ideas that were not relevant to the ASCI design and would not be a factor for the project moving forward. However, they were potentially patentable based on my computer architecture background. I would brainstorm with him and not the group. These ideas were not relevant for a discussion by the larger group. We filed a couple of disclosures based on these discussions. They eventually became patents as well. They were part of the six patents received for this work. We learned that one of these two disclosures was similar to one the other folks on the team had filed, so they were also filing separate disclosures. As a result, we all met as a team to determine how we could combine the ideas from these separate disclosures into one patent application.

The patent review board that made this recommendation was led by our second-level manager, who initially led the integration discussion meeting. We were all making recommendations for how to integrate, when the second-level manager had to leave to attend a meeting. Once he left, all the participants except my manager and I made it very clear they had no intention of integrating their idea with ours. As a result, we filed two separate patent applications. A couple of years later, a patent was issued for the application my manager and I filed. In addition, that patent was in the top 30% of all IBM Research patents issued that year, as determined by IBM Research's IP department. We received a supplemental patent award for this highly valued patent. The other team never received such an award for their work. In my opinion, not recognizing the value I brought to the table based on my different background was a tragic loss for them.

I filed two additional disclosures with my manager that became patents. I also filed a separate disclosure as the sole inventor that became a patent. These patents were based on ideas I had that were similar to the work I did on the ASCI Blue project but more focused on my previous work in research. One of these patents with my manager was ranked in the top 5% of all patents issued to IBM Research in the year of issue, according to the IP department. As a result, my manager and I both received a supplemental patent issue award worth thousands of dollars for this work. It was a great validation to me for my efforts.

I enjoyed the substantive work on this project and was truly contributing significantly. However, the work environment became untenable. I was not happy. It was time to move on, but I needed to learn how to navigate this delicate situation. I loved research and wanted to stay with IBM Research. My manager was very happy with my work, and I knew he would try to convince me to stay. I turned to my mentor, Fran Allen. I had lunch with her and told her the specifics of my situation. She advised me to go to my manager and share with him exactly what I told her. I did not think or understand how that would help. However, she had been at this for quite some time, and I trusted her judgement and wisdom. I followed her advice and was subsequently given the green light to look for other opportunities within research. This was the catalyst for my transition to a different research area.

I spent time talking to several different groups conducting research that was interesting. I was also keenly aware of market conditions at the time, and I saw a transition happening from hardware to software. Thus, I began to concentrate on software-oriented research, while maintaining a foundational focus on performance evaluation. At the time, Java—a system enabling the cross-platform development of applications—was the subject of intense focus in the research and development communities. I soon began to focus my efforts on Java server performance, becoming the project lead, then the manager, for this group. We published a paper on this work in the *IBM Systems Journal*.

During this time, I received both internal and external recognition for my work. I received numerous patent awards and was named an IBM Master Inventor in the research division. I was also invited to present my work on Java performance and parallel I/O at several universities, including the University of California at Berkeley and Rice University, my alma mater. I received an award for Research Leadership at the Women of Color Technology Awards in 1998 and the Golden Torch Award for Lifetime Achievement in Industry from the National Society of Black Engineers in 2000. I was profiled in several publications, including getting recognition as one of ten technology innovators by *Black Enterprise* (March 1998), the cover of the IBM Diversity brochure (Spring 1999), and *Diversity* magazine (June/July 2000).

My objective with this recognition was to make myself visible to the external community to encourage and inspire others who look like me to become research engineers. I have a passion for encouraging and inspiring people to live their best life. I was also very active in the research community. I wanted to use my influence to increase the ranks of women and people of color in the field.

I was elected (1995) and reelected (1998) to the Computing Research Association's (CRA) Board of Directors. I was the only Black female in this role with a seat at the table for years. In addition to my active participation in CRA's CRAW committee, I cofounded the Coalition to Diversify Computing (CDC) which was funded by three professional organizations and the National Science Foundation (NSF) to increase the ranks of people of color in computing research. I also participated in the NSF's research funding awards review panel, Morgan State University's Advisory Board, and the Cochair of IBM's Research Diversity Council.

I was an active participant in presenting and planning the initial Grace Murray Hopper Celebration of Women in Computing conferences. It was the brainchild of Anita Borg, the same woman I ran into in a women's bathroom at a technical conference several years earlier. I was the chair or cochair of sessions focusing on women of color, upon Anita's strong request. In addition, I cochaired the Program Committee for the conference in 2000.

I was invited to be a plenary speaker at the conference in 1997. My presentation was videotaped and became part of the collection of video conference presentations that was distributed by University Video Communications. In fact, sometime later Theryl, who lived in Seattle, contacted me. She told me she woke up that morning, turned on the television, and began channel surfing. She stumbled upon my presentation on her television screen. She couldn't believe it. This event has now become a very large conference for women in computing, with over 10,000 attendees to the annual event.

I was also the Program Committee Chair and member of several conferences on Java and supercomputing during this period. I was actively engaged both technically and professionally at the highest levels in my chosen field, and I thoroughly enjoyed every minute of it.

5

The Awakening

CHAPTER 11

I Didn't Know That

I was in my office one day in the late '90s reading my email when I came across one that got my attention. I was invited to attend the Women of Color Technology Awards conference, held in Baltimore. I quickly secured permission to attend this event, and I was excited about the possibilities. I vividly recall walking into the ballroom where the event occurred looking for the IBM table. I looked all around the room and saw signs for various companies, but I did not see IBM. I happened to be standing adjacent to IBM's table, and I did not notice it until someone seated at the table grabbed me by the wrist.

This African American woman said to me "Oh Sandra, I've been wanting to talk to you", as she patted her hand on the empty seat next to her. I sat down and she said to me, "I want to talk to you about becoming an IBM executive". My first thoughts were *who is this woman?*, and *you seem to know quite a bit about me, but I don't even know you.* My response to her was thank you very much, but I'm not interested in becoming an IBM executive. Her response was "ah hah". At this point the program started. We chatted off and on throughout the first session, and I still did not know who she was. During the first break, she left the room for a few minutes, and I browsed through the conference program. That's when I saw her picture, name, and a short bio. She was Nancy Stewart, the first Black female IBM Vice-President (VP). She was to receive an award later at the conference. I could not believe it! At that point, I did not know Black female VPs existed at IBM. While I was still not interested in pursuing an executive position, I was interested in learning more about her and her story. I spent most of my time with her during this conference, we got to know each other a little better. We also agreed to follow up a few days after the conference.

Over the next several weeks, I had a few conversations with Nancy. I learned that her office was in Armonk, New York, just a few minutes from my office in Hawthorne, New York. It was clear that this was a woman who did not take no for an answer. I was very happy with my work–life balance at the time. I was successful in a fulfilling career and active in my community. In fact, I was the President of my local Delta chapter. Most IBM and other executives I knew expended a considerable amount of time on their work and careers, and I was unwilling to do that given my full and balanced life. Despite this, Nancy tried several methods to convince me to at least consider executive opportunities. She was about to give up on me when she telephoned me in my office one day.

At the time I was going through some challenges with some of the women in my Delta chapter. Nancy detected this in my voice and asked me "what's going on?". When I responded, she asked "you're the President of your Delta chapter?" "Yes". "How many women are in your chapter?" "About 125". Then she said to me "anyone who can manage 125 highly opinioned, strong, Black women can be an IBM executive. In fact, it's probably easier to be an IBM executive than to manage 125 Black women". That got my attention. In fact, only a Black woman IBM executive could get my attention with that type of statement. At that point, I was willing to listen.

We scheduled a lunch meeting at a restaurant offsite from IBM's corporate headquarters. This became a two-hour business lunch. It was very enlightening for me. It was the first time I learned about the real IBM and generally how corporate America works. We had an engaging conversation. She asked me questions, and I answered. For example, she asked if I had stock options. My response was "no, that's something given to IBM executives, and I'm not an executive". Nancy looked at me startled, then placed her head in her hands and shook her head. I'm thinking, *was it something I said?* Her response was "ask your manager". We went back and forth like this for quite some time. Nancy informed me that based on my resume and accomplishments, I should be better positioned for IBM career advancement. I had no idea what she was talking about. However, given her reaction to my responses, I began to think something may have been amiss.

After lunch, I went back to my office building and straight to my manager's office. I asked him about stock options. His response was "this is something given to IBM executives". Now that I was better informed, I asked him to investigate it. Two weeks later, I received stock options. This was an eye-opener to me, very enlightening indeed. I had been with IBM about nine years, and I was completely oblivious to the details regarding career advancement, etc., within the company.

Granted, I was not interested in working outside of IBM Research. I loved my professional life as a researcher and was happy to continue with this work as a lifelong career. Promotion to upper-level management was not something I pursued because it would mean less work as a researcher and more work as a manager and executive, which was not very appealing to me. However, once enlightened, I became somewhat angry at my situation. Instead of focusing on what would have, should have, and could have been happening to me, I began to educate myself on the nuances of the IBM culture and forward-thinking moves for the future.

Nancy introduced me to several IBM executives shortly after our meeting. One by one, I met with each of them. The more executives I spoke to, the more enlightened I became. In addition, every single one of them became angry at my situation and what should have been happening for me but was not. In fact, one of them said to me, "you never heard this from me, but if I were you, I would check my market value". My reaction with each meeting was dumbfounded silence. It was an awakening experience that was a catalyst for a strong, passionate, and urgent desire to move forward and ensure I am fully recognized and rewarded for the positive impacts I made, and will make, for the company. I worked closely with Nancy, and several others, to start this journey.

I continued to conduct research with a focus on Java-related projects. I became interested in management and worked with Nancy on how to achieve this objective. I shared with my manager and others my management interests. In addition, another mentor advised me of another management opportunity in a development division. I applied for that position, conducted my due diligence on the nature of the work, and went on an interview trip. It was a good trip. I met some great people and had engaging conversations; however, it was not a good match for me. The hiring manager called my manager, as is customary, to advise him of this. I continued to look for other opportunities.

Nancy asked me for feedback on the trip, which I shared. She seemed perplexed about this, asking more detailed questions. I was curious about the questions. She informed me that my manager spoke to the research HR director and informed her that my interview was not very good. He advised that the hiring manager spoke to him about this and reported that I did not have good interview skills. Neither my manager nor the hiring manager mentioned any of this to me. In fact, I did not believe this was true. However, the HR director suggested that Nancy get with me and teach me how to conduct a good interview. This was insulting. One of the projects my Delta chapter offered to the Westchester County community was an interview skills workshop. My sorors and I did our due diligence on effective interviewing skills to offer this workshop. I was part of the team that put this together and implemented it. I know effective interviewing skills, and I shared this with Nancy. I told her I do not know why my manager received that feedback, but it was just not true. Despite this, she worked with me to improve my interviewing skills.

I later learned that Nancy happened to be in a meeting with this hiring manager in Armonk. She shared with him the feedback she received about my interview with him and his team. He was appalled. He said he did not provide that feedback and was angry that someone was untruthful when sharing his input. He and Nancy decided not to do anything about it, to my knowledge. However, Nancy asked him to help me if at any time in the future I came to him for help. In the meantime, I aspired to get a new management position as soon as possible and move from this manager and his ability to potentially harm my career. I am certain that Nancy and some of my other mentors worked to make this happen.

Shortly afterwards, I was promoted to manager for the Java Server Performance (JASPER) team. I successfully provided technical direction and led the technical team to quantify Java server performance, relative to legacy systems on IBM's server platforms. I worked across the research division with teams focusing on various aspects of Java research activities. We made some notable contributions to the early development of Java, based on quantifying Java performance and suggesting optimizations for IBM's offerings. This resulted in several papers and presentations. In addition, I was on the program committee for several technical conferences, including SC98, a supercomputing conference, and Java Grande 2000. I was also the Program Chair for IBM's Java Server Performance Workshop and Program Cochair for the Grace Murray Hopper Celebration of Women on Computing Conference (2000).

During this time, I received several IBM Supplemental Patent Awards. This included three awards each for coinventions that were in the top 30% of all patents issued to IBM Research in the year they were issued. I was the primary inventor of one of these three inventions. In addition, I received the IBM Supplemental Patent Award for a coinvention, with me as the primary inventor, that was in the top 5% of all patents issued to IBM Research in the previous year. (This was the top award I previously described.) I was also named a Master Inventor for IBM Research.

I attended IBM manager school upon my promotion. It was great to learn about the basic management techniques and tools available for IBM managers. I learned a lot during this class. However, it was this internal IBM education, coupled with the leadership training I received regularly as a member of Delta Sigma Theta, Sorority, Inc., that gave me a broader perspective and understanding of management. I was beginning to understand what Nancy meant when she said it would be easier to be an IBM executive.

I started getting more external recognition for my work in STEM. For example, I was featured in a 1998 *Black Enterprise* cover story on ten technology innovators entitled "The Black Digerati". I was the only woman featured in this story. Later that year, I was recognized for Research Leadership at the Women of Color Technology Awards. I was on the cover of the IBM Diversity brochure in 1999, and the recipient of the Golden Torch Award for Lifetime Achievement in Industry from the National Society of Black Engineers in 2000. For me, these external awards were more about visibility to encourage and inspire young people and others to pursue STEM professions, not about me.

Furthermore, my marriage was breaking down. I reached the point where it was untenable for me to continue in a marriage where

I was not happy. I made plans to file for a divorce. At the same time, I looked for IBM management opportunities outside of research and the New York Metro area. Nancy had suggested that a two-year assignment in another division would be a good opportunity for me. I looked for such opportunities, eventually landing a management role in San Jose, California. I quickly began the onboarding process to the IBM Silicon Valley Lab, including moving my belongings, car, etc., and searching for an apartment in San Jose. I was looking forward to a new experience and a new life, professionally and personally, on the west coast.

CHAPTER 12

California and Texas

S AN JOSE IS THE HEART OF SILICON VALLEY. I was moving there when technology companies were riding an unprecedented wave of success, and right before the bubble burst. Great apartments were difficult to find. I was told that if I found something to grab it right away because it would not be on the market for long. I found a comfortable one-bedroom in a complex just off the freeway and a few minutes from work, downtown, and the airport. I grabbed it. Thus, my destination location was secured, and I planned my move.

I was not in a great emotional state, given I was going through a divorce. IBM was a great help, as this two-year temporary assignment enabled me to keep my permanent New York address, it was home. I was paid extra for living temporarily in California, including a monthly trip to New York to "go home". It was a lifesaver for me, something for which I will always be grateful. It enabled me to travel to New York for divorce court when needed, and to pack up my things in the New York house when it was about to be sold, as I did not bring everything to San Jose. This minimized any issues I encountered with the New York divorce process while living in California.

I enjoyed my work as the Manager, WebSphere Database Development at the IBM Silicon Valley Lab (SVL). I successfully led a technical team in ensuring relevant functions and features were included in both IBM's application server offering, WebSphere Application Server (WAS), and its database offering, DB2, so they quickly installed and worked well as an integrated entity.

DOI: 10.1201/9781032724270-17

In addition, I developed an environment to test enterprise applications with Enterprise Java Bean components on WAS v4.0 and Windows NT. I used the environment to assist several customers in isolating issues with the applications and to publish white papers on this work, positively impacting customer sales. Also, during this time, a couple of patents were issued to me as a coinventor, and I filed a patent application.

My new environment in development was very different from my research experience. The people were friendlier, and I ran into women in the restroom. I could not believe it! After two weeks in an environment that was less hostile and stressful than research, I made the decision not to go back. I did not know what I would do after this assignment ended, but I knew I was not going back to research.

Later in 2000, I received a call from an editor at *Black Enterprise* magazine. They were planning a cover story on some of the top Blacks in technology. They contacted IBM who recommended me as one of their employees to profile. They asked me if I was interested, and I said yes, as I was still committed to being visible to encourage and inspire. I had a telephone interview with them the next week. A few weeks later, the magazine called again. They wanted to do a photo shoot with me for the article. They had a short time window to get this done, and they would call me later in the day on the time and date for the shoot. Right before I left for the day, on a Monday, the photographer called. The magazine scheduled the photo shoot for the next day at my IBM location.

At the end of the call, she informed me this would be a potential cover photo. I said *what?!?*. The magazine did not tell me that. They were planning three photo shoots with potential cover candidates. One of us would be selected for the cover. I began to panic. This was a Monday; beauticians do not work on Mondays. How was I going to find someone to do my hair and makeup for a cover shoot? I could not believe I went a little overboard with this. Anyway, I calmed down and did my own hair and makeup before going to work the next morning.

By this time, I was an experienced subject of photo shoots, and this worked like a charm. The magazine asked that I wear all black and sit on the floor, lotus style, for the photo. I specifically chose a necklace with a Delta charm. I wanted to advertise the fact that I was a Delta. A couple of weeks later, the photographer called and informed me I made the cover. I was excited, I was already sitting down, but I began to think about what that really meant. This would be a new level of exposure.

I was on the cover of the March 2001 issue of *Black Enterprise*, featuring the "Top 25 Blacks in Technology". I subscribed to the magazine and was waiting, with great anticipation, to receive my copy in the mail. I quickly learned that subscribers on the east coast received their copies first, and it gradually went west over the next few days. I started getting calls from family and friends on the east coast, then the Midwest, etc. I was a member of Delta's national Technology Task Force, and our upcoming meeting was in Washington, DC in a few days. I was hoping I would get my copy in the mail before the trip. I did not. The night before this trip, I went to the local Barnes & Noble store to see if they had received the new issue.

I arrived at the store and looked closely but could not find the latest issue. While I was looking, a young lady who I had never seen before came to the magazine section and stood next to me to look for a magazine. She said to me, "I bet you're not looking for what I'm looking for!" "What?" "*Black Enterprise*! My coworker is on the cover". "What? I don't think it's here". Then she became a little sensitive and agitated, asking me what I knew about this. "I'm Sandra K. Johnson Baylor, your coworker". She was so shocked that she ran out of the store, and I never saw her again.

The next day I flew to DC via the Dallas-Fort Worth (DFW) airport. As I walked through one of the DFW terminals changing gates, I passed by a store selling magazines. I had to stop suddenly because I saw a row of *Black Enterprise* magazines in the store with me on the cover. I was overjoyed! I went in, picked up 15 copies, then got in line to purchase them. I noticed the people around me began to look at me through the corners of their eyes but did not say anything to me. When I reached the cashier, he looked at the magazines in my hand, then me a couple of times before he said, "is that you?". I said "yes". "Oh, cool". Then I packed the magazines away and went on to the gate.

When I made it to DC for the Delta meeting, my sorors were all excited and wanted autographed copies of the magazines I had. I did this for our National President, Gwendolyn E. Boyd, but suggested to the others that we go to a local bookstore during the break to buy their copies that I would autograph. I wanted to keep the ones I bought for my closest family and friends. I had so many funny and interesting experiences while on the cover. The jeweler who made the Delta charm called to thank me for the free advertisement. Many of his customers had seen the magazine and contacted him. My mother called everyone in her address book. She was so excited. She told me that one of her high school classmates who lived in the Los Angeles area immediately went to a bookstore and purchased a copy. She told everyone in the store I was her relative, which is not true.

I attended a half-day conference in San Francisco with my good friend, Leola, who is older than my mother. After the conference, we went to a store and there was the magazine. Leola made the announcement, "we have a celebrity in the house!" as she raised the magazine over her head. *Oh no!* Everyone turned around to see me standing next to her, wearing the same outfit as in the cover photo. Someone asked her, "is this your daughter". Leola hesitated to respond, so I said to her "Leola?". She responded, "I'm so sorry I know your mother so I can't say yes, but I am tempted to say yes". We had a good laugh about it.

One more story. I was invited to speak at a Black Enterprise Conference later that year. During the opening reception, there were larger-than-life sized copies of several *Black Enterprise* covers, including mine. I thought I was being discreet as I walked through the crowd. However, everyone, including people I did not know, kept calling my name and talking to me like I was an old friend. I was not used to that type of recognition, and it made me very uncomfortable. However, I engaged as best I could, given the situation. This happened throughout the conference.

At one point, I was so uncomfortable that I left the conference area and went to another part of the Opryland Hotel Nashville, a huge edifice, to find solitude. I sat on a park bench when someone called my name. I got up, went to my room, and sat on the balcony to read a book. Someone walking on the sidewalk below called my name. I could not get away from it. Eventually, I went back into my room and closed the curtains. I was thinking, *I am getting a small taste of what celebrities go through when they are chased by paparazzi.* After a little while resting in my room, I made the paradigm shift to get used to this, for the conference, and went back to the day's events. Then I remembered how I thought I had just 15 minutes of fame when I graduated from college!

A few weeks after my cover girl issue, an IBM marketing contact reached out to me. She asked if I was interested in participating in an advertising campaign featuring IBM employees. Her team saw the magazine and thought I would be a good candidate. I thought about it for a while before I agreed to do it. It enabled me to have a new and different experience that I never even thought about.

The photo shoot for the campaign was in a Los Angeles studio and conducted by a temperamental photographer. I flew down to Los Angeles from San Jose in the morning. There was a stretch limousine waiting for me at the airport, to my surprise. I got in the car and was driven to the studio in Hollywood. When I arrived, I was taken straight to makeup where I sat in a chair while the makeup artist did my hair and face. *Where was this person for my cover girl shoot?* Once she was done, I went to the studio with lights and cameras everywhere. This was another level. The photographer snapped his fingers, and everyone jumped as he took pictures of me. It was a sight to behold. When he turned his head a couple of minutes, the makeup artist would come and dab my face or adjust my makeup. *Am I a star or something?* This was not going to get into my head; I was just playing with it. Once he was done, I went back to the limo that was waiting for me. I was taken back to LAX and flew back to San Jose. All in a day's work.

The ads appeared in many publications over the course of several months. This included *The New York Times*, *The Wall Street Journal*, *USA Today*, *The Economist*, *Fast Company*, *Golf Digest*, and *Smart Money*, among others. This gave my mother a thrill for many months. She was happy, so I was happy. It was all good.

As the end of my two-year tenure approached, I began to look for other development opportunities in management outside of New York and California. I learned about a great opportunity to manage a Linux performance team in Austin. I traveled there for the interview at the IBM Linux Technology Center and was offered the job shortly thereafter. I was favorably anticipating the possibilities.

Shortly after I filed for divorce, my high school sweetheart called me in my office. I recognized his voice immediately when he spoke. It had been several years since I had any communication with him. He said "I know you had a birthday a couple of weeks ago. I just called to wish you happy belated birthday". I thought, *really? I've been having a birthday every year for the past several years. Why are you calling me now?* However, my response to him was "thank you". I asked him how he got my office number. "Your mom gave me your business card". *I don't believe this, my mother!* We spoke for a few minutes, then I had to leave for a meeting.

Over the course of the next few months, we spoke regularly, for long periods of time. We got caught up on each other's lives and spoke about the future. I learned that he was also going through a divorce. After a few months, we started dating again, starting a long-distance relationship. I know the wisdom of avoiding starting a new relationship, especially when I am in the process of legally ending a marriage, although the relationship and marriage ended long before I started the divorce. If it was any other person, I would not have done that. However, this was my first love, a person I knew and had matured into a wonderful man. I trusted him.

My move to Austin was good. I decided to rent an apartment for a few months to learn about the various parts of the city before buying a house. My divorce would be final soon, and I was anxious to be free of the past and move forward with new possibilities, both professionally and personally.

As the manager of the Linux Performance department in the IBM Linux Technology Center (LTC), I led a technical team to successfully deliver on quantifying the impact and readiness of Linux for IBM's high-end, scalable mainframe computers months ahead of schedule. This major accomplishment enabled IBM executives, marketing teams, and sales teams to use our data to promote Linux and close deals. We worked with performance and other teams within IBM and the open-source community, leading efforts to facilitate this process. I served as a Linux performance evangelist, publicizing our efforts to establish, communicate, and negotiate direction and strategy within IBM, the open-source community, and customers. Our team successfully quantified that Linux is ready for the enterprise. As a result, Linux was widely adopted in high-end systems and is prevalent throughout the world today as a stable and respected operating system in this space.

As I thought about our work and its impact, I had a conversation with my team leader about writing a book on Linux performance. We made significant contributions to Linux for the enterprise, not just IBM machines, and I felt it was the right time to share what we learned in a book. He agreed and we got other members of the team to brainstorm on the book's contents. We created an outline for the book. At the same time, a publisher reached out to the team lead suggesting that he write a book on Linux performance. It was great, we did not have to find a publisher. I would be the editor-in-chief with a couple of team members as coeditors, including the team lead. The proposal was presented to Pearson and was accepted. Thus began our multiyear process to publish. During this time, the team lead stepped down from his editor role, and we quickly replaced him with another leader. *Performance Tuning for Linux Servers* was published in May 2005. Subsequently, Hungarian language and Chinese language translations were published as well as a paperback edition.

I worked with my team and others to file disclosures for future patent applications and submit papers to conferences. Since we were working with the open-source community, we had a time limit for filing patent applications with the US Patent and Trademark Office. Many of our disclosures were published on IP.com, and a few became patents. We also had papers published in internal and external conferences and on websites.

I have a passion for innovation and invention. During this time, I worked with three separate groups of IBMers to encourage them to submit disclosures for their ideas. The first was a group of African American female STEM Ph.D.'s at IBM. One of my IBM diversity contacts reached out to me to mentor these five to seven women individually, which I did. One common thread was to encourage them to build a portfolio of patents. I informed them that earning a Ph.D. in a STEM discipline meant that you have already contributed knowledge to our global society that may be patentable. Therefore, use this skill to continue this process. They were somewhat hesitant, so I suggested we get together and brainstorm. Most of them were based in Research Triangle Park, North Carolina. During a subsequent trip there, we did just that. That initial session turned into periodic sessions every month or so. We eventually filed several disclosures, most of which became patents.

The next team I worked with was a group of technical women of color in Austin. Once a month we would go out to lunch and brainstorm potential patent ideas. We submitted a few disclosures which became patents. One of these patents was only advanced in the internal IBM patent file process after a series of challenging events. One of the young ladies on this team had an idea related to intrusion detection. I encouraged her to lead the effort in writing up the disclosure and presenting at the patent review board. All three of the coinventors participated in the review via teleconference. We listened while the board raised issue after issue that, in my opinion, was successfully rebutted by this young lady. After a few rounds, the board finally decided not to pursue a patent on this idea. The young lady was very disappointed.

I suggested to her and the team that we take a couple of days to think about this, then get together for lunch to discuss the next steps. During the lunch, the young lady was adamant, she believed the idea was patentable and suggested we do something to move forward. She convinced me, so I reached out to an IBM Research contact who is a security expert. I explained the situation and asked for a recommendation for the best expert in research in this area. He introduced me to an individual, and I reached out to him. We had a teleconference where I explained the situation and asked if he was willing to review the paperwork and give me his professional opinion on patentability. After reviewing the information, he not only thought it was patentable but also suggested that we add an additional technical feature to make it a stronger patent. We included this feature in an updated draft and added him to the list of inventors, since the feature was his idea.

I went back to the patent review board with this new information from the company's best expert. They still said no. My female coinventors were perplexed, but I was unperturbed. I reached out to the IBM IP attorney who attended the patent reviews and was copied on all my email communications regarding this matter. I asked him to do what he needed to do to get this to a file. As a result, we filed this with the US patent office a few weeks later, and it became a patent. I was happy to teach these young ladies about a little more than patents.

The last group I worked with on patents while in Austin were mostly nontechnical IBMers. I attended a group meeting during a business trip to Poughkeepsie. There were several Austin IBMers attending the meeting. During dinner one night, our HR contact mentioned that she would never get a patent. My response to her was "why not?". She did not understand my question, but before we left dinner that night, we planned a happy hour event on a Friday evening when we were back in Austin. We had a few of these where we brainstormed over our favorite beverage, eventually filing a few technical disclosures. I guided them through the process, and they were thrilled! We eventually obtained a patent, and the HR contact was overjoyed. She mentioned she told one of her friends about the patent process she was going through. This friend mentioned to her she was never getting a patent. When my HR friend obtained that patent, she gladly took a picture of the first page and sent it to her friend. I told her that she could put "Inventor" on her tombstone if she chooses.

During this time, I also worked with my mentors to plan a career path for me to become an IBM technical executive. At the time IBM had three technical leadership positions: 1) Senior Technical Staff Member (STSM); 2) Distinguished Engineer (DE); and 3) IBM Fellow, the highest-ranking position. In addition, Nancy mentioned that she spoke to several HR and other IBM contacts about my ability to become a member of the IBM Academy of Technology. This was an internal entity modeled after the US National Academies. Existing Academy members select new members through a detailed selection process. At the time Academy members represented the top 1% of all 200,000 plus IBM technical employees. Members are significant technical contributors to IBM, making a favorable impact to IBM's growth, revenue, and brand. They are well respected within the IBM technical and executive communities.

I decided to seek IBM Academy membership. I began discussions with some of my technical mentors, including Mark Dean and Fran Allen (both IBM Fellows) about its membership process. I was able to get them and a DE to sponsor my Academy membership. I worked with Mark, my primary sponsor, on my package. He submitted it to the Academy database once the membership process officially started.

Shortly afterwards, I received an email from an IBM colleague, and former IBM Research manager, informing me he was coming to Austin and invited me to dinner to catch up. When I lived in San Jose, and he in Berkeley, California, we did this from time to time, so this was not something out of the ordinary. We met at a local Austin restaurant and ordered our meal. Then he went right to work. He mentioned he saw that Mark had sponsored my Academy membership. "What could he have been thinking! You don't measure up". *What?!?* "I know you have made some great accomplishments but not at a level for Academy membership. I'm here in Austin because I'm a member of its leadership team meeting here. We spent time looking at the database of candidates". He mentioned one candidate had accomplished this, and not me; and another candidate had accomplished that, and not me. "I just wanted to get together to share this with you, as your friend, so you won't be disappointed when you don't make it".

I was taken aback and speechless. It took a while for me to hear what he was saying because it was so unexpected from him. I had known and worked with this man for years, I could not believe he felt this way. He had the unmitigated gall, the boldness to invite me to dinner, and share this with me face to face "as a friend". This was so wrong in many ways. I do not recall what I said to him after his comments; however, I remember staying to eat the meal. I left right after I finished eating—call me anything but late for dinner. I remember thinking on my drive home, *they are just a bunch of good 'ole boys, who needs them!* I calmed down and kept moving forward. For decades, I told no one about this episode.

A couple of the members of my Linux Performance team and I wrote a paper on our strategy for improving Linux kernel performance and scalability and submitted it to the internal IBM Academy conference on Performance Engineering Best Practices. It was held in Toronto in the middle of the Academy membership cycle in which I was a candidate. One of my coauthors was the lead for this work, and I asked him to attend the conference when the paper was accepted. However, he did not want to go. I tried to encourage him to participate and explained the importance of this type of visibility to his career. He was unmoved and did not want to go. I reluctantly went instead.

It was a great conference, and I made several new IBM contacts. For example, there were three Japanese attendees who attended a few sessions together. During a break, I went to them and introduced myself, telling them I was born in Japan. They were delighted about this, asking me where in Japan. We had a good conversation, and for the rest of the conference, I would chat with them from time to time. I learned later that many of these conference attendees were members of the Academy; however, there was no indication of such on their badges.

I presented our paper, and it was well received with a great discussion afterwards. On my way back to my seat, I passed by one of the audience members who had just heard my presentation. He stopped me and mentioned it was a great presentation; I thanked him. He then mentioned my name and asked, "where have I heard your name before?". I looked at his name tag and immediately recognized him as the IBM Fellow who hosted me when I attended an IBM Academy meeting years earlier as a guest. (The guest program was designed to introduce future potential Academy members to its membership so they may build a network of Academy members aware of their contributions. Guests are nominated by existing members to attend the annual IBM Academy meeting. At the time, I was not fully aware of this program and did not know who nominated me. It was only years later that I discerned that Fran Allen, the Academy President at the time, nominated me as a guest attendee.) I reminded him that he was my host as a guest at a previous Academy meeting, in Ft. Lauderdale, Florida, and he remembered.

A few months later, I sent out an email communication to my IBM network informing them I had changed my name. This was my way of announcing that my divorce was final. The notice was sent out on a Friday evening, and I received a phone call from one of the email recipients the following Monday morning. She congratulated me and mentioned she knew it was a long time coming. I agreed. We talked about a few more things when she mentioned something that indicated we were talking about different things. I thought she had called to congratulate me on my divorce. I finally asked her, "what are you talking about?". Her response, "the Academy, you were elected!" *What?* "I was elected?" "Yes!". I could not believe what I was hearing. She mentioned that I would get an official notification later in the day.

I ended the call totally confused. Weeks earlier, this *rascal* convinced me that I would not be elected. I had already accepted that and did the paradigm shift mentally. Now I learned I had been elected. I was excited but at the same time in disbelief. The mental vacillation I experienced was amazing. This ended when I received the official congratulatory email from the Academy President.

Wow! I was elected! I thought about the people I met at the Performance Engineering Academy conference, the IBM Fellow, the three Japanese attendees, and others. I knew the Fellow was an Academy member, as are all Fellows. I later learned the Japanese employees, and others I met at the conference, were also Academy members. I thought about the fact that I had two IBM Fellows and a DE as sponsors, which was unusual for a candidate. I thought about the fact that I was not planning to attend the internal Academy conference but reluctantly did so when one of my team members was adamant about not attending. I thought about the Bible verse, "the steps of a good man are ordered by the Lord"—Psalms 37:23, NKJV—and I thanked God for ordering my steps!

My first annual Academy meeting as a new member was held in Toronto. I recall flying to Toronto via Chicago from Austin. I had some time between flights, so I went to the food court at O'Hare Airport for lunch. As I sat down with my food, I saw off in the distance another IBM Fellow, Joan Mitchell. I met her years earlier at an internal IBM conference. We were both panelists during a session on patents. Joan was with a couple of people, so I waved to her and sat down to eat. When I finished, I went over to speak. We chatted a bit and learned we were on the same flight to Toronto. I went on to the gate and boarded the plane at the appropriate time. It turned out Joan was seated in the same row; she sat near the window and me the aisle. We talked for the entire flight and took ground transportation together to the hotel.

The first event for this meeting was an opening dinner. The official start of the event was scheduled for the following morning. Newly elected Academy members are inducted in a ceremony during this opening program. I attended the opening dinner early; I needed to leave early to make it to the rehearsal for the new member induction ceremony. As I was leaving, I saw that *rascal*, who so passionately informed me I would not make it months earlier, eating dinner. I diverted straight to him, coming from behind. I tapped him on the shoulder. He turned around and saw me while he was chewing and was about to get up. I said, "Oh no, you don't have to get up, I'm going to the induction ceremony rehearsal. I just wanted to stop by and say hi". I then left the room.

The following year I worked with my management to put together a promotion package for STSM. I reached out to Joan Mitchell and others, asking them to support my promotion by writing letters of recommendation. All were happy to do this. Joan also asked for a copy of my resume, and I was happy to share it with her. She wanted to ensure she accurately described my work. I worked with her and others to put together a comprehensive package of my work, focusing on its significant IBM impact. At the time the STSM position was an appointment at the IBM business unit level. For me, this was the Systems and Technology Group (STG), the unit that developed and offered the IBM mainframe machines and systems, for example, the AIX and Linux operating systems. Existing technical leaders in STG reviewed the packages and provided recommendations to executive leadership, which made the appointment. I went through this process, and in July 2003, I was promoted to STSM. I was the first African American woman to be promoted to this IBM technical leadership position, yet another milestone for me and IBM. This was not just exciting for me, but the Black technical employees in the company, particularly throughout the United States, were happy and excited for this milestone.

As STSM, I became the Linux Performance Architect at the IBM LTC. I interacted with IBM server brands, pSeries and zSeries mainframes, etc., and middleware teams to lead efforts to address common Linux performance issues, advocated Linux performance issues as a factor in hardware design guidance, worked with the Linux distribution partner liaisons to address Linux performance issues, advocated for quality Linux performance in the open-source community, and led efforts to set general and specific Linux performance strategies, through IBM-wide performance councils and related avenues. I gave executive and customer presentations on Linux performance and the LTC and worked with customers to address their Linux performance issues. I became a member of the LTC technical board and was one of the LTC leaders to set the strategy and technical direction for the center. This was an influential technical leadership position, and there was no one in the company who looked like me in such a role.

I continued to file patent applications, have previously filed applications issued, and publish papers during this time. In fact, six patents were issued, with me as a coinventor, during my tenure in the LTC. I also continued to be profiled internally and externally for my work and to make professional contributions. For example, I participated in various technology advisory review boards, panels, and task forces. I was profiled in "CyberRhythms: Black Innovations in Technology", an exhibit at the Chicago Museum of Science and Industry, January 17 to March 2, 2003, *NSBE Magazine, Essence,* and *Ebony* magazines and BlackEngineer.com. I received the YWCA of Greater Austin Woman of the Year in Science/Technology Award in 2002 and the Black Engineer of the Year Award for Outstanding Technical Contribution in Industry in February 2005.

Furthermore, I participated in the IBM Innovators Tour in China and Australia. I was one of four technical leaders to travel to Shanghai, Beijing, Melbourne, and Sydney to discuss technical leadership at the top universities in these countries. We were a hit. There were many questions for me and my work on Linux performance. There was significant interest and focus on Linux in China during that time. It was a very rewarding and educational experience. As a team, we found time to tour Tiananmen Square and the Forbidden City in Beijing before traveling to Australia.

After a couple of days in Melbourne, our tour ended in Sydney. I took a few more days to vacation in the city and in New Zealand. I am a fan of the "Lord of the Rings" movies, which were filmed in New Zealand. When I saw the beauty of the place in the movies, I wanted to find a way to get there and personally see the country. This was my chance! I spent a couple of days touring Sydney, including walking around the city, enjoying a beautiful sunset dinner cruise, and visiting its world-famous Opera House.

Then I flew to Auckland, New Zealand, and conducted my own walking tour of downtown. I took a Lord of the Rings tour of parts of the Northern Island. Next, I flew to Christchurch to tour the Southern Island. I went on a boat ski tour and a train ride through the mountains. It was breathtaking. My spirit was filled just by wallowing in the natural beauty of the place. The people were friendly, the food was good, a very important point for a Louisiana girl, and I have never seen so many sheep in my life! When I dreamed of traveling as a teenager looking up at the summer night sky in my backyard, I never imagined this. My mind did not even think of anything outside of the United States at the time. This was beyond my wildest dreams!

For several years, I was one of four IBMers who worked with Career Communications Group as part of an IBM collaboration on Black Family Technology Awareness Week. I was available to travel throughout the United States to raise awareness of the advantages of leveraging technology for Black families. I received professional media training for this program, then traveled the country visiting community centers and schools to raise awareness as well as to encourage and inspire. I participated in radio and television interviews, live and recorded. I was included as part of the conversation in print media and other media channels to get the word out.

When I sent Joan Mitchell a copy of my resume to enable her to prepare a good recommendation for my STSM promotion, she did that and more. Shortly after I sent her my resume, she called me at home on a Saturday morning. This was unusual, but she was very excited. Without saying hello, she went straight to the point. When she saw my resume, she thought I would be a great candidate for IEEE Fellow. This is the highest membership grade for the Institute of Electrical and Electronics Engineers (IEEE), a professional engineering society. She reached out to a former IEEE President, who also happened to be the current IBM Academy President, to get his perspective. His response was "Not only is she a good candidate, but I am also willing to sponsor her candidacy". All before she reached out to me that Saturday morning.

Joan informed me she got him to sponsor my candidacy for IEEE Fellow. *What?* She asked me to go to the IEEE website and make three lists, IEEE Fellows who: 1) you are confident will give you a favorable recommendation, 2) may give you a favorable recommendation, and 3) you know but do not want to ask for a recommendation. At the time there were no African American female IEEE Fellows. This was not something I thought about pursuing. My thoughts were, *lady, you mean well, and I appreciate your passion, but this is not going to happen to me, or anyone else who looks like me, anytime soon.* At this point in my career, I had fought many battles to become an IBM technical leader. I was somewhat familiar with the process from a female perspective and assumed it would be more difficult as a Black woman. I was not willing to fight this battle. However, Joan's enthusiasm was so contagious I went along with the program and proceeded to prepare my lists.

Joan provided me with her successful IEEE Fellow nomination package, which I used to prepare mine. In addition, I carefully prepared my first list to ensure I had a substantive number of references who were external to IBM. Over a period of several days, I would receive emails from Joan informing me of another person on my first list of fellows who agreed to be a reference. I was pleasantly surprised. Next, my primary sponsor, the IBM Academy President and IEEE Past President, Joan, and I scheduled a meeting to sit down and review my nomination package line by line. The meeting was held just prior to the official opening of the Academy's annual meeting. Line by line, he would ask me questions like, "Were you just a member of the team or did you lead the team?". "I led the team". "Then make sure there is clarity here that you actually led the team". We spent nearly two hours on this review. Given that he was very busy with the Academy, I could not believe he spent this time with me. I am forever grateful to him and Joan for supporting me.

I knew from working on the CRAW committee that many individuals that submit such IEEE packages are not elevated during their first attempt. In fact, as part of the mentoring process the women conducted with female candidates for this professional recognition, they prepared them by emphasizing that this will be a multiyear effort. I therefore was not disappointed when I did not make it the first time. I worked with Joan to change a few minor things and resubmitted my nomination package the second time. This time I made it! I was elevated to IEEE Fellow, class of 2006 "For contributions to the design and performance evaluation of computer systems". I was the first African American woman to reach this level in the IEEE Computer Society, another first. I was mistaken about my potential for this elevation; Joan made a believer out of me!

About a year after my STSM promotion, I received a call from my manager informing me of a new opportunity. He described the role of Chief Technology Officer, Global Small and Medium Business (SMB) in IBM's STG business unit. I was the top candidate for this position. *What?!?* He described it to me during our conversation, asking if I had any questions. I did not have any. I assumed this global position several days later.

In this role, I worked to align IBM's STG products and technologies with SMB-specific solutions. I worked closely with IBM's global STG development teams to drive SMB execution plans that leverage IBM's innovative technologies. I also worked with IBM business partners to understand their customers' pain points and options for enabling IBM offerings to be easy to use, integrate, manage, support, etc. I connected with the development technical leaders for

IBM's global offerings to include the right functions and features to facilitate this "easiness" for customers. In addition, I worked with IBM business partners in resolving technical solution issues and in developing SMB marketing strategies for STG. It was a highly visible technical role that enabled me to travel the globe. I was galvanized! I was also aiming for a promotion to the next IBM technical level, DE.

I went through some transformations in my personal life while living in California and Texas. The duration of my divorce process was longer than two and a half years, with it officially ending a few months after moving to Texas. Several months before my divorce was final, my high school sweetheart, who I had been dating, stopped all communication with me. There was no explanation. I was ghosted, and I did not see it coming. He was someone I trusted with my heart at a time when I was vulnerable. It felt as though he stabbed me through the heart, and it was extremely painful. I was done with him! It was a challenging and stressful process for me, and I drew strength from my faith. In fact, my spiritual journey as a Christian during this time paralleled my divorce process. My faith in God increased, and I became more keenly aware of the spirit world.

As a teenager I had premonitions of the future, what I now know are visions, but did not quite understand what was happening. I told no one, as I did not want anyone to think I was losing my mind. They stopped after a couple of years. Near the end of my divorce, and almost 30 years after they stopped, I started having visions again. I began to see things and sometimes strongly sense things. I had Christian friends who enlightened me on my experiences, primarily based on biblical text. It was truly a transformation that I continue to experience.

While in California, I regularly attended a local church and was active in the San Jose Alumnae Chapter of DST. We hosted several programs to uplift the community. I also reconnected with Leola in San Francisco, visiting her and her husband Earl several times. We went on shopping sprees, out to dinner, plays, shows, and artistic events. We generally enjoyed each other's company. I also became friends with some of my IBM coworkers, and we had multiple excursions out to lunch, and a few dinners, and other places during my two-year tenure.

My move to Texas enabled me to be closer to family. As a result, I had many weekend and holiday visits to Darlene and her family in the Houston Metro area, or they would visit me. I got to know my niece and nephew, who were young children at the time. My family was so excited for me as I bought my house in Austin. In time, my niece and nephew considered it their weekend getaway. They each had their own room and sometimes would go straight to their rooms when they visited.

During this time, I also went on two divorce trips to Las Vegas; one long before the divorce was final, although I thought it was eminent at the time. I went on the second trip after the official, legal end of the divorce process. During the first trip, when I announced to my family that I was taking a divorce trip to Las Vegas, MaMe and Kimberly invited themselves to join me. They felt they needed to celebrate this event as well. During my second trip, my good friend over the years, Shirley Hinton, joined me. She was retiring from IBM after 36 years. She was celebrating her retirement and I, my divorce. Shirley, who lived in North Carolina at the time, was on a business trip to Austin the day I bought my house. She appeared at my new house with a bottle of champagne, and we celebrated by going out to dinner. It was wonderful.

I actively looked for a church in Austin that enabled me to learn more about my spiritual experiences while growing in my faith and strengthening my gifts. I found and became a member of such a church. I also became active in the Austin Alumnae Chapter of DST. I was actively engaged with my church and sorority, planning and participating in many community-based activities. I socialized with a few church members, a couple who have become lifelong friends, coworkers, and sorors. Also, every year I attended the Delta National Convention or Regional Conference where I reconnected with many sorors I had met and worked with throughout the country or found new sorors to connect with. My life was full.

CHAPTER 13

More Enlightenment— Why Are You Not a DE?

S EVERAL MONTHS AFTER MY PROMOTION TO STSM, I had a conversation with Mark Dean regarding my promotion to the next level, DE. He thought I could make it to DE in two years. I was very surprised. This was a position that was revered in the company, I thought it would take more than two years to get to the next level. In his opinion, I should have been promoted to DE soon after I left IBM Research. He said that I was doing the type of work that DEs do, for the most part and could not believe I had just made it to STSM. Mark was on the corporate DE committee and knew the successful DE process very well. If he sincerely believed that I could be promoted to DE in two years, then I could not argue with him. He mentioned that I would need my second-level manager's support on this and suggested I have a conversation with him about supporting me in this endeavor and putting a plan in place to make this happen.

A couple of weeks later, my second-level manager had a business trip to Austin. I initiated a meeting with him to discuss this plan. Prior to meeting with him, I sent him a note, stating that I wanted to discuss working with him on a plan to get me to DE in two years. I included a summary of the work I had done up to that point and mentioned to him this would be the basis for putting a work plan in place to target a promotion to DE. He came to my office and closed the door to begin our discussion. The first question he asked me was "What on earth makes you think you can get to DE in two years?" I mentioned to him that I thought it would take three or four years; however, after talking to Mark, he convinced me I could do this in two years. He replied that since Mark Dean thinks you can get there in two years, I will work with you to make this happen. However, I will talk to Mark to get his input on this. I said to him, "By all means, speak to him".

I was apprehensive about this manager. Shortly after I first took on the CTO role, he shared with me his thoughts about me in this position. He stated that he worried about me in this CTO role. It was a huge responsibility with a broad impact. My response to him was,

> Well, I just presented a status report to our business unit's Senior Vice-President (SVP), Rod Adkins, and his directs. The feedback I received from them was I was doing an outstanding job, that my presentation was better than the other newly appointed CTOs who presented.

What this former manager was really saying was he thought I was way out of my league and did not think I could do this job. My response was *really, who cares what you think because your boss and his boss think I'm doing a great job*. He got the message and just slightly shook his head. This manager had his preferences for people on his team, whom he wanted to support for promotion to DE.

I was excited about reporting at this new level. I participated in the staff meetings of my new manager and learned about the processes, procedures, roles, and responsibilities of these high-level executives. It was very educational. It also became clear that it was a good decision to have the CTOs report to the VPs. It cuts the red tape in getting things done. CTOs had a responsibility for impacting change at the development level in STG, and it is much easier to do when you report to the executives responsible for that.

During the spring of the year leading up to me preparing my DE promotion package, I learned quite a bit about the DE promotion process. I learned the specifics of the requirements for promotion by participating as part of a special corporate team evaluating this process. As a result, I was aware of the requirements for promotion to DE and knew that I met most of them. I had about a year to fill in the gaps. I spent the next several months working tirelessly, long hours for months completing the work I planned for the year and making a significant IBM impact. This filled in the gaps in my promotion package. I had dropped everything else I was doing and devoted virtually every waking moment to my job. I was completely dedicated and committed to this effort. I was also hopeful about the prospect.

In the Fall 2005, two years after my mentor first mentioned that I could make DE in two years, I prepared my promotion package. It was a very complete and exhaustive package, with references from both technical and line executives, just as was recommended. In fact, everything that was recommended for promotion to DE, I had done. I did, however, have what I considered to be two holes in the package: technical awards and performance evaluations that are typical for DE candidates.

In fact, during the summer prior to the formal promotion process, a targeted set of women and underrepresented minorities were asked to put together DE promotion packages to be reviewed informally by a set of individuals on the corporate DE promotion review board. This was the feedback I received for this process. A question was raised about my lack of formal technical awards. I was really upset by this because as part of the process for putting together this package, it became very clear to me, or to any unbiased person reviewing this, that I should have received at least one formal technical award in my career. My documentation showed several papers and patents that I worked on with other individuals on a specific project. I was an integral contributor to the work on this project. I was also a cowriter and coinventor of papers, patents, and other documentation associated with the project. Yet, other coworkers and coinventors received formal technical awards, and I did not. I turned it around and asked my manager, stating that I agree with this reviewer, and asked, where is my technical award for doing this work? I did not get a definitive response.

I know that I earned the award I did not get. Now, to have this be one of the reasons that there is a gap in my promotion package was very disheartening. At the time the award was given to my coworkers, I was presented with an informal award; one that was lower in status and value. I did not understand the implications of not receiving the more formal (and monetarily higher) award at the time. My thinking was, well they shafted me this time; there will be other awards in the future. I did not worry about it and therefore did not fight for it. I was naïve at the time.

I still went forward to pursue the promotion. My manager and I both understood that no one candidate was going to have all the requirements. While these were gaps, they did not translate into an insurmountable obstacle. The DE promotion process is hierarchical. First, the candidate must pass an evaluation of DEs, Fellows, and line executives from the employee's business unit. In my case, this was STG. The second level is the IBM corporate DE evaluation board. Not all candidates would pass the business unit review.

During STG's evaluation of their DE packages, I learned that I was named an IEEE Fellow. My mentors and I were really excited about this recognition. This is because the membership grade of IEEE Fellow is the highest honor bestowed upon its members. It is an internationally recognized honor. Over the years, my mentors shared with me that getting top external recognition for my IBM work is very helpful to my career as I work to advance within the company. Since one of my mentors, Joan, suggested that I mention the fact that I had applied for recognition as an IEEE Fellow, she was very happy to share with the STG DE evaluation team that I was recently named an IEEE Fellow. (Joan was a member of this team.) Joan informed me they were very impressed by this external recognition. In fact, external to IBM, elevation to IEEE Fellow is far more globally recognized in the profession than promotion to IBM DE.

I was one of the DE candidates from STG, who was recommended to move to the corporate DE review board. I passed the first round. I was really getting excited at this point, as I had everything going for me. A candidate's nomination package is assigned to a reviewer on the corporate DE review board. That person is responsible for conducting due diligence, ensuring the candidate did what is stated in the nomination form. In addition, the person is responsible for checking all the references. The corporate nomination packages were due in early December, and the candidates were to be notified in early to mid-February. I waited two months for notification.

I knew of additional African Americans who had put together DE promotion packages and made it to the corporate level for review. We supported each other and shared our promotion packages so that each of us could enhance our package. Early in February, I began to get subtle messages about the status of my nomination. First, one of my closest friends informed me that they had a conversation with a member of the DE corporate promotion board and was informed that I got the promotion. I was excited about that. In addition, another colleague came to me during a top awards program for Black engineers. He informed me that only one of the Black candidates was promoted, and that person was attending the conference. Since I was the only one attending the conference, I assumed it had to be me. That made me more excited. The next day, another colleague sent me an instant message. It stated that they could not tell me what happened with my DE nomination, but they had just spoken to someone on the corporate DE evaluation board, and that I would be very happy about it. They went on to state that I should plan a party. So, with three different pieces of information from three different sources, all from different individuals on the corporate DE evaluation committee, I was extremely hopeful that I had gotten the promotion. However, I knew this was all hearsay.

I saw my manager during this February event. He gave me no indication of the decision regarding my DE promotion. Since I already knew that others were being informed, I asked him about this. His response was he was waiting to get the official word before telling me specifics. I was okay with that. About a week later, he sent me an email stating that he wanted to speak to me the next day about my DE candidacy. During this time, I was excited that I got the promotion and was thinking about the kind of party I would have. This would be a first for a Black woman at IBM, and it required a significant celebration. I responded to my manager that I was looking forward to the discussion.

The next day, February 23, 2006, I looked forward to the call with great anticipation. However, my manager began to explain to me some of the things that came up during the due diligence done by the executive who had my package. He was focusing on things that were not quite positive, so I was trying to figure out what was happening. After a few minutes, it became clear that I did not get the promotion. My manager shared some primary reasons why, but they made no sense. For example, I spent too much time promoting myself outside of IBM. Instead of spending my time promoting Sandra, I should spend time making an IBM impact, helping IBM grow its revenue. *Are you kidding me?*

I was offended by what I heard. I spend time promoting myself? Not once did I go out and seek any of the external recognition I received. It all came about because IBM, an outsider, or one of my mentors, suggested or encouraged the recognition. In addition, this kind of positive publicity helps IBM, although it is difficult to quantify its impact. I learned the *rascal* was also a member of the corporate DE review committee. As a result, I had my suspicions about what really happened.

I did not receive any good, constructive feedback regarding things I could do to make my package stronger for a future promotion. Had I received such, I would have responded favorably, although still disappointed. I would have seriously considered the feedback, made the appropriate plans, and then worked to implement them and come back in a year or two with a stronger promotion package. Instead, I was insulted. My manager mentioned that several high-level IBM executives, including Rod, tried to address this matter. They decided it was better to back off and work with me to prepare a better package in the next year. *Better? Based on what?*

One thing I know is this; I earned a promotion to DE during that cycle. It is my opinion that for many African Americans who have sought advancement and upward mobility in corporations across the United States, for many African Americans who have been trailblazers in their endeavors in corporate America, they fully understand that race may play a role in situations such as this. I knew I was not alone in this regard, but it still hurt my heart, to my very core. I kept telling myself, this is 2006, not 2056. Advancements take time. Yes, you are suffering from this nonsense; however, you are paving the way to make it easier for others behind you. This is what trailblazers do. On the other hand, I was thinking this was unacceptable! I earned this, and I should go to bat and fight for it. I was not happy with this situation, and I began to think of IBM in a different light. At this point, I did not know what to do.

All my hard work, for 17.5 years, resulted in this. I put my heart, soul, and an overabundance of working hours into this. This result threw me off guard. For all its shortcomings, I loved working for IBM. However, this experience was the catalyst for reevaluating my relationship with the company. My view of IBM forever changed on February 23, 2006. I went home that evening thunderstruck. I love eating with all my heart; however, for the first time in my life,

I could not eat. The smell of food made me nauseous. The more I thought about what had happened earlier in the day, the angrier I became.

I thought about my high school sweetheart. We had not communicated in years. He knew about my aspiration to become an IBM DE, and my maniacal focus on making it happen. When we were dating, he asked me to let him know how things turned out with this promotion, no matter what happened with our relationship. I called him that evening and told him that I did not get the promotion, and the ludicrous rationale given. I told him that I could not believe IBM would do such a thing. It was clear to him that I was devastated by this news. He was very supportive and began to encourage me. He mentioned that I should not worry about IBM. He said he knew in the future I would do something in my life that is much bigger than anything I would do at IBM. Having heard just about as much bad news as I could at that point, I was desperate to hear some good news but not half-truths and lies. However, I would cling to those words in the following months; they became my future hope. Suddenly, our connection was cut off. He was on his mobile phone, so I assumed we just lost the connection. I unsuccessfully tried to call him back. I made a mental note to call him the next day. His words were medicinal to my spirit.

I had difficulty sleeping that night but managed to get a few hours of sleep. In the morning, I got up, dressed, and went to work. I did some menial tasks, as I was still astounded and could not think straight. During my lunch break, I successfully reached my high school sweetheart. While he was warm and supportive the previous night, this day he was nasty and rude. He was outright hostile to me, and I could not figure out what was happening. He finally said to me, "I'm seeing someone else, and out of respect for her, please don't ever call me again". *What the hell?!?* I was so shocked, I froze. For several seconds, I said nothing and neither did he. I finally said to him, well, have a good life, then I hung up. It was a mistake to call him, what was I thinking! Since that conversation, I have never reached out to him for support.

To say that my life as I knew it was changing was a gross understatement. Professionally, all my hard work was apparently not good enough for IBM DE promotion decision-makers. I felt as though I hit a concrete wall. Then the man I at one time thought was my soulmate, totally insulted, disrespected, and marginalized me on a personal level. This was a man who had never, ever spoken to me in that manner, when he knew I had been bitterly disappointed professionally. How could he have done such a thing? How can you beat a person so effortlessly when they are down? I felt as if someone had backed me up and run me into the same concrete wall again the next day. I was on the edge of brokenness.

My whole body was in severe shock, and it affected me physically. I could not think or eat. I could not even walk straight. It took every ounce of energy I had to pack up the things in my office, go to my car, which I did very slowly, and make the ten-minute drive home. When I arrived, I put my things down and slowly made it to my bedroom. I just laid on the bed and stared at the walls and ceiling all afternoon and evening. I did the same thing all night long. I barely moved. My spirit was on life support. I could not believe the events of the past couple of days and was too afraid to think about what would happen next. Shock, disbelief, excruciating heartache, pain, bitter disappointment, numbness; I felt all of these with great intensity.

I tossed and turned throughout most of the night. I called a couple of friends; they were dismayed and tried to comfort me. I thought about getting all my IBM clothing and taking it to Goodwill. It enabled me to calm down enough to get a couple of hours of sleep. I woke up that Saturday morning hopeful. I got a garbage bag, then went through all my closets. Any piece of clothing that had IBM on it went in the bag. I took it to Goodwill with great anticipation. Once the donation was done, I went back home and washed my hands. Next, I went looking for all the pictures I could find in my house of my high school sweetheart. Most of them were stored away. I ripped them up, threw them in the trash, and put the trash out of my house. I went back in and washed my hands again. It was so refreshing and energizing to have washed my hands of IBM and that guy. I felt empowered but still weak.

I was at a crossroad. I no longer considered IBM my family. Yes, I still consider IBM to be a good company, with great people. I still consider quite a few people who are employed by IBM my family. IBM was my employer. I signed a contract to provide a service for a fee. As long as both sides were happy with the conditions of the contract, we had a wonderful working relationship. However, at this point I was not happy, I did not get what I earned. From that point forward, I would not work such long, hard hours, denying myself a full, wholistic life, for an entity that did not appreciate my value. I was at a level where I could demand that, and if I did not get it one place, I would go elsewhere. I wanted to go where I would be appreciated, celebrated, and not just tolerated, or worse.

I was still in shock and weak. I was not able to get much rest, and I was still unable to eat. I turned to my faith to get me through this. On Sunday afternoon, my prayer partner took me to lunch after church. I told her that I was not sure if I was going to be able to eat, but she took me anyway. We went to a Souper Salad restaurant, and I was able to eat a little salad. However, I devoured their gingerbread cake, one of my favorite items at this restaurant. I was slowly on my way back to eating food again.

That Sunday evening, I met with my pastor for spiritual counseling. He was astounded and extremely supportive of me going through a healing process. He mentioned he had known me for several years, and he had never seen me this shaken and embattled. He understood this had deeply impacted all aspects of my life. He mentioned that I had some type of warning from God that something like this would happen. He reminded me of a prophetic word I received at the end of 2005; that I would have to start looking for some new opportunities. This startled me, as I only remembered this prophecy when he reminded me. However, I was so focused on finishing my projects and putting together a successful DE package that I had forgotten about it.

During this session, my pastor stated that as I had this prophetic word, God has something better planned for me. Yes, it hurts, and I cannot understand why any human being would do what that man did to you but understand that God has something better for you in the future. You just be strong, hold your head up, and wait on God. In the meantime, I'll keep you in my prayers. These words were very comforting.

At the end of the conversation, he shared a story about his daughter who was ten years old at the time. She had to write an essay in school on a prominent African American. She chose to write about me. He said that she stood up in class and announced that a member of her church is the first Black woman to get a Ph.D. in the entire world. He said he had a talk with her teacher to inform her and his daughter that was not quite right. Dr. Johnson is the first African

American woman to get a Ph.D. in electrical engineering. (Actually, it's electrical and computer engineering.)

When I went home, Darlene called. She mentioned that her daughter and my niece, Brianna who was 11, had to write an essay on what she wanted to be when she grew up. Darlene, who had no idea I did not get the promotion, wanted Brianna to read to me a certain part of her essay, but she did not want to do it. Darlene read it to me instead. Brianna wrote that she wanted to be like me when she grew up. She went on to explain my professional accomplishments in detail. Neither I nor any other member of the family told Brianna these details, so we assumed she did some research on the Internet to get this information.

Both stories were extremely heartwarming to me, particularly at this difficult time in my life. This is because some of the feedback I received from not getting the promotion was that I should spend less time promoting myself externally, and more time positively impacting IBM. I was doing it to be a role model, particularly for young African American girls. Prior to that Sunday evening, I had little or no direct feedback that I was impacting these girls. Then in one evening, I learn that I was positively impacting not only my pastor's daughter but also my own niece. Despite the hurt and pain I was feeling, this was heartwarming, and it brought tears to my eyes. I knew this was no coincidence but a direct message from God to just ignore the nonsense from the IBMers about self-promotion. I had to keep making myself visible externally. God showed me how it was positively impacting those close to me. I was to just keep doing what I was doing. I found profound comfort in this.

I made the decision to leave IBM. I contacted headhunters, those who focused on executive recruiting. I began preparing for a move, as most likely I would leave Austin. I began to collect a few moving boxes; I went to the post office to obtain change of address forms. I had set my mind on leaving IBM and Texas.

During this ordeal, I had one-on-one conference calls with the executives who worked to try to save my promotion to get their input on what happened. During a call with Rod, I was extremely angry with IBM and alluded to the fact that I was about to leave the company. He then asked me, very forcefully, not to leave. He said I was very close to getting the promotion. He said they were not going to wait two years but to put me up for promotion during the next promotion cycle. He said to me, "if you don't make it next year, I will personally help you find a job somewhere else". I was very surprised by this, and it caught me off guard. I didn't respond to this, I just thought about it. However, from that point on, I knew I had a deal with him, which incidentally, I did not hold him to. This is because I later learned my true purpose and destiny, and it is not IBM.

I landed an interview with Google. My technical background is the performance evaluation and optimization of supercomputers. I also had a background of improving the performance of the Linux operating system on high-end enterprise servers. Google is a company that builds massive computing farms, all running on Linux. They were very much interested in speaking to me. At the time, Google was known for paying top dollar for the best engineers they could find in the world. I was therefore very excited about the interview. My view was that IBM made a big mistake, and I'm about to go and sell my services to a great company who pays top dollar for my expertise. Before I even traveled to California for the interview, I was mentally making plans to move back to California.

I spent one day at the Googleplex in Mountain View, California. During one of the morning interviews, I was told that Google searches the world for top talent in computer science and engineering. I then examined the large crowd of people sitting outside on this beautiful day having lunch. There must have been at least 2,000 people having lunch. I saw two African Americans, both very young, probably right out of college. I didn't see anyone that appeared to be Hispanic. I began to think, search the world for top talent, and you can only find a couple of African Americans? You cannot find Hispanic employees in a state with a very large population of Spanish-speaking people? I began to think that if I did this, I may be jumping out of the frying pan into the fire. I began to seriously think about this.

Then during my last interview, the interviewer asked me several technical questions about Linux. Now here I was, a Linux performance expert, who was editor-in-chief of a book on Linux performance, and I could not answer a single question. Of course, I knew the answers to these questions, but at the time they were asked, my mind went completely blank. It was very frustrating to me, because this guy did not think I knew what I was doing, I knew the answers to these questions, and I was not nervous. He asked question after question; my mind was blank. I began to think there was something else going on. There was only one other time in my life when this happened. It was during my first Ph.D.-qualifying oral exam. My mind was so blank then, that if they asked me my name, I would not have been able to correctly state my name.

While this was extremely frustrating, and I initially did not understand what was happening, I walked away from the interview knowing that I was not going to get an offer. I was still devastated because I didn't know what to do next.

I had dinner that evening with Mark Dean, and I told him about this. His response to me was maybe corporate America is not in your future. He stated that no matter where you go, there will be people who will think you are a threat to them. There will always be those who believe you do not have what it takes. At your level, they could put obstacles in your way anywhere you go. I knew there was some truth to these statements.

Now don't misunderstand me; I was, and always have been, a fighter. However, I had reached the point in my life where I questioned whether this was worth fighting for. I began to ask myself, *is this something you want to do for the rest of your career and life, or is there something else that is different, better, with a greater positive impact on the world, and more rewarding? Do you really want to spend more time and energy fighting to reach a level that may not be your purpose and destiny?* I loved the work I did; however, I also loved doing many other things. I began to seriously think about my alternatives. I eventually concluded that corporate America was not in my future, not because of any obstacles I encounter, but because God had other plans for me. I had no idea what these plans were, but my faith in God grew stronger because of this process, and I knew he had something else for me. Whatever that "something else" was, I was sure *it* would be my purpose and destiny in this life.

During this same time, I was experiencing a serious spiritual struggle. Everything I had known, all my hopes, dreams, aspirations, my centers of focus were annihilated. I did not know what I was going to do. All I knew was that I was going to leave IBM and the state of Texas. I had won an iPod in a raffle the previous summer that I only used sparingly. I began to download spiritual songs on the iPod. For several weeks, then months, I would go to work, come home, eat a little something, then read the Bible, pray (many times prostrate on the floor), and listen to the gospel songs on my iPod. On many occasions, this happened all night long. I would only get two to three hours of sleep. It was during this time that I was drawing closer to God. It was a spiritual journey that I had never known. It was this power of prayer and spiritual songs that literally saved me from the brink of insanity. I believe I had done everything humanly possible to get the promotion, and the love of a man—what was I thinking regarding him. It all came down; it was sudden and unexpected. I had no other place to go but God. My love for him, and my commitment to him, became stronger. It was Him who healed my heart with his healing balm.

There were a couple of songs that were special blessings to me. They were *I Gotta Believe*, by Yolanda Adams, and *Stand* by Donnie McClurkin. There were times when I didn't think I would make it through the night. These songs really ministered to my spirit and soul. They became my theme songs throughout. During some of the difficult nights, I would pray to God and then play these songs, they were very medicinal.

During the first few weeks of my healing process, one of my deeply spiritual church members came to me to talk. She pulled me to the side and said to me: you are going through a terrible ordeal. You feel as though something was taken away from you, something you earned. She said: I was feeling this in my spirit, and I prayed to God about it. I told God I wanted to go and talk to you about it. God's response was, no, leave her alone, do not talk to her. I will take care of her.

This was a surprise to me. I thought I had done a good job keeping what happened to me under wraps, and I did. This woman saw what was happening to me in the spirit, although it was clear that she did not have a clue what she was saying to me. In fact, while she was articulating this to me, she was examining me very closely, to determine if she heard God correctly and to observe how I would react. I kept a poker face during most of the discussion, and she was expecting some kind of reaction from me. She wanted to see some sign that she was not out there on a limb. I said to her, you are right on the mark, thank you for your words. She seemed relieved that she did not make a fool of herself.

Around the same time I went through my spiritual recovery process, one of my protégés began sending me email about the pastor of the church she had joined after her recent move to Research Triangle Park (RTP), North Carolina. This pastor was also a Ghanaian traditional leader, with a kingdom of over 2 million people in this country in West Africa. He was also very well educated, with an undergraduate degree in electrical engineering and a couple of doctorate degrees. He speaks over 13 languages, was an international businessman and consultant, and an evangelical minister. He has established churches throughout the world, over 100 churches on 5 continents. He also has dual citizenship, as an American and a Ghanaian. His name is His Royal Majesty, King Adamtey I (HRM), the Suapolor of the Se (Shai) people of Ghana. When my protégé first learned of HRM's vision for his people, she was really excited about it and thought it would be good for him to meet me. She was very enthusiastic about this, and she kept sending me emails about him.

I read these notes but was too deep into my healing process to give this any serious thought. I was willing to meet with him, if need be, as I didn't have any idea what God had in store for me. I was willing to meet and listen to just about anyone. In the meantime, I just kept doing my IBM work. After a couple of months, I received word from my protégé that HRM would be traveling to Dallas on business. He wanted to know if I would be available to have dinner with him on a specific date. I checked my calendar and was available to drive up to Dallas from Austin for this engagement. The date was set. In the meantime, HRM asked for a copy of my bio, which I forwarded to my protégé. I asked her to give HRM's assistant the contact information for my assistant to handle the logistics of this dinner meeting. Several days later, I was about to leave my office for a meeting when the telephone rang. I was at the door, trying to decide whether I should answer the phone. I looked at my watch and saw that I had a few minutes, so I went back to my desk and answered the telephone.

I heard a male voice with an accent I could not recognize. He said, "Hello Dr. Johnson, this is His Majesty". My response was, "his who?" I thought this was a joke. Then after a couple of seconds, I realized that this must be HRM. He laughed in response to "his who?", so I knew he had a sense of humor. "Hello, Your Majesty, how are you". The very first thing he said to me after our initial greeting was this: "There are over 40 known slave castles in Africa, and of that number, about 33 are in Ghana; so, chances are, you are a descendant of a Ghanaian, and it is time for you come home and help your people". At this point, I sat down at my desk and forgot about the meeting I was planning to attend. What do you say or do when someone says that to you? I wanted to hear more. HRM mentioned that he was very much interested in meeting me for dinner in the coming weeks. He asked me a few questions, such as "tell me a little about you". I was beginning to think I was being interviewed for a job. Anyway, it was about a 10- to 15-minute call, but it piqued my interest.

I conducted research on slave castles, learning about the sad story of one of the largest, the Elmina Castle, in Elmina, Central Region, Ghana. Here, still standing, is concrete evidence of a staging place for Africans awaiting transport to America. It was a component of the transatlantic slave trade. I wanted to visit that place. I also began to do research on Ghana, and on HRM. The more I learned about Ghana and HRM, the more interested I became in their story, in his story, and why specifically does a man, a king no less, wants to talk to me when he appears to be one of the busiest people on the planet. I began to ask my protégé more questions about him. In the back of my mind, I began to wonder if this was the link I was waiting for. Is my destiny and purpose somehow connected with HRM? Well, I knew I would more than likely find out once I met him.

I was still recovering during this time, still very much angry with IBM, but I did not let that hinder my work ethic. I continued to work hard and be very productive; however, I did cut back on the number of hours I spent working for the company. I became more productive in the process. I was also still in disbelief with my high school sweetheart. Friends began to tell me that he would contact me and apologize. I knew this would not happen, at least not anytime soon. They did not hear how nasty he was on the telephone. I was convinced that my future was greater than my present. I did not know exactly what I would do next; however, I was looking forward to the meeting with HRM.

I never again pursued an IBM promotion to DE. Shortly after I did not get it, I sat down with an IBM executive who was passionate about working with me to put together another DE package and try again the next year. He informed me there were others who were appalled at my situation and would be working with us to make this happen. As he looked at me while discussing this, he suddenly stopped. He looked me in the eye and said, "You don't want to do this again, do you?". I said, "no I do not". This was my way of informing my supporters that I was done. I knew I could have pursued this and more likely than not been appointed the next year.

However, I had moved on and was amid a paradigm shift. It was a spiritual process for me, an awakening. It took every ounce of strength, faith, positive energy, and quiet resilience to traverse it; enabling a soft power that came from within. At some point while going through this process, I knew that promotion to DE, and subsequently to IBM Fellow, was not my purpose or destiny. I did not know the specifics, I just knew that these positions specifically, and IBM generally, were not my future. Thus, I let it go and initiated a new, peaceful journey to find my life's purpose. One lingering concern I have, even today, as I am writing this memoir in the Summer 2023 is this: *there has never been and there is currently no Black female IBM Fellow.* To my knowledge, this is true for *all* global technology companies.

6

The Move

CHAPTER 14

Technology in Africa?

O N THE MORNING OF OUR FIRST DINNER MEETING, HRM telephoned me at home. I did not recognize his voice and thought it was someone with the wrong number. I was getting ready for work. He mentioned he was looking forward to our dinner that evening and prayed that I have a safe trip to Dallas. He also gave me his personal mobile numbers and asked me to call him if there would be any delay. I went to work for a half-day and headed for Dallas just after noon. I planned to spend the night in a Dallas hotel, so I went there to rest before getting ready.

I called him when I arrived at his hotel, then waited for him in the lobby. A few minutes later, he came from behind and introduced himself. We went to a local seafood restaurant and after ordering our meals, HRM began a general discussion about his thoughts and views about life. He first mentioned that kings do not go out in public to have dinner, especially alone with someone they do not know. *What?!?* However, he said sometimes he breaks protocol if he knows it will assist him in helping his people. It was evident that he loved his people and would do anything for them. I was thinking, why does he think having dinner with me is going to help his people?

As he continued his discussion about his view of life, I could not believe what he was saying. The dinner with HRM was in September 2006. The previous month I was the invited speaker at the summer commencement program at the University of North Texas in Denton. As HRM espoused his view of the world, he was reciting over 90% of my commencement speech, a significant portion of it

DOI: 10.1201/9781032724270-20

word for word. I knew there was a minimal chance he was aware of the nature of my commencement speech. However, there he was, reciting it.

It was a surreal moment for me, one that was repeated throughout most of the evening and left me with my mouth wide open many times. His whole mannerisms, the phrases he would say, *etc.*; this was all very similar to mine. In fact, at one point he recited word for word a couple of nuggets from my book *Inspirational Nuggets*. I never encountered anyone like this, and it really got my attention. I was trying to figure out what exactly was happening. Was this God trying to tell me something? Did this have something to do with my destiny? I was beginning to think it did. I mentioned all of this to HRM, but I do not think he really grasped what I was saying.

He began to ask a few questions about my career, and I shared a few things with him. He had not seen a picture of me and therefore thought I was much older. After having met me, he was very surprised and excited at the accomplishments of someone who was relatively young. He asked me if I had ever been to Africa, and I said no. He was so amazed that he said to me, "how is it that God would raise up someone like you, with your accomplishments, to prepare you for a task to do on a continent where you have never been". *What in the world is he talking about?*

He said to me,

> I want to introduce you to Africa, and the African people. They will love you and respect you, much more than IBM could ever do for you. The people, particularly the women, will be so inspired by you. They need to know that someone like you exists.

A chill went through my body when he said this to me. I was thinking, "how does he know how IBM has disrespected me? How does he know what IBM has or has not done for me?" However, as I began to think about this, I thought about the fact that he is a pastor and a consultant to corporations in several areas, including gender-related issues. I therefore assumed that he did not know my specific situation. There was no way in the natural he could have known, as I told only a very small number of people; my protégé who connected me to him did not even know about my IBM situation. However, given his experience as a spiritual advisor and a corporate consultant, he would know how someone like me with my credentials is treated in corporate America.

At some point during the dinner, HRM shared with me his vision for creating a Silicon Valley in Ghana. He said he has 1,000 acres of land in his kingdom that he will dedicate to this project, and he wanted my assistance in making it happen. I didn't quite grasp what he was asking as I was listening to him discuss many things. However, I thought this was an interesting concept and wanted to learn more about it. Sometime later, I asked him "what is your strategy for creating this Silicon Valley in Ghana?" His response was "I was hoping you would tell me". It was only at this point that I understood what he was asking. HRM only had the vision, a grand and glorious vision. He wanted me to take the lead to make it happen. I said to him in kind and respective words that this type of task requires many people to work full time to have a realistic chance of success. I already have a job, and I could not do what he was asking for with my time-demanding job. He asked if I was going to work for IBM forever, and of course I said no. He then asked about my plans once I leave IBM. I had not even thought about this. He asked me to think about it.

He took this a step further. He made it clear that he understands this would be a long-term project, around the order of seven to ten years for success. He did not want any misunderstanding of what he was asking of me. He made it clear that he was expecting me to leave IBM at some point in the future and work on this project full time. He was not going to set a time frame for my departure from IBM; he would leave that up to me. In the meantime, he suggested that I think about working on this as a volunteer, until I leave IBM at the appropriate time. I said to him that I would think about it. This was happening so fast that I needed time to think this through.

We continued to have discussions throughout the evening. I asked several questions of him, regarding his kingship, being a senior pastor, successful business activities, *etc.* I was trying to figure out how one person was able to do all that he had accomplished. He also behaved like a king. The way he walked and talked, the way he sat down at the dinner table, like he was seated on a throne. His mannerisms, *etc.* were all those of a king. While I had never met a king before, up close and personal, his behavior reflected my knowledge of a king's behavior. In addition, he was very wise, and that came through loud and clear throughout our discussion. However, he was very personable, humble, and genuine, which was very refreshing for someone of his stature. We finished dinner, and I took him back to the hotel.

We sat in the lobby and talked more. He had a copy of my bio, which he proceeded to read in front of me, word for word. He read a little, then stopped to ask me questions about what he had just read. I answered, then he would read a little more. He repeated this process until he read the entire one-page bio.

He was intrigued by the whole patent process, and how an individual's company, in my case IBM, received the full benefit of the patent, and not the employee. Yes, the employee did get a modest award for patents filed and issued and other potential awards as part of the patent process; however, the employee would not fully benefit from the patent. Even the significant supplemental patent awards were not comparable to the revenue some companies receive in patent licensing, or the additional benefits from cross-licensing. Those rights are signed away on a legal document by every employee on their first day of employment, before they do any work. He could not understand why anyone would be willing to do such a thing, as he thought this was unfair. I tried to explain to him there are tradeoffs, including time and expenses, in getting a patent and then protecting your rights once you obtain a patent. He was just not buying this concept.

HRM then reached the bottom of my bio, where it references me being an IEEE Fellow. Since he is an electrical engineer by training, he knew what this meant. He became very excited and mentioned that I must be one of the few Black women to have achieved such an honor. I responded that I was the only Black woman in the whole world who was an IEEE Fellow at that time. This Ghanaian king, ruler of over 2 million people, this honorable, wise king was very impressed. I could not believe what was happening. Just seven months prior to this event, I was completely devastated by the IBM technical and line executives' decision not to promote me, based in part because they felt I was too busy promoting myself externally. Here I was, seven months later, with a real wise African king in awe. This was yet another surreal moment for me.

In fact, it took me several weeks to intellectualize what happened that evening. It turned out to be the precipice to a series of unexplainable events in my life. In the following days, I began to pray about whether HRM and his vision were part of my destiny, and if leading this Silicon Valley effort was a significant part of it. I knew better than to completely dismiss this idea, as when God has a task for you, he will provide you with what is needed to get it done.

I decided that I could not lead such an effort. It would require too much work, more than I was willing to do at the time, and I was still going through a healing process. While I was doing much better, at least professionally, I was still not completely healed, and I was still waiting on God. I proceeded to think about others, many very close to retirement, who had the credentials that would encourage HRM to ask them to take the lead with his vision. During my subsequent conversations with him, I began to share with him some of these people. After a couple of telephone calls, he said to me, "I don't want you to go and find someone else to lead this effort. I want you to lead this". I did not have a response for him, so I said nothing. He asked me to keep thinking about it, which I did.

A few weeks later, I had lunch with a protégé from another technology company in Austin. He had been with his company for over seven years and was beginning to get frustrated with his lack of advancement at the rate he felt he should have been moving. I asked him a series of questions to determine if he had really thought about this issue. One of the things I said to him was this: "You have been with your company long enough to understand the culture and how things work; let me ask you this; given your situation with this company, what do you want to do in your professional life?" My protégé was Nigerian, and his response was, "I want to go back to my home country and build a technology park". I responded, "You want to do what?" I could not believe what I was hearing. Here is a young man from a West African country telling me that he wanted to go back home to create a technology park. Since I was at a stage in my healing process where my eyes and hears were open to hearing from God, I knew this may have been one of those times where God was working on me through this young man. I asked him, "So how would you go about making this happen?" For the rest of our lunch meeting, we went back and forth on how to successfully build a technology park in West Africa. I had just met this guy a few weeks earlier. Here I was, having my first strategy session on how to build a technology park in West Africa. I did not believe this was a coincidence and began to think that God was really speaking to me through this young man.

I was excited and in awe at the prospect. However, I knew that I needed more information to fully understand what was happening. In the meantime, HRM was beginning to suggest that I move to North Carolina and be close to his offices in RTP, volunteering with his nonprofit corporation to initially make this happen. My initial response, which I quickly articulated, was "I'm not moving anywhere. I like Austin and I plan to stay here". He did not respond; he was just very quiet. He then said, "just think about it".

At that point I was thinking, this man or king or whatever you call him must be out of his mind if he thinks for one minute I'm going to move anywhere. Again, I was still going through the healing process, still waiting on God for direction in my life, and trying to understand if the recent set of events was the answer I was waiting for. I just kept going to work, reading the Bible, praying, and listening to spiritual songs as I went through this process, getting closer and closer to God.

In October 2006, I attended a women's awards banquet, sponsored by the YWCA of Austin. I was a presenter for an award, having been an award recipient in a previous year. I sat next to a woman, who was receiving an award that evening for Entrepreneur of the Year. During dinner, I learned that she was a fellow Stanford alum. In fact, we were there at the same time earning graduate engineering degrees, she in chemical engineering, and I in electrical engineering. We exchanged contact information and decided to have lunch at a future date.

We were able to make it happen in early December. Once we arrived at the restaurant and ordered our meal, she went right to work. Her first question to me was "Sandra, why are you still working for IBM, they are not treating you right?" I looked at her in amazement. How could she possibly know how IBM was treating me? She saw my expression and responded,

"Oh I don't know the exact nature of what's happening to you at IBM; however, I worked in corporate America for 15 years before I left and started my own company. I concluded the *boys* were not going to give me what I know I earned, so I decided to leave and use my ethnicity", she was Hispanic, "to my advantage by starting my own company".

Before I had an opportunity to respond, she continued by saying,

[Y]ou know there is a lot going on in Africa; you should consider leaving your company and starting a business in Africa; with your credentials and skills, you can become a consultant and charge people $250 an hour; you should also create a nonprofit organization, something technology related to help the people of Africa advance in technology; so yes, you should do both for profit and nonprofit companies.

Again, before I had a chance to respond, she went on to say,

[Y]ou know, Austin is probably not where you need to be to do this Africa thing; you need to move somewhere on the east coast, a place that is not that expensive, because you will not have a lot of money initially; but someplace where it's easy to go back and forth between West Africa and the US.

What?!? This was only the second time I met this woman, and she's talking to me about leaving IBM and doing something in Africa. She did not know HRM. I did not lose site of the fact that this lunch was two weeks after the lunch with my Nigerian protégé, where we discussed strategies for creating a technology park in West Africa. At this point I stopped the woman, as I was afraid of what she was going to say next. I said to her, "I'm going to name three cities on the east coast; you let me know what you think about them". The first city I mentioned was "New York City". She said, "well it is on the east coast, and it is easy to get back and forth between the US and West Africa". She mentioned West Africa, not East Africa, not South Africa, not Central Africa but West Africa. "However, it's too expensive to live there, so I would rule that one out". I said, "Ok, how about Washington, D.C?" Her response was, "Well it is also easy to go back and forth between the US and West Africa from Washington; however, it would still be too expensive for you to live there, for what you want to do". I took a deep breath and said to her, "The Raleigh/Durham area". She got very excited, her eyes grew bigger, and said, "That's it, that's it!" Then she looked me in the eye, changed her body to a power position, pointed her index finger, and deepened her voice to slowly say, "You need to move to Raleigh", moving her finger with each word. Then she changed her body to her previous position, and her voice went back to her normal tone.

At that point, I got it. I had this surreal feeling it was not this lady speaking to me but a higher authority letting me know the next direction for my life. There were additional lunches and a dinner with others, where I learned there was a Ghanaian prince who had just joined IBM who also wanted to focus on technology in Ghana. I learned about the work another protégé was doing, working with a technology incubator. One of the things she did was assist new business owners with business plans. These individuals approached me, with no prompting from me.

After additional prayer and spiritual focus, I finally got it that my destiny was to leverage my technology background to assist in a collaborative way in building technology infrastructures, not only in Ghana but throughout the sub-Saharan Africa as well. This would be a momentous task, but something I knew was ordered by God, so it would be a success. Yes, it was going to be difficult and challenging, but in the end, I knew it would succeed in due season.

I suddenly had a newfound excitement about planting seeds to assist the people of Africa in driving globalization through technology. I was energized by the thought that this would change millions, if not billions, of lives in the long term, raising the standard of living of the African people and assisting in restoring the continent to the majestic greatness God intended it to be. This was the opportunity of a lifetime, to truly have an impact on changing the world. This seemed more important and impactful to me than helping IBM increase its revenue, market share, and value to its stockholders. So, from the pain, insult, and disrespect of being denied an earned promotion, to the most heart-wrenching personal dilemma I ever experienced, to weeks and months of studying God's word, prayer, and worship, I came to understand my destiny and purpose in this life. This is how I picked up my mantle to do the work I believe I was put in this world to do.

I contacted HRM and informed him I would help him with his vision, first as a volunteer, then we will see what happens next. I also said to him that I would move to the Raleigh/Durham area. I was still spending considerable time at night lying prostrate, in what became my prayer room, in prayer and meditation. I came to the place spiritually where I was prompted to do this. I would move in the August/September time frame, 2007. In the meantime, I would make monthly trips to the RTP area and work with the people in the Life for Africa office, HRM's nonprofit organization we would use as the initial vehicle for making this technology park happen.

In the subsequent weeks, I brainstormed with HRM about how to do this. He suggested that we host an African Technology Conference in the summer of 2007 and invite technology professionals from around the globe to come to Ghana and brainstorm on developing a strategy for building this technology park. He knew that I had experience in chairing and birthing conferences, as he had read and remembered my entire vita. He therefore asked me to make it happen. I assumed this role, again on a volunteer basis. We later changed this date to the summer of 2008 to allow adequate time to plan and host a world-class conference.

I soon learned that IBM was beginning to have a focus on Africa. IBM was planning to use Africa as one of its focus topics for its Global Innovation Outlook (GIO) for 2007. When I learned of this endeavor, I quickly contacted the leader of the effort and informed him of my efforts with this technology park in Ghana, and with the African Technology Conference. He became very excited about my work and began to pull me into the plans for IBM's GIO Africa initiative. I got HRM involved, and IBM invited him to attend one of the GIO Africa deep dive sessions.

I also introduced HRM to many of my technology contacts and mentors. As a result, HRM was invited to speak at the recognition dinner for the Top 100 Most Important Blacks in Technology, as part of the Black Engineer of the Year Awards Conference in February 2007. He gave a riveting, impassioned speech at this event, where he asked the audience to assist him, and me, in developing a Silicon Valley in Ghana, then replicating it throughout sub-Saharan Africa. The audience, which consisted of some of the top technology executives in the world who are of African descent, was speechless and gave him a standing ovation before and after his speech. It was truly heartwarming to witness.

I moved to North Carolina (NC) in August 2007. I was able to lease my house in Austin and find a brand-new house to rent in NC. Also, I had the type of job at IBM where I did not have to physically be in Austin. I set up a home office in NC for my IBM work. I was hopeful about taking my first step toward my purpose and destiny; however, when the movers left my Austin house and I had finished cleaning it prior to my renters' arrival, it was a little difficult for me to leave. I overcame that fear, said a prayer for my safe travel, and started my trip.

I had a beautiful drive to North Carolina. I started out on a Saturday afternoon, driving from Austin to Shreveport, Louisiana. I stopped at a hotel for a good night's rest and then drove on to Atlanta the next day. I went through northern Louisiana, Mississippi, and Alabama before entering Georgia. I had a great lunch stop in Meridian, Mississippi, and spent the night at the Marriott Marquis Hotel in downtown Atlanta. That Monday morning, I woke up, had a wonderful breakfast at a Waffle House just outside of Atlanta, and then headed east to North Carolina, via South Carolina. My entire trip was a beautiful, sunny drive with absolutely no rain, and my car was just heaven to drive. I arrived in Cary in the afternoon and went to the rental office. I picked up the keys to the house I was renting and drove to the house. I had never seen the house, as I had a good friend check out several rental houses for me since I was unable to travel there to examine them myself. It was a beautiful four-bedroom house with granite kitchen countertops and stainless-steel appliances. I loved it. The movers came the next day and delivered my things with nothing broken or lost. By the end of the week, I was all moved in, except for the boxes I placed in the garage. I made this move effortlessly, and I was ready to start my new life. Shortly after my move to NC, I became a member of HRM's church. He became my pastor.

I quickly connected with IBM colleagues and friends who had moved to NC prior to my arrival. This included my good friend, Shirley Hinton, who I worked closely with in the Westchester Alumnae Chapter of DST. She was the first Vice-President of the chapter during my tenure as President. We worked closely together during this time, and we were already friends prior to that. Shirley was also an IBMer. I also met friends at my new church and the Raleigh Alumnae Chapter of DST.

I continued to contribute with innovation and invention at IBM. While I went through this move and transition process, I submitted approximately 15 disclosures, some of which became patent applications and others were published on IP.com. In addition, I was a coinventor on a couple of patents that were issued. I also received a formal Outstanding Technical Achievement (OTA) award for my CTO work. This was a highly regarded technical award for making a significant IBM technical contribution. OTA winners were invited to the annual Corporate Technical Recognition Event (CTRE), held for top technical employee contributors.

This was my second invitation to CTRE, the first was when I was elected to the IBM Academy of Technology. It was a wonderful event both times. Employees attend business meetings during the mornings, where they are recognized for their technical achievements in the prior year. The afternoons were dedicated to recreational activities. Each employee, and an adult guest, selects from a plethora of activities such as horseback riding, water sports, or spa activities. I chose spa activities, as they were fabulous. It was wonderful. However, during my second CTRE event, one of the attendees came to me, and with disdain in his face said to me, "What are YOU doing here?". *Oh, how rude,* I thought to myself. My response was, "I'm here for the same reason you are here, I received an OTA award last year". *In fact, I'm sure my contribution was more significant than yours!* He just huffed and walked away. My thought was, *God, help him.*

I continued my work as a global CTO in STG. I worked to align STG products and technologies with small and medium business (SMB)-specific solutions. I worked closely with IBM development teams to drive SMB execution plans that leverage IBM's innovative technologies. I evaluated the feasibility and viability of emerging technologies for the mid-market (medium businesses). I also collaborated with IBM business partners in resolving technical solution issues and in developing mid-market strategies for STG. I worked with IBM marketing teams as part of this effort.

I traveled to Europe and Asia, consulting with many of IBM's mid-market customers on their pain points and other issues. I used this knowledge to work directly with STG's development teams globally to ensure our offerings were enhanced to address these customers' concerns. This resulted in many technical discussions with technical leaders on understanding our offerings and how they can be enhanced for this purpose. I traveled to China—Shanghai and Beijing—during one of my customer visits, also speaking to IBM's China development and research teams.

I recall a meeting with the research team, where one of my IBM colleagues was describing to me the technical details of his ongoing project. As I conversed with him, I described my understanding of the details. As I was articulating this, I noticed he became animated. He was moving around in his chair as though he was about to boil over. I thought, *"What's happening, why is he doing that?"* I did not mention anything to him about this, I just kept talking. When I was done, he said to me, "That is not quite what we are doing. However, what you described is a better technique that we did not think about. Since your idea is better, I think we should work to file a patent application on this". I was surprised, and he was excited. A few weeks later, while working with the China team on the details after I returned to the United States, we filed a disclosure on this work. It went through the IBM patent process in China.

I also worked closely with IBM's marketing teams that focused on the mid-market. Together, we created programs to work with IBM business partners, which focused on this market. I provided input from the technical development's perspective, while also learning about how IBM markets its offerings. It was an educational experience.

I continued to receive external recognition for my work. I became a Distinguished Engineer with the Association for Computing Machinery, a professional computing organization. I was recognized with awards from the IBM Austin Black Diversity Network Group. National recognition included being named in the "Top 100 Most Important Blacks in Technology" and receiving the Summit Heritage Award from the IT Senior Management Forum.

I conducted research on technology parks around the world. I learned that successful parks leverage stakeholders from academia, government, and industry. They work closely together, collaborating to facilitate innovation, invention, and creativity. I made several trips to Ghana during the time we were planning the technology conference. I worked to build the network of stakeholders for the park and the conference. My first trip to Ghana, and Africa, was in the Spring 2007. I made sufficient progress in building a network of stakeholders; however, the most memorable part of my trip was a visit to a slave castle on the Atlantic coast.

The Elmina Slave Castle is in Elmina, Ghana, right on the Atlantic Ocean. The castle was used to imprison the captured slaves before they were placed on slave ships for their transatlantic voyage. This castle was the largest of its kind in sub-Saharan Africa and globally. It was built by the Portuguese in the 17th century, and they occupied it for 155 years. The Dutch then attacked the Portuguese and took over this castle, maintaining control for over 200 years. The British were the last to occupy the castle, having control for 85 years until 1957 when Ghana became an independent nation.

I was very moved by this experience. The castle was built on a bed of rock on a cliff overlooking the Atlantic Ocean. It was a beautiful day, with a vibrant blue sky, but that in no way tempered the strong feelings that came over me during the tour. There were several dungeons used to keep the slaves; the smell of death was still there, hundreds of years later.

Our tour guide shared with us intricate details of the history of this stone castle. The women were repeatedly raped by the guards and the governors of the castle. The governor had a large living quarter on the castle's third floor, overlooking the Atlantic. When he felt the need, he would call the guards to bring him women to rape in his quarters. These women had not bathed in weeks, but that did not matter to him. He would pick one, and the guards would bring her to the governor's bedroom, aka rape room. Any woman who resisted the governor or the guards would be chained to cannons and left outside in the hot sun or rain for days. This was to discourage other women from resisting.

At this point I began to weep, as I could not bear the reality of standing on the site where my ancestors began the suffering that we still experience today, though to a lesser extent. I had to step away from the rest of the tourists, as I was the only African American there among the various Ghanaians and multinationals on the tour. They were not visibly impacted as I was, but on the other hand, it was my ancestors who suffered from this evil. I sat on the steps of the castle leading to the governor's quarters, listening to the waves of the ocean, feeling the gentle breeze, and trying to come to grips with the reality of the situation. I could feel the spirituality of the place, and I began to see very short, but real, visions and images of the slaves in these very quarters. I could hear their cries and feel their anguish and hopelessness. It was surreal.

I also visited a chamber used to keep the slaves who rebelled against their imprisonment. All they knew was they had been captured and were kept in horrible conditions. They had done nothing wrong and could not understand why this was happening to them. They fought for their freedom. As a result, they were placed in this chamber. It had no ventilation, and at most ten slaves were kept there at a time. They were given no food or water. They stayed there until they all died. Therefore, some of them were there around dead, rotting bodies until they died too. As I entered this chamber, and the door was closed, I felt a sense of hopelessness. I prayed for the souls of all who died there.

I was shocked to see two churches in the middle of this castle. One of the churches is directly above the women's dungeon, where the women were consistently raped by the guards. There is a Bible verse on the sign above the door of the church, "This *is* my resting place forever; Here I will dwell, for I have desired it" (Psalms 132:14, New King James Version). I was angry and appalled at the reality of this situation.

One of the former governors of the castle was only there for a short time. He died of yellow fever several months after he arrived. There is an encryption, written in positive text, about him on the rock in the castle right above his burial place. I felt a strong desire to spit on this burial site, or at least stomp on it; but I resisted that urge.

We went on to see the path of no return. A very dark path from the dungeon to a narrow opening, where only one individual at a time would pass through to the outside and be placed on the awaiting slave ship. I also saw a branding room, where the slaves were branded with cargo numbers to keep track of the "stock". I went through the path of no return and stood on the ledge, about five feet above the ground. There I stood, frozen in the moment, looking at the Atlantic Ocean and all its beauty. The calming force of the wind and waves could not veil the horror and evil of this place, nor the depth of my pain and anguish in knowing what happened.

Throughout the tour, I found myself in a constant battle. I was extremely angry, frustrated, and hoping that all those guards, governors, and others who worked there went straight to hell. On the other hand, I know that God is in control. While we do not always understand why this evil happened to our ancestors, I know that He is still on the throne.

As I stood near the edge of this cliff and gazed at the beautiful Atlantic Ocean before leaving, I thought about the slave ships that were present hundreds of years ago. I began to see them in a vision. I thought about the long voyage our ancestors made to reach the Americas. I thought about the horrible things that awaited them there, and the unjust things that we are still experiencing today. I thought about my own experiences, particularly my recent experiences. I know there is a reason why God enabled me to experience those events during that time in my life. It is tied to my destiny. That I, a descendant of the thousands who passed through this place, have returned. Not just to visit, have a moving experience, and go back to business as usual in America. I could never do that again.

This was my eureka moment. There is a stone near the entrance of this castle that describes the anguish of those who were imprisoned in this place, the charge to never repeat such atrocious injustice, and a desire for the descendants to return. It was confirmation that my destiny is to be one of those who return, to help rebuild this beautiful continent, and restore Africa to its greatness. To bring Africa to its rightful glorious place, by being one of those leading the globalization drive through technology. There I stood, taking it all in. I prayed for the souls of those who perished there and through the middle passage, and for those who survived and landed in America. I prayed that all those souls are resting in a place where there is no sorrow, pain, or any of the horrible things they experienced. I also knew that as long as I live, I will be guided by a light to live out my destiny that He has shown me; to work tirelessly and passionately; to travel to Africa many times and help my people, after being away for so long.

When I had dinner with HRM and his associates later that evening, he mentioned one thing that stuck with me as I pondered the events of the day, "Love your enemies". This helped me with my dismay and anger regarding the events of the day. Yet, I could not unlearn how our people were stripped of their dignity and freedom. It is something that moves me and drives me every day I am on earth.

CHAPTER **15**

The Middle East
and Africa

I CONTINUED TO MAKE TECHNICAL contributions to the company and professionally. I was a coinventor of six patents issued during this period. In addition, several disclosures were written to initiate future IP. A few were filed as patents while others were published on IP.com. I addition, I coauthored a technical book chapter on 3D data centers in synthetic worlds and became a member of a new patent brainstorming team. Joan Mitchell, one of my mentors, asked me to become a part of a small group of her mentees for this purpose. She wanted to introduce me to other current and future IBM technical leaders, as well as educate her mentees in the technical pipeline on the patent process.

I believe Joan was also conducting due diligence to learn what happened with my DE process. When I informed her that I did not get the promotion, her response was "I'm sure it had nothing to do with your race". I did not expect that response from her. We had never discussed race in any of our conversations. I did not respond to that remark; however, I disagreed with her and knew she was speaking from an unenlightened perspective. During her due diligence, she asked many people I collaborated with over the years of my work and their assessment of my abilities. As the months progressed, she became more agitated and concerned about what she was learning and beginning to understand. It was during this

DOI: 10.1201/9781032724270-21

time that she asked me to join her patent brainstorming team. She wanted to learn firsthand about my technical abilities, thought processes, etc.

One of Joan's mentees, a White woman, was promoted to DE the next year. Joan was incensed. I recall a telephone conversation when she informed me of her protégé's promotion. She could not understand how this woman could be promoted and not me. (We were both happy for her achieving this milestone.) Joan said that my credentials were much stronger, and my IBM impact much greater than hers. Joan questioned, "How could she be promoted to DE and not you?". I did not respond to her; I just allowed the words to be in the atmosphere. I believe it was at that moment that Joan reluctantly and uncomfortably understood what I, and those who look like me, have known and lived with our entire lives. I had already moved on, focusing on my purpose. However, it was enlightening for me to see how this White woman who was naïve about such matters came to an uncomfortable understanding of the lives of some of her fellow Americans.

Joan and our team filed several invention disclosures over a few years. Most of them resulted in the issuance of patents sometime later. During one of the disclosure reviews, only I and a coinventor were available to defend our idea via a teleconference. The evaluator was to decide on filing a patent application, publishing on IP.com, or closing the process. He was very condescending and insulting as part of our discussion. I ignored his extraneous remarks and focused on his substantive arguments. My young coinventor was about to share a few unpleasant words with him about his behavior. I quietly sent him an instant message online, asking him to restrain himself and let me handle the evaluator.

He calmed down and let me talk. The evaluator was ruthless and petty, but I continued to focus on the substantive issues he raised. Over time, I addressed every issue to his satisfaction. When he realized that he had no other issues, he reluctantly made the decision to file. After we ended our conversation with him, my coinventor immediately called me and asked how I could let the guy talk to me like that. I told this African American male that the evaluator is a gatekeeper. We just needed him to open the gate. I informed him we had a choice of patent review teams for submitting the disclosure. We know how this review team operates now. So, once he opened the gate and decided to file, we will not go back to him or his team again. I said to him, "let this be a lesson to you to keep your eyes on the prize". I did not follow up and have a discussion with the evaluator's management regarding his behavior. I discerned this was not a fight worthy of my time.

In addition, I was very active with IBM Academy activities. I co-led the Performance Engineering Conference since my induction, the same conference where I presented a paper while being a candidate. I also co-led a couple of Academy studies. For one of them, I attended the event where the facts and findings were presented to IBM's CEO. I was actively engaged and impactful as an IBM technical leader.

I knew my purpose and destiny were to help drive the economies of Africa through technology. As a result, I attempted to find IBM job opportunities on the continent. The 2007 IBM Global Innovation Outlook (GIO) had a focus on Africa. This was around the time I began to personally focus on the continent. I was asked to participate in the planning activities for GIO Africa. I actively engaged in a deep dive session in Atlanta and attended the GIO Africa results presentation in New York.

I continued to focus on Africa in my volunteer work outside IBM. I was also connected with IBM's Africa focus while doing impactful work. I spent time as an STG assurance architect, then moved into new roles in business development and university alliances. This enabled me to work closely with the STG sales teams. I led technical teams to close joint development agreements, and other similar deals, with industry partners. I also focused on developing collaborative partnerships between universities in sub-Saharan Africa and those in the United States and globally in areas of mutual interest.

IBM's Africa strategy became a significant component of its future growth plans. More activities, including opportunities to do international assignments on the continent, were initiated. I started looking for international assignment opportunities in Africa. I learned about at least two opportunities within an 18-month time frame and had discussions with the relevant contacts about them. On these occasions, my resume was forwarded to individuals in

Johannesburg, South Africa, for review and comment. Each time, I did not get a response.

I tried another approach. I discussed my aspirations with Rod. He informed me of the creation of some new roles, including opportunities on the continent. He suggested I connect with a couple of individuals he recommended, which I did. I learned about the role with a geographic scope of the Middle and Africa (MEA). It was a business development role, very different from the research and development roles I had in the past. I applied for it and was offered the job after a great interview. However, I was apprehensive about accepting the offer. It required a move to Dubai, United Arab Emirates (UAE), or Johannesburg, South Africa. After some due diligence regarding the advantages and disadvantages of these two options, I chose Dubai.

In January 2011, I had a conversation with one of my girlfriends, Angela, about a potential vacation together that year. She focused on a party cruise or Dubai. I said to her, "I'm not feeling Dubai". While I was aware of Dubai and its many tourist attractions, I had no desire to travel to the Middle East, especially for a vacation. I wanted to do a spa vacation, but she was not interested. We agreed to plan separate vacations.

The spark that initiated the Arab Spring occurred a couple of weeks earlier. It began with Tunisia, then Algeria, and on to Egypt, Libya, and Syria. I had some concerns about moving to Dubai in the middle of the Arab Spring. I discussed them with Mark Dean. He said the United Arab Emirates is fine. Yes, while there are some historic events happening all around the UAE, in other parts of Arabia, the UAE was a safe place. He emphasized this by informing me that he was in Dubai on a business trip, and everything was fine. I discussed this short-term assignment in Dubai with others who had just completed or were completing a similar assignment. They convinced me that Dubai was a safe place, and a very different place than the United States.

I accepted the offer. In doing so, I changed the type of job I had and moved from research and development to business development in sales. I would also move from the country and culture with which I was most familiar, the United States, to the UAE. Furthermore, I would move to Dubai in the Middle of the Arab Spring. While I would not be physically based in Africa for this role, my territory included all of MEA. My manager informed me that this would be 100% travel, including several countries in Africa. I was excited about this opportunity. I now had a new role, region, and culture, and of course, the opportunity to travel to several countries in Africa. In fact, I would be fostering relationships with technology business leaders and government entities focused on technology. This was awesome and in line with my purpose and destiny.

How was I going to explain this to my mother? Here I was about to move halfway around the world, to Arabia and a Muslim country, in the middle of the Arab Spring. Every time I thought about calling her about this, news of the unbelievable activities occurring throughout the Arab world would fill the airwaves. What was I to do? After a couple of weeks, things quieted down a little, and I called her. I told her I had a new job in Dubai. She was not very familiar with Dubai and wanted to know more about the place. I gave her some background, and she began to get excited for me. I informed her that I would be traveling throughout Africa. Then I informed her of the geographic location of Dubai, in the United Arab Emirates in the Middle East. I was thinking she would be concerned about her daughter moving to Arabia at that time. Her response was "I know where it is". I was very surprised. She was aware of the location when I first mentioned it to her. She was not the least bit concerned about my safety in this region. Her thinking was if I was going to move there, then I must be confident about my safety. If I was okay with this, then she is also okay.

She did, however, have some questions for me. First, how would I be able to communicate with her while there? I informed her we could communicate via Skype. I would have my nephew, her grandson, set it up for her on her laptop and show her how to use it. Next, when would I be buying a ticket for her to come and visit me. Again, I was taken aback. It is one thing for me to go into a potentially dangerous situation. It was another thing for my mother to do the same. She was not the least bit concerned. This was an opportunity for her to learn about other parts of the world. I clearly had underestimated my mother. She was as interested in learning about new parts of the world, firsthand, as I was. In fact, I am my mother's daughter. My quest for adventure, to go out and learn about new and different things, about other parts of the world, came from her; amazing!

A few days later, I had another conversation with Angela. I informed her that I had a new job based in another country. I told her I would be moving to Dubai for a two-year assignment doing business development in the Middle East and Africa. Her response was, "not Ms. I'm not feeling Dubai! You're moving to Dubai? I can't believe this!". I said yes, I am moving there in a couple of months. She was aware of my passion for Africa. Once I began to share the specifics of the role with her, she was really excited for me. Then she remarked, "now I know we are going to have a vacation in Dubai". I asked her to give me some time to get acclimated and then we'll plan a vacation there.

As part of my due diligence in learning about how to develop successful technology parks, I knew I would have to develop a community that includes all the stakeholders. This would be universities, technology business owners, entrepreneurs, the relevant government entities, etc. This would be contacts not only in Ghana but throughout Africa as well. As I thought about a technology park, I knew this would be a momentous task that would require significant funds to travel throughout the continent and meet the right people. I had no idea how I could facilitate such a task and became frustrated. Two years later, I got this role in Dubai requiring me to do just that, at IBM's expense. This was something that would be mutually beneficial to IBM and to me and my post-IBM plans. This was a divinely opened door for me, creating the path for me to walk through, and I knew it.

Once I accepted the position in IBM MEA, I initiated the Dubai onboarding process. Applying for work and residence visas was a multistep process. I needed to get my highest degree attested, send documents to the US State Department in Washington, DC, submit documents to the UAE Embassy in DC, then send everything to IBM in Dubai to apply. Part of the degree attestation included obtaining documentation from the NC Secretary of State's office. Once I received them from that office, I sent the information to the US State Department in Washington, DC and waited a couple of weeks for a reply. At the same time, there were threats by members of the US Congress to shut down the government due to their inability to agree on a budget.

The State Department sent the entire package back to me indicating it was incomplete. I took it back to the NC Secretary of State's office and was told they gave me the wrong information. I obtained the correct documentation from them and drove to Washington to personally submit everything to the State Department. I could not wait another two weeks, especially if the government would shut down.

I contacted a college friend, Joanne, who lived in DC to connect with her while being in the city. I made it to her home a few minutes before she arrived from work. I sat on the swing on her front porch and waited for her. It was a wonderful evening, and I enjoyed the view. A few minutes later, she drives up in her convertible. It was refreshing to be driving around Washington in a convertible on a gorgeous April evening. The weather was perfect. We had dinner in a downtown Italian restaurant. Joanne knew the Matre'd and the chef, and they took care of us! It was a genuinely heartwarming evening as we celebrated life itself and my new international opportunity.

Joanne had just completed several months of chemotherapy after a colon cancer diagnosis and was cancer free. She had a positive attitude and outlook throughout her experience. We celebrated her life that evening. It was so good to see her looking fabulous!

I arrived at the State Department early the next morning and was able to get my application processed in 15 minutes. Next, I drove to the UAE Embassy to submit my package. They checked to ensure I had all the correct information, which I did. They informed me that they would mail the final document to me within two business days. With that, I was done with my business in Washington at 10:15 AM.

I started my trip back to North Carolina. It was a beautiful morning, and I had a relaxing drive home. I waited a couple of days to receive the package from the UAE Embassy, which I received on time. I sent the complete package to the IBM HR team in Dubai to initiate the processing of my residence and work visas. I sent everything to them via express mail; however, it took several days for them to receive it. This was because the UAE weekends are Fridays and Saturdays, which delayed their receipt. (The package arrived on a Friday; however, it was another two days before it was received.) By this time, I knew I would not be receiving the documents needed for me to fly to Dubai to begin work on May 16. I had to wait until the preliminary processing was complete in Dubai before I could get on a plane. Once the HR team received my package, they submitted everything to the authorities in Dubai. They informed me that they would have the documentation for me to fly to Dubai in seven days.

It was during this process that I first learned that any time frame mentioned to you is a suggestion or a recommendation. In fact, it is unlikely to be complete in the time frame quoted. It will happen when it happens. I was not fully aware of this until I was on the ground in Dubai, so at the time I thought seven days really meant seven days. After a few days, I received the documentation then arranged to take the next flight to Dubai. I arrived on Tuesday evening, May 24, my first trip to Dubai. I reported to work on Wednesday, May 25, 2011.

My first day in the office was good. It was the typical signing of legal documents, etc. While I had been an IBM employee for nearly 23 years, they were spent entirely in the United States. I was a new IBM Middle East and Africa employee. I had to go through "annual" processes that I had just completed a couple of months earlier in the United States.

I scheduled an AIDS test the next day. At that time, the UAE did not allow anyone to be a resident who has AIDS. Every residence visa applicant must take an AIDS test at a government medical facility, paid for by the applicant. I spent the morning getting this test and the afternoon going back to the facility to get my results. Next, it was time to complete the process for getting my residence and work visas. The HR team informed me it would take seven days—does this sound familiar? This time I did not take it literally. However, to my surprise, it only took one week. I was told by many of my peers that I was lucky. They were unaware of the drama I experienced to get to Dubai.

Since I had to turn in my passport and wait these seven days, I could not leave the UAE. This was not an issue, as I proceeded to look for a place to stay, open a checking account, etc. I continued with the onboarding process as I awaited my final documents. Prior to departing for Dubai, my financial advisor suggested I get a UAE bank account with an America-based bank. I went to a Citibank branch location a few days after my arrival to open a checking account. They gave me an application to complete and informed me that I needed my permanent residence before they proceeded. Once I received this within a week, I went back to Citibank with this documentation. They informed me that someone would contact me in a couple of days with my account information.

Citibank did not contact me, so I contacted them. They informed me that they would investigate this and get back to me. After a couple more days, I received an email from them asking a plethora of questions. For example, where have I lived for the past 10 years, how long have I worked for IBM, they wanted documented proof that I worked for IBM during this time frame, and many other similar questions. I picked up the telephone and spoke to them, as I was trying to understand why they were asking me all these questions. I just wanted a checking account. In fact, in the UAE it is the law. An employer must pay their employees by depositing payroll into their checking accounts. If I did not have a checking account, I could not get paid. This was not only for payroll but also for any payment, *e.g.*, travel and degree attestation expenses. I was motivated to get a checking account ASAP.

Citibank was unable to explain to me to my satisfaction why they were asking me all these questions. In fact, they were offended that I had the proclivity to ask. I do not believe they were used to a woman being so firm with them. Yes, this was Citibank, but I was in the Middle East, a society more misogynistic than in the United States. They stopped communicating with me for a couple of weeks. This is despite telephone calls, emails, and visits to the local branch office where no one would help. I am not making this up. This is what happened.

IBM's banking was via Citibank. I connected with the IBM finance team and asked them to please contact their counterparts at Citibank and ask them to create a checking account for me, and they did. The Citibank folks stated they would investigate my situation and ensure I would have an account opened for me. A few days passed and still, I had no checking account.

In the meantime, the IBM HR team was contacting me every other day asking me if I had a checking account. I kept them abreast of the checking account drama. They informed me that they wanted to pay me for my housing and other expenses, even before the regular payroll cycle kicked in for me, but they could not until I had a checking account. I informed them that I wanted a checking account more than they wanted it for me.

Finally, after six weeks, four trips to Citibank branch offices, and several communications between the IBM and Citibank finance teams, I received an email communication, congratulating me on receiving a Citibank savings account. A savings account? Are you kidding me? I didn't ask for or want a savings account; I wanted a Citibank checking account. I gave the IBM team my savings account number so I could get paid. I would worry about changing this to my checking account later if I ever received a checking account.

I inquired about getting a checking account. I went back to the Citibank finance team via email and voice mail, with no response. I could not believe I was going through all this trouble just to get a checking account, and after six weeks I still did not have one. I went to a different Citibank branch office to inquire. They checked the system and could not understand why I did not have a checking account. However, they were not able to determine from the system whether a checking account for me was eminent. However, they assured me they would investigate it. I did not believe them.

A few days later, I received a call from a courier service informing me they had my checks. They wanted to know if I wanted them delivered to me at home or the office. I wanted these checks ASAP, so I said work. At the time, I was not sure if these were checks for a savings or checking account. It was only after I received the checks, examined the account number on them and compared it to my savings account number that I knew I had a checking account. I never received a communication from Citibank congratulating me and informing me that I had a checking account. This is certainly not the way any bank should treat its customers, particularly a large global bank like Citibank. I made the mental note to close both my US and UAE accounts once my tenure in Dubai was completed and I returned to the United States, which I did.

Once I had a checking account, I went back to IBM payroll to give them my checking account number, asking them to deposit funds into that account and not my savings account. IBM obliged, and there were no issues. Finally, after nearly seven weeks, I had a checking account. I was paid (payroll) for the first time at the end of July 2011, over two months after I first arrived in Dubai. I was finally in the system and on track for regular monthly payroll payments, as well as any travel expense reimbursements or other payments.

In addition, once I received my Citibank UAE checking account, I set up online banking for the UAE accounts. I had already created a Citibank checking account, including an online account, in the United States. Once I had online accounts in both countries, I did all my banking online, including paying all my bills in the United States. (I do not think my lawn maintenance guy in NC ever knew I was living out of the country for over two years.) I love online banking. It is a great equalizer. It doesn't matter if you are male or female or if you ask challenging questions as a woman in a misogynistic society; online banking just focuses on banking. It was great. I was also able to transfer funds easily and quickly from my UAE and US Citibank accounts. In fact, once I initiated the transfer from my UAE to US accounts, the funds were available immediately in my US account. In addition, the fees for the currency exchange were very low.

My first role in Dubai was as a Business Development Executive. I was still part of STG but on the sales team. I worked with IBM business partners throughout the Middle East and Africa to develop new solutions to bring to market. My focus was primarily on countries in Africa, some of which included Ghana, Nigeria, Senegal, Kenya, Tanzania, Uganda, Tunisia, and South Africa. I also collaborated with partners in the UAE. I worked to close many agreements with partners in these countries to go to market with IBM offerings.

In addition, I attended the IBM Global Sales School in Johannesburg, South Africa. This required a couple of trips to South Africa in the early months of my time in Dubai. It was another opportunity to learn about closing deals with partners and customers. This was very different from my technical training, and I loved the challenge. One session of classes there was held during the week of Thanksgiving in the United States. One of my classmates, a German on assignment in Johannesburg and his wife invited me and other colleagues to their home for dinner. He did not know it was Thanksgiving in the United States; however, I arrived at his home to a feast. It was primarily meat. There was a variety of grilled meat everywhere and just a small amount of salad. That is how I learned that South Africans, and I later learned Namibians, love to eat meat. I announced to everyone that it was Thanksgiving in the United States. I thanked the hosts for enabling me to have a wonderful Thanksgiving feast.

While I worked in Dubai as part of a sales team, I still maintained my technical roots, as always. I had regular conversations with the STG technical lead for the Middle East and Africa. I had previously sponsored him as a candidate for membership in the IBM Academy and communicated with him about that. I did not meet him until I arrived in Dubai. From time to time, he would come to me to brainstorm about a technical issue. He worked to hire an IT architect for my sales team, so I collaborated with him on the hiring process. I also had regular meetings with this newly hired architect once he came on board.

While I was on assignment in Dubai, seven patents were issued, with me as a coinventor, in the United States. These were for applications that were filed prior to commencing my work in MEA. I thought about ideas that may be patentable while on assignment; however, there was no official IP process in MEA. As a result, I set out to create one. I conducted my due diligence, talking to the legal teams in MEA and Europe. I put together a proposal and submitted it to the relevant IP team. I later learned that an IT architect on assignment from IBM in Austin and based in Johannesburg was asking about the patent process. The proposal was approved, and a short time later the IBM Middle East and Africa Patent Review Board was announced with me as the Chair, and my Johannesburg colleague as the Cochair.

There has been an increased focus on emerging markets with low-cost, high-quality workers with abilities to drive new innovations. The most untapped markets of this global economy are on the African continent. With its increased levels of foreign direct investment (FDI), favorable business climates, relatively stable governments, and expanded trade, Africa is now a change agent for its economies and people. Further, with its vast resources, most notably young people, its governments focusing on information and communications technology growth strategies, the unique ability for unprecedented creativity and innovation, and sustained economic growth rates, Africa is a continent on the precipice of transforming regions and changing the world through innovative technology.

There is a significant interest in the favorable growth opportunities in this diverse market. It derives from technology and other industries, investors, educators, industry analysts, the media, and nonprofit institutions.

Africa is a very large continent, both geographically and in population, with an estimated 1.46 billion people in 2023. In fact, the countries of the United States, Spain, Portugal, Belgium, the Netherlands, Germany, France, Eastern Europe, China, Japan, Italy, Switzerland, India, and the United Kingdom can all fit within the continent—including Madagascar. It is rich in a plethora of natural resources such as gold, platinum, copper, diamonds, gemstones, natural gas, and oil. Africa consists of 54 countries. I met quite a few people throughout the continent and learned about its diverse cultures and languages during my travels.

I met business leaders throughout the continent during this role and the next. For example, a Ugandan government official introduced me to this young man who is enthusiastic about Africa. He is the founder of many companies, including a technology company. I recalled meeting with him and the CEO of his technology company at a luxury hotel in Dubai, which has many of these hotels. We were so excited and passionate about Africa that we spent hours discussing possibilities. I met with this young CEO on other occasions in Dubai, one on one, and Uganda. I eventually signed a joint development agreement, on behalf of IBM, with his company, and we collaborated on some projects.

A few months later, I was in Kenya on a business trip. As I prepared for breakfast on the morning after my arrival, I noticed a magazine on the table in my hotel room. There was a cover story on Africa's youngest billionaire. This magazine was underneath other magazines, so I just saw the title, which intrigued me. I picked it up and saw the young man. It was the same person I spent hours with discussing Africa's promise. What a surprise!

Some of the most aesthetically pleasing sites I have seen on earth are in Africa. For example, during one of my trips from Kenya to Johannesburg, I took a walk down the aisle on the plane while in flight. On the way up the aisle, I looked out the window and saw Mt. Kilimanjaro, the highest mountain in Africa. I have picnicked along the beautiful shores of Lake Victoria, the largest lake on the continent, and took day trips to a wonderful resort at the base of Mt. Kenya, the second-highest peak on the continent. One of the most beautiful cities I visited is Cape Town, South Africa. In fact, during my first trip there, as I sat on the Victoria and Alfred Waterfront near the Atlantic and Indian Oceans celebrating my birthday with cake and ice cream, I seriously thought about buying one of the condos overlooking the Atlantic Ocean. With Lions Head, Table Mountain, Robben Island in the distance, Cape Point—where the Atlantic and Indian Oceans meet—and the wine country close by, the natural beauty of the city is breathtaking.

I had many eventful experiences during my travels in MEA. One that comes to mind was during one of my numerous trips to an African country. I usually reserved a flight departing in the morning to such a country. I had a routine where I would arrive a couple of hours ahead of the flight's departure and have a fabulous meal in the Emirates business class lounge at the airport. Then I would find my way to the gate, board the flight, and have another fabulous meal in route. On one of these mornings, I entered the airport and ran to enter the elevator to the lounge before it closed. I stood next to an elderly Black man who looked at me and asked where I was from. My response was "the United States". He said, "Which state?" "North Carolina".

I was about to ask him where he was from when I noticed a tall man on the opposite side of the elevator staring me down. He appeared to have something in his ear with a chord going down his neck into his shirt. I looked at him and thought *why is he looking at me like that?* He finally said to me, "This is the President of Zambia". I was shocked but tried not to show it. I realized the tall man was his security guard. I turned to the man—President Michael Sata who was standing directly to my left—and said to him, "Hello Mr. President, it is a pleasure to meet you". At this point, the elevator door opened, and the President walked to the first-class lounge with his bodyguard. I recalled a few years earlier when I bought my house in Cary, NC, on Presidents Walk Lane. At that time, I said to my friends that means I will be walking with Presidents—they thought I was joking, but this was something I sensed. Six months later, I met with the Ugandan President Yoweri Museveni. This was my second President encounter, and I could not believe it.

When I was not traveling to a faraway country, I spent time exploring Dubai and the UAE. I quickly learned that the native Emirati were not very friendly to the expats living in the country. The women rarely spoke, and the men seemed to be slightly more friendly. From my conversations with IBM colleagues and other friends, I learned they had similar experiences. However, one of my American friends who was friendly by nature befriended a group of them by obtaining a tailor-made national Emirati outfit for men. The locals initially thought he was one of them when wearing it. The fact that an American went out of his way to befriend them in this manner was endearing to some of them. They invited him to social and other events. I learned much about the Emirati culture and lifestyle through his experiences.

I learned about the small minority of Black Emirati when I was having dinner one evening. There was a Black man in full Emirati attire sitting with what appeared to be his family. This was a rare sight for me, and I could not help but stare at him. At one point, he noticed me staring so I quickly turned away but found time to observe him for the remainder of my dinner. I later learned that Black Emirati were descendants of captured Africans who were brought to the Middle East by the Arabs as slaves. In fact, this started before the Europeans captured Africans and brought them to the Americas to be slaves.

During my first few months, I would work during the week, which was Sunday through Thursday, and be a tourist on the weekend. I explored every part of the city. I visited the beaches along the shores of the Arabian Gulf, downtown Dubai with the Burj Khalifa, the world's tallest building, and the Dubai Mall. That mall is so big that I got lost twice during my first visit, and I hardly ever get lost. With so many shops and restaurants, I had a fabulous experience every time I visited. It also hosts The Dubai Fountain, which is water dancing to music, like the fountain at the Bellagio Hotel in Las Vegas. I visited the gold and spice souks (markets). I visited the Burj al Arab, the world's first seven-star hotel, and only one of two. It was over the top.

I also visited the Dubai Financial District with some of the best restaurants in the city. I strolled down The Walk in the Dubai Marina area and shopped in the Dubai Marina Mall. I visited the Mall of the Emirates within the first few weeks of my arrival. I remember sitting at the food court eating lunch when I saw off in the distance what appeared to be people traveling down a hill. When I got closer, I saw it was a ski resort in the mall. There were people all in winter clothing taking a lift to the top and skiing down. I saw children making snowmen in the snow. This was very surreal.

Dubai has a plethora of five-star hotels with great restaurants, and I wanted to patronize as many as possible during my tenure. I made my mark. After some time, I settled on regularly relaxing with friends at some of the happy hours sponsored by some of the opulent hotels in the city. I regularly attended a jazz club on the top floor of the blue Address Hotel, one of the anchor hotels at the Dubai Mall.

I lived in a high-rise apartment in downtown Dubai with a good friend, Sharon. We had an outstanding view of the Burj Khalifa in the middle of our balcony. It was breathtaking to see every night. We later moved to a high-rise apartment in the Dubai Marina area with awesome views of the Arabian gulf. I loved walking through the marina area every morning on my way to the Dubai Metro stop on my way to work.

I was happy to partake in some of the most luxurious spas in the world. The opulent Talise Ottoman Spa at the Jumeirah Zabeel Saray Hotel on The Palm was heavenly. The Palm is a man-made island, in the shape of a palm tree, that is part of the city. There are many residences, hotels, and restaurants on The Palm. I had coworkers who lived there and hosted many parties I attended. I also patronized many restaurants at The Atlantis, at the top of The Palm. One of my favorite Dubai restaurants is Pier Chic. It is slightly off the coast with an awesome view of the city. The seafood at this restaurant was soul satisfying. It was part of the Jumeirah Al Qasr, another opulent hotel with a fabulous veranda. Sometimes I would go to that veranda on beautiful Dubai weekends and have afternoon tea, by myself or with a friend. I also loved going to the Ritz Carlton on Jumeirah Beach Road for afternoon tea.

Since I was in Johannesburg during my first Thanksgiving holiday in the Middle East, I planned to celebrate the holiday with a friend, Linda, once I arrived back in Dubai. We had a great lunch on one of the top floors of the Burj Kalifa. It was a fabulous view of the city and very memorable. The Christmas holiday season was very festive in Dubai. There were holiday decorations all over the city, especially in malls and other shopping venues. There were no religious decorations but plenty of Christmas trees, scenes of Rudolph and the other reindeer, Frosty the Snowman, and other secular decorations. I did some of my Christmas shopping in the malls, as I prepared to travel home for the holidays.

The most memorable events during my time in Dubai were their New Year's Eve celebrations. For ringing in 2012, a group of mostly Americans rented a suite at a hotel on the beach along the Arabian Gulf in the Dubai Marina area. We had a party and played great music and cards. Just before midnight, we went down to the hotel's exclusive beach for the celebration; we knew there would be celebrations up and down the Arabian Gulf. The hotel staff gave each of us a glass of champagne as we walked onto the beach—yes, in Dubai. They launched the fireworks from a vacant lot adjacent to the hotel. The whole sky lit up as they went off. It was magical, something I had never experienced before. We then danced the night away on a dance floor situated on the beach for the occasion. We danced to music from a live Mexican band playing pop oldies but goodies. It was fantastic. The next time, ringing in 2013, we attended celebrations in downtown Dubai. It was a well-orchestrated show that was mesmerizing. Dubai really knows how to put on a great show.

Angela and I finally had our Dubai vacation in March 2012. Sharon joined us for some of the adventures. We visited several landmarks in Dubai and had dinner at the Al Muntaha, a Michelin-starred venue on the 27th floor of the seven-star Burj Al Arab hotel. It had a fabulous view of the city, and the food was exquisite. We went to a party with IBM colleagues, a jazz club, a dessert Safari, and tours of Abu Dhabi and Dubai. We spent the opening night of the 2012 Dubai World Cup horserace viewing dignitaries attending the elaborate event from the balcony of our hotel suite situated opposite the venue. We witnessed the fireworks overlooking the Arabian Gulf to end the event. It was several days of pure delight!

I learned interesting details about Ramadan, experienced by some, during my stay. Each day, Muslims fasted during the day, then broke the fast with a feast, an Iftar, at sundown. Much of Dubai was shut down during the day; however, IBM and many technology companies were in Dubai Internet City. This was a special zone where businesses, including restaurants, remained open. However, they covered the windows so no Muslim could see us eating during our snacks and meals. Curtains were installed in the IBM snack area also. We were not allowed to eat or drink in public, not even water. Iftars were open to the public. Restaurants throughout the city had Iftar specials, and I did partake in several Iftars during Ramadan.

Christian churches were active in restricted areas in Dubai. I recall one Friday morning celebrating Easter, when several new Christians were baptized in the Arabian Gulf. It was a moving experience for me. Afterwards, Sharon and I had a wonderful brunch and ruminated on the events of the day.

I also used my time in Dubai to visit the other emirates in the country. The UAE has seven emirates. In addition to Dubai, I visited Abu Dhabi, Sharjah, Ajman, Ras Al-Khaimah, and Fujairah with friends and colleagues. We visited museums and beaches and took general tours of the emirates.

When I was nearing the end of my tenure, I initiated a discussion with Mark about my next opportunity. He was the Chief Technology Officer (CEO) for IBM Middle East and Africa and informed me there was a critical need for a CTO, under his leadership, in Central East and West Africa (CEWA). He mentioned I would be a good candidate for the role and asked if I was interested. I said yes, and we began the formal process for me to apply. Several months later, I was offered the role. I would be reporting to him in Dubai, as well as to the General Manager for IBM CEWA based in Nairobi, Kenya. I moved to Nairobi in January 2013 to assume the CTO role. I was finally living on the continent.

I was part of the IBM CEWA leadership team, which covered the countries of Ghana, Nigeria, Kenya, Uganda, Rwanda, Ethiopia, Tanzania, the Democratic Republic of Congo (DRC), and several others. I led the technical sales team in this part of Africa, working with customers on technical prototypes, resolving significant issues, and managing customer relations from a technical perspective. I spent my first few months in this role primarily traveling not only throughout the region but also to countries in Southern Africa, e.g., Harare, Zimbabwe; Lusaka, Zambia; Lilongwe, Malawi; Maputo, Mozambique; Windhoek, Namibia; and the island of Mauritius, working to address IBM customers' technical issues. I traveled to South Africa where many members of my technical team, as well as the sales colleagues who accompanied me on these trips, were based. I had very passionate, professional discussions with CEOs and other executive leaders of some of the largest companies in these countries and many industries, including the finance, telecommunications, and government sectors. I worked with them to resolve their technical issues. I was also able to connect with their technical leaders, many of whom were very young. I became a mentor to several of them. In addition, during my Nairobi-based assignment, three patents were issued in the United States with me as a coinventor.

I recall a few occasions where the systems of the top banks in the countries went down for several days. They were critical situations where my IBM colleagues and the customer's leadership worked closely to address the issues. They were challenging times, and at one point I had to contact the top global IBM support executive in the middle of the night in the United States for help. We were able to resolve the issues and learned quite a bit from those experiences.

I worked to bring together the technical teams into a cohesive entity. I personally connected with many of them as I traveled around the continent. I helped them to view their role as an opportunity to have a great career and to think bigger and broader. I encouraged them to be diligent in maintaining their technical competence throughout their careers.

I made new friends throughout the continent with IBM colleagues, customers, and partners, smoothly building a social network. I had many dinners with friends in Kenya, Ghana, Nigeria, Ethiopia, South Africa, Namibia, and other countries where I learned about the country and the culture. I connected with my American friends in these countries to talk about our experiences on the continent. It was especially endearing with African American contacts. Many lived in Nairobi, and I regularly had dinner with them to discuss our passion for Africa and our IBM work.

I recall early one Saturday morning when an American colleague, Karen, called me very concerned. I was in Accra, Ghana, for the week and took an overnight flight back to Nairobi. I arrived at 5:30 AM local time and slept in late that Saturday. I went to the gym at my apartment complex and came home to take a shower. My plans were to go to the Westgate Mall next, have a nice brunch, then shop for groceries for the week. The mall was not far from my apartment in the Westlands area of Nairobi. I heard the phone ringing multiple times while in the shower and quickly got out to answer it. Karen said, "Where are you?" My response was "I'm in my apartment". She said, "Oh thank God!". I said, "What's going on?". She said, "Turn on your television".

This is when I learned about the Westgate Mall terrorist attack that was ongoing. I was shocked. Had I not slept in late from my overnight flight, I would have been there. In fact, I would have been at the restaurant where the terrorists first attacked and killed many people. After learning about this attack, I stayed home and ordered in. It was frightening. The attack lasted four days, with the terrorists killing 67 shoppers. The IBM leadership team implemented our plan to reach out to everyone to ensure they were safe. All my people were safe at home. We had a small number of people in the mall at the time, for several hours, but they were safely removed from the mall by security. I reached out to my family in the United States to inform them of the attack and let them know I was safe at home. I was happy to have reached them before it became a major international news event.

We were cautious after this terrorist attack but eventually returned to our regular business activities. Several months later, a group of IBMers from the United States came to visit several large customers. One of them asked me in a somewhat condescending tone how I could stay here given the mall attack. My response was that I was no more afraid of a mall attack in Nairobi than a mall attack in the United States by gunmen. She thought about it, recognized the similarities, and did not mention it again.

I quickly learned about the technology startup ecosystem in Nairobi. The city is a hub for brilliant technology entrepreneurs. The iHub is a popular innovation hub and hacker space in the city. I started spending much of my free time at this hub, talking to budding entrepreneurs. I was excited about the many brilliant young people and their ideas. Moving forward, I learned about similar entities in the largest cities in Ghana, Nigeria, Rwanda, and other countries around the continent. I visited them as well. It was clear to me that the African technology potential was enormous. The young people just needed the right sponsors, mentors, and funding to make it happen. I also knew instinctively that helping these young people is part of my purpose. I nurtured many of them while being there and continue to do so.

I was also fully aware that I was traveling throughout Africa, meeting CEOs and technology leaders in various industries, and with government and university leaders. I thought about how just a few years earlier I became frustrated on how to make this happen. Now I was doing it at IBM's expense. Amazing.

I spoke at many events focusing on women in technology. Many global technology companies with locations in Nairobi, as well as some of the top companies in the country, like Safaricom, had some efforts focusing on increasing the number of women in technology.

It was heartwarming to speak to the women, from little girls to adults, about their potential in technology.

I thoroughly enjoyed my time in Africa. In addition to my job and some of the personal trips mentioned previously, I tried to spend at least an extra day exploring the countries I visited. For example, during one of my trips to Dar es Salaam, Tanzania, I arranged for a weekend trip to Zanzibar before flying back to Nairobi. I took a ferry which crossed a portion of the Indian Ocean to Zanzibar. I had a villa right on the ocean, and it was very relaxing. I went back to Zanzibar on two subsequent occasions. I spent a few extra days in Mauritius after business trips there. The island reminded me of Hawaii in its natural beauty and friendly people. I also spent partial days touring Lilongwe, Malawi, and Windhoek, Namibia. I walked along closed off streets parallel to the Congo River in Kinshasa, DRC, and watched the awesome sunset after a long day of passionate technical discussions. It was a great way to cap off a challenging day.

For some of these countries, the official language is not English. For example, in Mozambique it is Portuguese, and in DRC it is French. I always traveled with an IBM sales colleague who spoke the language. I therefore had interpreters in these countries.

I also enjoyed living in a city and country full of people of the Africa diaspora. From people on the streets, in advertisements, television shows, to news anchors, government officials at all levels, corporate CEOs, airline pilots, and copilots, etc., all were Black. Never had I experienced this, and it was soul satisfying. I also blended in with everyone else. If I did not speak and reveal my American accent, I was one of them. In fact, sometimes as I shopped, I would say something, and the people around me would be shocked. They thought I was a native and told me so.

I flew Kenya Airways, based in Nairobi, when traveling throughout the continent. Every flight consisted of a Black crew, from the pilots to the flight attendants. It was like a subtle validation of what I knew but had not quite witnessed on this scale, Africans of the diaspora are highly capable and brilliant. Many of us do not get the opportunity to fully utilize our potential. This experience was medicinal for me. It is something I think about often, especially when I encounter obstacles in the United States.

CHAPTER 16

What's Next?

A FTER SEVERAL MONTHS in Nairobi, Mark Dean, who was my manager in Dubai and the CTO for MEA, retired. I would be getting a new manager soon but continued to aggressively connect with clients throughout the region. A couple of months later, two individuals were appointed as CTOs in MEA, one with a focus on IBM's software group division. He was a good friend and was based in Nairobi. The other CTO was based in Dubai, and I would report to him.

Throughout my IBM career, I maintained good relationships with my management. We did not always agree, and I may not have been happy with certain situations and outcomes, but I always maintained a good rapport with them. I was not encouraged by the initial conversation with this new CTO. I perceived him to be arrogant and condescending. I discerned that he would be difficult to work with; however, as a professional, I would work to make it happen. I would continue with my present work and would do so until my tenure was up in October 2014.

A couple of months later, this CTO came to Nairobi on a business trip, and I hosted him. It was a challenging experience. A simple example I'll share relates to the Nairobi traffic. We planned to visit a customer at a given time. I suggested that we leave early due to the Nairobi traffic. He rebuffed me, insisting the Nairobi traffic would not be a problem. Keep in mind this was the man's first trip to Nairobi, and I had been living there for several months. We left later than I recommended, and we were late for our customer meeting. And so it went, independent of the topic.

DOI: 10.1201/9781032724270-22

Slowly over the next several months, this adversely impacted my mindset. By the end of 2013, I was miserable and seriously considered expediting my next move. With the new CTO, I had the same role and responsibilities; however, I was no longer treated as a valuable member of the team. I went home for Christmas with the objective of having a good holiday and ruminating on alternatives for my next opportunity.

While at home, I decided I would leave IBM and start my own company. I spent time thinking about the specifics of what type of company, *etc*. I knew I wanted it to relate to technology and Africa. I thought about the contacts I made over my three years in MEA and the critical need for deep technology experts with many of IBM's customers. I focused on creating a technology consulting company, with initial clients in Africa. At this point, I did not share my plans with any IBMers or our clients. I conducted due diligence on how to start a company. I even bought the book *LLCs for Dummies* as part of this process while Christmas shopping at home.

While I was home, the HR Director in Nairobi called and informed me that my contract with IBM CEWA would be terminated early. He had informed my IBM US manager so the two of us could start searching for my next IBM US opportunity while I was home. He suggested that we come together and agree on my departure date from Nairobi once I get back from the holiday break.

I was ecstatic, overjoyed! The fact that I did not have to wait until October was a burden lifted. This was my confirmation from God that it was my season to leave IBM. I was happy and proceeded to make my post-IBM plans. I had a Merry Christmas.

I traveled back to Nairobi a few days after Christmas. Karen and I had planned to spend New Year's Eve in Zanzibar. The plans were made prior to the Christmas break. We had difficulty booking a flight from Nairobi to Zanzibar, as this was a popular destination for New Year's Eve travelers. As an alternative, we made plans to fly to Dar es Salaam, then take a ferry to Zanzibar.

The Zanzibar Archipelago is semiautonomous with Tanzania. It is located west of mainland Tanzania, which is on the African continent. The Indian Ocean borders its east coast, while the Zanzibar Channel separates Zanzibar's west coast from the mainland. Its turquoise blue waters and white sand beaches are mesmerizing while its historic largest city, Stone Town, is its capital. The trip to Zanzibar was exciting. The flight to Dar es Salaam was great, and the ferry to Zanzibar was fantastic on a picture-perfect New Year's Eve. Karen and I were on the top level, basking in the sun for a treat. I was also reading *LLC for Dummies* during the 1-hour and 45-minute ride covering 46 miles.

We stayed at the Zanzi Resort for three nights. It is a beautiful, secluded boutique resort in the northwest part of Zanzibar. It is between two military properties so it's relatively safe. We arrived in the evening and were greeted with coconut juice, inside a freshly cut coconut. The staff was very friendly and catered to our every need. It makes a big difference, and it was delightful!

Our villa had its own private swimming pool and gazebo with a bed, with an awesome view of the Indian Ocean. It was very private, secluded, and peaceful. The villa was like a comfortably sized apartment, with a large bathroom and great amenities. The sofa in the living room area faced the ocean. You could see the outside patio, private pool, and gazebo from this sofa. The view was breathtaking. We had our own private beach. The food was fantastic during our stay. Most of the fruit was fresh, cut from the fruit trees on the property. They included mangoes, bananas, coconut, *etc.* I read *LLCs for Dummies* during this trip while Karen swam in the pool. I also brainstormed with her for potential names of my company, settling on SKJ Visioneering, LLC.

Karen and I took a walking tour of Stone Town. It was amazing. We walked the wonderful cobble-stoned streets and visited the Anglican Cathedral of Christ Church. It was built at the site of the largest slave market in East Africa, a place that held captive Africans for the Arabian slave trade. The altar of the church was built at the site where the slaves were whipped prior to being sold and transferred to Arabia. It was surreal and reminiscent of my visit to the Elmina Slave Castle in Ghana.

It was a memorable trip. I was able to think, relax, reflect, ruminate, and prepare for a great 2014. It certainly had an incredible start.

When I arrived back at work the first week of January 2014, I went straight to the HR Director's office. I was so happy that I brought him a gift. He did not know how to handle this; he thought I would be upset. I did not mean for him to be uncomfortable, as he was very helpful to me. I thought, *at some point in the future you will understand my excitement.* We agreed that I would close out my activities by

February 14 and then go back to the United States. I spent the next six weeks doing just that, both professionally and personally. Some of my IBM colleagues were very upset; however, I assured them it was a good move for me. I had several goodbye parties hosted by colleagues, friends, and mentees. It was a wonderful sendoff! I keep in touch with many of them.

It was with great anticipation that I looked forward to the end of my tenure in Nairobi. I recall closing out on the car I had during my stay, along with my driver, Jacob. The wife of the rental car company's owner was sorry to learn of my pending departure. On my last day there, she gave me a big box of Kenyan tea. There was only one other day when she was that excited. It was when I had a passionate discussion with her husband about the rental rate. He was being unfair and was not relenting. After I got his IBM contact involved to settle the issue, the owner finally relented. It was interesting to see how excited his wife was to see me stand up to him. I became her friend.

After 13 months together, including driving me to and from work and numerous Kenyan road trips, I said goodbye to Jacob on February 14 when he took me to the airport one last time. He was a good driver and a great friend. In fact, when Jacob described me to his wife, she became my surrogate mother. She would give me eggs every week to ensure I had a good breakfast every morning. I kept a few Kenyan shillings (currency) and gave the rest to Jacob when he dropped me off at the airport. This was quite a bit of money for him. He was so excited that he could now take his wife to dinner for Valentine's Day and have a fabulous time. It was hard to say goodbye to Jacob, but it was heartwarming to see him so happy.

My long flight back to the United States was relaxing. I flew through Dubai and was in premium class on the flight to JFK. I arrived in NC relaxed and ready to focus on the next chapter in my career.

I went back to the same department I was in when I departed IBM US. I was given 60 days to find another IBM job, or I had to leave the company. I looked for other IBM opportunities, while at the same time preparing to start a company if I did not find anything that appealed to me. I was looking for opportunities that had an Africa focus. Since I had just left the continent, I knew it was unlikely I would find something like that within IBM, but that is what I wanted. I did not find anything and left IBM in April 2014.

For nearly 26 years, I worked for this global technology behemoth. I had amazing opportunities to leverage my innate, God-given talent and honed skills to be innovative, inventive, and creative, becoming a global technology leader and CTO. I was also recognized as one of the top professionals in my field. All while living a life beyond my wildest dreams, traveling throughout the world, broadening my horizons, and learning about new and interesting places and cultures. I was fiercely independent, and it was an amazing journey and chapter closing. However, a door was opening for more opportunities to have a greater global impact. I walked into it with great anticipation!

7

Amazing Opportunities

CHAPTER **17**

Entrepreneurship

I REGISTERED SKJ VISIONEERING, LLC as a company in North Carolina in the Spring 2014 and was ready for business. My objective was to provide technology consulting services globally, focusing on customers in sub-Saharan Africa. I had previously conducted due diligence on how to operate a consulting services business and moved forward to implementing the strategy and plan I prepared. This included registering my company with the relevant US entities, enabling me to secure US government contracts.

I reached out to many of my contacts throughout the Middle East and Africa. I traveled to Kenya, Ghana, and Nigeria to connect with some of them in person. I quickly learned that while there was a significant need for someone with my deep technology skills to serve as an advocate for businesses when securing enterprise technology goods and services, most of them were not willing to pay for such services. I thought about other alternatives for leveraging my skills for the benefit of the African Diaspora. I had to pivot.

I thought about mobile money, a financial account tied to a mobile phone number. It is pervasive and popular, with over 60% penetration in sub-Saharan Africa with significant growth opportunity. It is very popular in some African countries, as well as several emerging countries globally. Most of the populations in these countries are unbanked, they do not have bank accounts. However, a significant fraction of the population has mobile phones. In Kenya, the largest mobile phone service provider, Safaricom, offers mPesa, its mobile money offering. It is the most popular method for any type of transaction involving funds. I used mobile money during my tenure in Kenya. It was amazing to see how few people used cash in a cash-based society.

In addition, I experienced the pain of transferring funds from the United States to Kenya and other countries in the region during my vacations. It was very expensive and, in some instances, challenging to make this happen. There were situations where the transfer times were prohibitive. I therefore focused on a money transfer or remittance offering. I would target those in the west who send funds to family members and friends in emerging countries, starting with those in sub-Saharan Africa.

I try to stay current on innovative, trending, and impactful technologies. During this time, blockchain was at the peak of its hype. I conducted research on blockchain technologies; not cryptocurrencies but blockchain. I engaged with the blockchain community, reading technical and other publications on the technology, writing blogs on the topic, speaking at universities and public venues on the subject, and attending blockchain conferences. After several months of extensive due diligence on blockchain, I made the decision to use it as the foundation for my mobile money transfer application. I brainstormed about the specifics of leveraging blockchain technology for this type of application and invented methods for implementing components of such a design. I filed two patent applications for this work. This would provide my company with IP protection for my efforts.

I designed the application, denoted geeRemit, and started its implementation. geeRemit enables senders in the west to deposit funds into the mobile money accounts of receivers in sub-Saharan Africa. I included features in the design that further secured geeRemit's social benefit. It enables senders to save a percentage of the transfer fee in a bank account controlled by them in their country, initially the United States. Funds would be deposited into this account with each transfer. This enables the sender over time to save for a future life-changing event for the receiver, *e.g.*, starting a business or paying school fees. As an alternative, the sender would choose to donate the funds to a charity in their country or to carefully selected charities in the receiver's country. The sender would also have the option to choose both. The transfers would leverage blockchain technology. While this due diligence work was done via

SKJ Visioneering, LLC (SKJV), my plans included creating a separate company for geeRemit.

While attending a local tech startup event, I learned about the provisional patent application with the US Patent and Trademark Office (USPTO). This enables one to secure an early filing date and requires a corresponding non-provisional patent application to be filed within 12 months. Filing a non-provisional patent application is relatively expensive. A patent attorney or patent agent is strongly recommended for such filings, and their fees are high, in addition to the filing fees charged by the USPTO. However, fees for filing a provisional application are nominal, under $100. I filed my two blockchain inventions as provisional applications. I had 12 months to connect with a patent attorney to file the non-provisional application.

A couple of months later, I listened to an IP attorney on a panel at a conference briefly mention the USPTO providing a free service to some inventors. I spoke to him after the panel and learned the details. He mentioned that there is a very long waiting list for this service. Since I had already filed a provisional application, I probably would not get to the top of the list in time to use their service. However, he suggested that I reach out to the local law schools where I lived, as many of them offer such services as part of an IP clinic.

I made the mental note to reach out to a couple of law schools when I returned home. However, a good friend of mine called me the weekend before I was to call the schools. I had not communicated with her in several months, so we spent time catching up on each other's lives. During the conversation, she briefly mentioned she was going to stop by the IP Clinic at the law school where she had recently graduated, North Carolina Central University (NCCU). I asked her "what did you say?" She repeated, "the IP Clinic" at the law school. I explained to her my dilemma. She immediately sent me the link to their IP Clinic website application for this service. She instructed me to complete it ASAP, as there may be a demand for the service. I completed and submitted the application the next day, and by the end of the day, I was accepted into their program. They informed me that they would reach out to me in a couple of months.

After several months, I received an email from the NCCU IP Clinic informing me that due to resource constraints, they would not be able to help me in a timely manner. However, they wanted to transfer my application to the Cordoza Law School at Yeshiva University in Manhattan and wanted my permission to do so. I said yes. A few days later, a contact from Yeshiva called to inform me of the Cardozo/Google Patent Diversity Project. It is designed to partner with law firms across the nation to provide pro bono IP services to women and people of color because they are underrepresented as inventors in this country. I was elated! I completed an application and was accepted into the program. They matched me with a law firm in the Washington, DC area, and I worked with them to file the two non-provisional patent applications within the allocated time I had. Subsequently, I used this firm as a continued participant in the Cardozo/Google Patent Diversity Project. I filed 11 additional patent applications based on the ideas I had while implementing geeRemit.

I investigated the lifecycle of technology startup companies, which generally includes development (ideation, innovation, prototyping), startup, growth and expansion, maturity, and exit. I conducted due diligence on the various types of funding sources for these stages, some of which include bootstrapping, crowdfunding, family and friends, angel investors, accelerators, customers, and venture capitalists. I focused on the early stages and read extensively on the topic. I tapped into the startup ecosystem where I live in the Research Triangle Park (RTP) area in NC. I networked with entrepreneurs, angel investors, mentors, and coaches, both locally and nationally. I leveraged the numerous local, regional, and national governmental and other agencies that assist startup founders, including the North Carolina Small Business Technology Development Center. I attended many webinars, seminars, and conferences for startup founders, particularly those focusing on technology startups.

I created the business plan for this new company, which partially included the results of a study of the remittance market, particularly in sub-Saharan Africa. I decided to raise funds from the public to initiate my company's operations. My first geeRemit fundraising effort was rewards-based crowdfunding through ifundwomen. com. This enabled the company to raise debt-free capital while providing funders with a nominal gift. On August 2018, I used part of the funds to formally create Global Mobile Finance, Inc. (GMF), the business entity for geeRemit. I kept SKJ Visioneering, LLC as a separate technology consulting company. I used the remaining funds for initial GMF operations and continued geeRemit development.

While developing geeRemit, I conducted research on funding sources for GMF operations, development, and other areas of strategic direction. I pitched to dozens of angel investors and investor entities locally and around the country. After some time, I applied to accelerator programs, focusing on those that did not require an ownership stake in GMF. My objective was to seek GMF funding while minimizing the GMF ownership stake of funders.

This was a tremendous and enjoyable learning experience. Having started this journey as a highly experienced global technology professional, I avoided several pitfalls that a younger person would not see coming. I quickly learned that the ecosystem is not designed for startup company success, most notably for people of color focusing on sub-Saharan Africa. For example, while many investors in the RTP area were impressed with my corporate background, they were not very knowledgeable about Africa and therefore passed on the investment opportunity. I knew I had to broaden my focus to investors around the country or globally. However, in such instances, I was required to fund my travel to pitch to them. In addition, founders are expected to present using pitch decks that are created professionally. While I get and understand this, it is a catch-22 cycle for startup founders with minimal funding resources.

While I did bootstrap and raised initial funds via crowdfunding, I did not want to use these funds to travel around the country, pitching to investors or pay graphic artists exorbitant amounts to create the best pitch deck on earth. However, given that I had accumulated a wealth of airline miles on various airlines, I minimized my travel and hotel costs. I also leveraged my network to create a great pitch deck. In addition, I wisely used the advice and feedback I received to optimize the quality of the services I needed and minimize the costs. My business negotiation skills were a significant asset in this regard.

I participated in two accelerator programs and a startup educational workshop, all in the Fall 2018. The "Ready Set Raise" (RSR) accelerator program for female founders was designed to "support and advance high-growth, pre-seed startups in North America". It was hosted by the Female Founders Alliance (FFA) and its founder, Leslie Feinzaig. RSR was a six-week primarily virtual program, with the final week in Seattle, Washington. This intensive program consisted of a cohort of eight company founders. We experienced extensive coaching and preparation for pitching to angel investors at the end of the program. Each coach was a successful angel investor committed to this program. The intensive program enabled us to optimize our pitching skills and presentation. In addition, we were provided with a professional graphics artist, who created exceptional pitch decks for us. I used this deck for a couple of years afterwards, it was well-developed.

The last week in Seattle consisted of talks and panel discussions for individuals representing various parts of the startup ecosystem. They shared words of wisdom and advice that were very helpful and informative. Near the end of the week, we pitched to investors and had a final pitch to the public at the downtown Seattle iMAX theater. This was followed by an outdoor reception that was very well done. All these services were provided to us free of charge, including our lodging for the week. We only had to pay for our travel and a few meals during the week.

This event was very good for me. I learned much during the process and connected with like-minded women from various fields of endeavor. The most exciting outcome was this: GMF secured a $100K investment from an angel investor in the Seattle area, Dennis Joyce. In fact, he was one of my coaches during the RSR six-week accelerator. One of the facts we learned during this program was that many founders pitch to dozens or hundreds of investors before they secure an initial investor. They wanted to lay the groundwork for us to understand that this would be a long journey but stay the course. For GMF, our journey to this initial investor was a short one, and I was thrilled!

Next, I participated in the Founder.University workshop, with a focus on women and people of color in San Francisco, California, in November 2018. This free workshop was sponsored by Jason Calacanis, a successful technology angel investor based in the city. Dennis strongly encouraged me to apply for and attend this event, and I was happy to do so. The workshop included expert presentations on various aspects of the startup focus. Example presentations included pitches and presentations, business planning and strategy, driving viral growth, term sheet negotiations, mergers and acquisitions (M&A), equity crowd funding, financial diligence, and CTO strategies. Also, a subset of the founders, including me, pitched to Jason and some of his professional contacts. We also had networking receptions during the two-and-a-half-day event. The final day was an offsite hiking event in a park in Marin County, just across the Golden Gate Bridge from San Francisco. It was a bright and sunny day for an exciting hike, culminating in an incredible view of the Pacific Ocean. It was an excellent team-building activity.

The final accelerator program for GMF was the Business of Blockchain Commercialization Lab, sponsored by Springboard Enterprises. It is a nonprofit organization "with the mission to accelerate the growth of entrepreneurial companies led by women through access to essential resources and a global community of experts". This event was held in Times Square in New York City in December 2018 for a couple of days. It included a series of speakers and panels discussing various aspects of blockchain technology and startups. In addition, each cohort pitched to potential investors and other experts attending. I learned more about the startup lifecycle and processes while growing my network from various discussions during this event. Near the end of the event, a couple of women approached me expressing an interest in investing in GMF. They asked if I would be back in NYC soon. I had a scheduled pitch to an angel investor group there several days later, so I scheduled a lunch meeting with these ladies as well.

The location of this event was a building in Times Square. The reception area was just outside our meeting room. It was all glass from floor to ceiling and had a magnificent view of Manhattan. In fact, the ball which drops every New Year's Eve was just a few feet away with an eye-level review from this area. I took a picture of this view and posted it on social media. Within minutes one of my former IBM colleagues, Caroline, who lived in Manhattan, posted a comment, inviting me to dinner if I was available. That very evening, I had dinner with Caroline and her husband, Jacques, at their apartment in Greenwich Village.

A networking and recognition reception was held for the Springboard Enterprises cohorts and other stakeholders at the midtown law offices of one of the sponsors. We completed our program a couple of hours before the reception was to begin. I had been thinking about how I would find the time to go and buy my favorite chocolate, Teuscher, during this visit. Teuscher of Switzerland has a store in Rockefeller Center near the ice-skating rink. This was my opportunity. It was a crisp fall evening as I walked to Rockefeller Center looking for the Teuscher store. It was early December, and I had forgotten about the fabulous Christmas decorations in and around Rockefeller Center during that time. Since this chocolate store was in the middle of it all, I walked right into it.

It had been years since I experienced the magic of the Christmas season in Manhattan. The streets were closed to traffic, and people were there from all over the world taking it all in. The excitement on their faces, both children and adults, was contagious, and I began to lighten up and enjoy the moment. The tree was magnificent, as always.

My GMF pitches during this time went very well. I was able to discuss GMF's objectives, the remittance market opportunity, competitive landscape, sub-Saharan specific issues that geeRemit targets, how geeRemit operates, our go-to-market plans, our GMF team, and projected milestones. The investors knew that our team was strong and experienced, especially with me as the leader. However, I discerned some biases from our conversations.

For example, I had an extensive discussion about GMF and geeRemit with a couple of investors. They asked me all sorts of questions regarding the company. Have you thought about this? Have you thought about that? The who, what, why, when, and how, plus more. I expected all of this and was prepared with well-researched and reasoned responses. First, their body language projected their surprise at my responses. It was amazing to watch how people who thought they were being discreet but instead visibly demonstrate their surprise. At the end of our intense discussions, they mentioned how impressed they were with my responses. They informed me that most of the founders they had conversations with did not have a well thought-out vision, strategy, implementation plan, *etc.*, for their company. They complimented me on my well-prepared and articulated discussion and how pleasantly surprised they were.

I thanked them but was also perplexed. They knew I was not a typical founder of a tech startup. They knew my background as a former IBM CTO with decades of experience with a large global company. Yet they were still surprised? *Are you kidding me?* I was talking to highly successful, accomplished women, one a woman of color. This is just one typical example of many of my experiences. In fact, while conducting my due diligence in 2018, I learned that for startup companies founded by women, 39% are privately held, 20% of them have greater than $1M in sales, and they employ over 9M people. However, they only receive 13% of angel investor funding and 2% of VC investments, with 0.2% for women of color. In fact, in 2018, women of color received on average $36K from investors, compared to $1.3M for White males. While the numbers have improved slightly in 2023, they are still significantly less than parity.

Yes, I participated in accelerator programs that resulted in success regarding funds raised and valuable knowledge and experience regarding the process. However, I still encountered obstacles. For example, I applied for funding with a local funding entity. The feedback I received was that my team, especially me as the CEO, was exceptional; however, they were apprehensive about investing in a region they knew little about. In addition, I reached out to another local program about funding, and they were eager to work with me. They were preparing to apply for funding to the National Science Foundation (NSF) to continue with an ongoing program, the one I inquired about. They needed highly regarded references to include in the application and asked me to be a reference. I was happy to do so. They applied and received additional funding. When I approached them afterwards to apply for the program, I was told that GMF did not qualify. I did not see that coming, but I took it in stride and moved on.

I continued to fundraise for 18 months, conducting over 25 pitches to over 100 angel investors and investment entities. I was by and large unsuccessful in this endeavor and became frustrated. I consulted with some of my advisors and mentors about this, and we concluded that I needed to find a different type of investor, one with a global mindset who could see the value of a rising African market. I set out to look for such an investor. One method was my post to medium.com on April 2, 2020, part of which is included here:

> GMF did not get additional investors; however, there was a clear pattern emerging. The investors had a well-defined methodology for evaluating startups. Some of this included ascertaining the strength of the founders or leadership team, the market opportunity, the value proposition for geeRemit versus its competitors and the market traction. GMF's strengths were exceptional with some of these metrics but limited in others. The prevailing feedback was the need for GMF to have market traction.

The geeRemit minimum viable product (MVP) is ready, but it is pre-market. We need funds to start the pilot and plan its commercial product launch. Remittance is a highly capitalized industry, with the need to comply with regulations and pre-fund financial accounts. While many investors see GMF as a potentially great opportunity, their investment methodologies preclude investment now.

I did a reset to examine the issue and devise a plan for moving forward. The investor-founder relationship is like a marriage. One must determine the qualities of a potential partner, then seek to find the individual or entity best suited for the journey.

GMF is a social enterprise. We likely need super angel investors who: 1) are global thinkers; 2) believe strongly in the trailblazing founder who has a decades long history of success; 3) look for a return on investment with a tremendous social impact that is just as valuable as the financial metric(s); 4) are seeking startups with significant financial growth potential; 5) are investing for the long-term, not necessarily a 3–5 year time window; and 6) understand this may have more risks than those of other startups, but is passionate about the potential. GMF is seeking enthusiastic visionaries who understand that facilitating game-changing success is a risky path full of significant obstacles, but tremendous success potential. Those who do not just focus on what cannot be done but facilitate collaborative thinking about innovative methods to overcome the obstacles and blaze new trails. GMF is looking for these non-traditional investors.

We have one such investor and are working to connect with others. In the meantime, we have launched a trailblazing local public offering (LPO), an equity crowdfunding campaign in North Carolina. It is designed to raise funds to enable us to get to market by launching the pilot, then the commercial availability of geeRemit. We will then get the successful market traction needed to have discussions with non-traditional and other investors. Please join us, together we can make this happen!

I did not get takers. I proceeded with the North Carolina LPO campaign and raised about $30K in a year. In addition, I received a $25K grant from American Express, in partnership with iFundWomen of Color, with its "100 for 100" program to "invest in the future of Black women entrepreneurs in the US". This was a welcomed surprise. I was very appreciative of AMEX's grant and my iFundWomen networking contacts! However, overall, it was a very tough sell for GMF and me. I expended a significant amount of time and resources for this purpose. This was very frustrating, yet I continued to move forward with the vision.

I applied for, and was accepted into, the local NSF's Innovation Corps (I-Corps) program, hosted by the University of North Carolina-Greensboro and North Carolina A&T State University. This enabled me to conduct geeRemit customer discovery. I was able to get input from potential geeRemit customers. We had conversations with dozens of them regarding the use of geeRemit, soliciting their feedback on potential features. We learned that over 92% of them would use geeRemit, and of those, 92% were willing to pay a 2% premium to facilitate donating funds to a nonprofit that transforms lives, a planned geeRemit feature. Some of the comments from this discovery included: *this is a gamechanger; this is a journey of transforming lives; I am very attracted to this; this is absolutely a differentiator;* and *this resonates with my values.*

In parallel, I hired a local software development company to complete the development of the geeRemit MVP. Also, based on the customer discovery, I formed a marketing team to develop a marketing plan to secure early adopters to participate in a geeRemit pilot. Previously, we successfully obtained a money transfer license (MTL) in Georgia. Therefore, we were only able to transfer funds from Georgia until we generated enough funds to secure MTLs in other states. We completed geeRemit's development and successfully transferred funds to Ghana and later Kenya from Georgia.

We launched a comprehensive marketing plan, targeting Kenyans and Ghanaians in Georgia. However, while our metrics showed we were reaching our targeted audience with the message, we were unsuccessful in getting our targeted senders to act. We regrouped and brainstormed about our next action. Unfortunately, time was not on our side, as we were low on funds. After conversations with the board and mentors, I decided to pursue more fundraising via investors or finding a buyer. Neither option came to fruition, and after running out of funds after six months, we dissolved the company.

While we were unsuccessful with selling the GMF vision to our targeted customers, I learned a fair amount in the process. I have no doubt I will use this knowledge for something greater, and I'm looking forward to it. I still have my technology consulting company, SKJ Visioneering, LLC, and l was looking forward to working with customers on emerging and existing technologies, like cybersecurity and generative AI, as well as IP and technical writing. I was excited as I looked forward to a favorable, impactful future.

CHAPTER 18

Ups and Downs

IN SEPTEMBER 2016, my financial advisor invited me and a guest to a fundraising event. He bought a table for the affair and invited some of his clients to attend. I gladly accepted, reached out to my good friend, Sheila, and asked her to join me; she accepted. When we arrived, I introduced Sheila to my financial advisor. He then introduced me to his other guests who had arrived, Leonard Hango and his daughter, Lenore. Leonard is a native of Namibia, a country in southern Africa, just northwest of South Africa. He is also a seasoned software developer. Since our advisor knew my passion for Africa, my travels throughout the continent, and my STEM background, he thought it would be good if we met.

When our advisor mentioned to Leonard that I had lived in Africa and I was in STEM, he immediately asked if I had traveled to Namibia. Leonard could not believe it when I said "yes". He said there were few people he met who had even heard of Namibia. So here I was, someone who not only was aware of Namibia as a country, but I had also traveled there. He asked where in Namibia had I visited, and I responded, "Windhoek", which is the capital city. We talked about the hotel where I stayed, the Hilton, which he knew well. I also told him about the great people I met there and the tasty food. Leonard was ecstatic.

Next, we started talking about our STEM careers. He was at the point in his career where he was thinking about changing his technical area of focus. He suggested that we get together at another time to discuss some attractive technical areas of focus for him to

DOI: 10.1201/9781032724270-25

consider. This is something I love and do all the time with people, so I was happy to oblige. We exchanged contact information and decided to connect later. At that point, the fundraising program started, and I spent most of the evening chatting with Sheila. It was a marvelous affair.

I connected with Leonard a couple of months later. We had lunch at a local restaurant in a shopping center in Chapel Hill. I recall driving in the parking lot looking for a place to park when I saw him walking toward the restaurant. I recall noting that he had an interesting type of walk. It was natural and rhythmic. I could not quite put my finger on why I thought about this, it seemed to be something slightly out of the norm that consciously registered with me.

We had a good professional discussion about our careers. He gave me a good overview of his work, then I began to ask him questions about the types of technologies and work actions that interested him. We did not complete our discussion by the end of our lunch, so we planned to meet again.

Over the next few weeks, we met a few times and continued our discussions. During this period, our conversations gradually moved from strictly professional to mostly professional to sometimes professional. Every now and then Leonard would say something that was interesting and piqued my curiosity. I would turn my head slightly and think about it and then gaze at him. The way he thought about things and approached life was different, it caught my attention. After a few meetings, I began to think deeply about some of the nonprofessional things he had discussed. Gradually, these continued meetings shifted to something disparate. I could barely understand why or what was happening.

Also, I never initially ask people about their personal lives when we have professional discussions. If they choose to discuss this, I will have the discussion with them. During our initial meetings, we never discussed our personal lives. I knew of his daughter, Lenore, but nothing else. I did ask about his home country, Namibia, sometimes, and I learned about some of his family during that time. However, I didn't even know if he was married or single. (No, he was not wearing a wedding ring, but not all married people wear rings.) It was not something that interested me initially.

I had been single for a long time, and I was enjoying every minute of it. I was fiercely independent and felt free to get up and go anywhere I wanted, any time I wanted. I founded a tech startup company and had a consulting business. I worked from home and was active in my church and local and professional communities. I had friends and family locally in the United States and all over the world that I connected and socialized with. For example, I hosted an *I Love Me Some Me* Valentine's Day party for my single-lady friends one year. We had great food, a must for this Louisiana woman. And of course, my favorite chocolate, Teuscher's, and a selection of beverages. (I am still trying to find something like that great wedding wine that Jesus made at the wedding in Cana in Galilee.) We also had pampering activities and music. I asked the ladies to bring their favorite nail polish so we could give each other pedicures. One of my friends is a licensed manicurist. I did not know that until she brought her equipment to the event. So, we had professional pedicures. I had peace in my house every single day. I lived alone, but I was not lonely—I was lonely when I was married and sharing a house with my first husband so many years earlier. At this time in my life, I was happy and living my best life.

It was not on my radar to find a man, start dating, and get into a relationship. Now do not misunderstand me, I was not against relationships. I was not so angry with my past relationships that I did not want one in the future. When anyone asked me about it, I would say "not today, but I don't know what tomorrow may bring". I was happy and comfortable with who I was as a person. I was having fun with Sandra. So, when I had these meetings with Leonard, my approach was strictly professional. On the other hand, Leonard had a different mindset.

I recall a conversation with Leonard, one that I typically have with anyone when we discuss professional goals. I asked him, "what do you ultimately want to achieve or do professionally?" Then we would discuss where you are currently and proceed to create a roadmap for moving from where you are to your ultimate destination. Leonard responded by stating that he was in the middle of a divorce and wanted to focus on that before he could concentrate on his future professional objectives. I certainly understood that.

Leonard started calling me from time to time, and it appeared as though he just wanted to talk. I was thinking, *why is he calling me now? We are not talking shop.* I never asked him that. Instead, when he called and asked me a question, I would sit down and start talking to him. I was not paying attention to what was happening, including why I continued talking to him. It had been over a decade since I had dated anyone, and I was a little rusty about the process. Then everything came together in my mind during dinner at a restaurant one evening. Leonard mentioned his desire to help young men, especially those raised by a single mother. He felt that if he shared with them his story, it would be an opening to connect with them. I asked Leonard, "what is your story".

Leonard's response, a summary of his story, was astounding. He grew up in South West Africa, a colony of South Africa. Its name was changed to Namibia when it became an independent country in 1990. He grew up in apartheid. At the age of 17, he had enough of being treated less than human and left the country in the middle of the night, crossing the border into Angola to the north. He settled in a refugee camp, then another and another. He bartered for food and nearly starved to death a couple of times. Many of his friends died of starvation. He was shot at when trying to escape. The bullets missed him, but some of his friends were shot to death. He wandered for ten years in refugee camps. Then one day, a woman representing a US foundation came to his camp's office to talk. She had him, and others like him, come back the next day to take a test, like the SAT or ACT. The next day, she called his name and a few others, informing them they were getting scholarships to go to college in the United States. He flew to the United States, first class, and enrolled at Morehouse College. Upon graduation with a computer science degree, he was awarded a graduate school fellowship and earned a master's degree in computer science from Atlanta University.

Leonard went through the gory, horrible details of this experience. I was in awe as I was sitting down listening to him tell this horrible and heartwarming story. I'm thinking, *what?!?!* He was so cool and calm about it, telling it nonchalantly. Many of his own people betrayed him and his friends. Some of them are still living, mostly in Namibia. He has no hatred, malice, or animosity toward them. I was thinking, *how could you not have strong emotions for someone who betrays you like that?* He was then, and still is, one to look past such atrocities with a measure of forgiveness that enabled him to move on and have a wonderful life.

It took time for me to process his story. I began to think acutely about him as a human being, looking at every aspect of what I knew of his life. I thought, *what an amazing character this man has, he is a good man, I want to get to know him better.* We continued to have more conversations, deeper conversations about life in general, our lives, goals, objectives, etc. We spoke regularly and met for lunch or dinner from time to time.

Amid these conversations and dinners, Leonard invited me and a few of his friends to a play about the genocide of the Ovaherero people of Namibia at the hands of German soldiers in 1904–1908. It was showing at the theater on UNC-Chapel Hill's campus. Leonard suggested I meet him and other friends for dinner at his house, then travel to the theater to meet a larger group of friends. He gave me his address and advised me to walk into his house through the garage when I arrived. I did just that and ended up walking into the house of a young couple with a small baby and a house full of boxes. I was clearly in the wrong house. The couple took it all in stride and invited me to stay and help them unpack, as they had just moved in. I politely declined and called Leonard. I typed an incorrect address into my mapping app. His house was down the street.

Once I walked into Leonard's house, I saw he was in the kitchen, wearing an apron and cooking dinner. It was clear that he knew his way around the kitchen. He introduced me to some of his closest friends, Edwin and Minnie. This couple was sitting down having a conversation with him while he cooked. I sat down with them, after offering to help Leonard. During our discussion, it appeared as though I was being interviewed. I did not bring this up during our engaging conversation, but I was sure of it. After dinner, we went to the theater where I met more of Leonard's friends.

The play was amazing in telling the chilling story of the Herero people, and how about 80% of them were annihilated. Many starved to death at the hands of German soldiers in the early part of the 20th century. Germany had colonized South West Africa. The leader of the Hereros led a rebellion against German rule, killing about 100 German settlers. Germany retaliated with the genocide. It was a learning experience for me and Leonard's friends, as many of us were unaware of this German genocide.

Leonard, Edwin, Minnie, and I went back to Leonard's place after the play and discussed it for hours before leaving for the night. It was a wonderful, memorable evening, and I still look back over it with fondness. Edwin and Minnie's interview led me to do likewise.

Several weeks later, I encouraged Leonard to host a dinner at his house and invite a couple of my friends over. Mary Ann and Elijah, a seasoned, elderly couple, had assisted Leonard when he prepared and hosted a reception for his older sister, Penny. She, and their sister Mweenda, came to the United States from Namibia for Lenore's high school graduation. Penny worked for the President of Namibia, Hage Gottfried Geingob, at the time. Once he learned of Penny's trip to the United States, he assigned her some tasks to do during her stay. Leonard and I worked to assist her with these tasks, including preparing for a reception. This enabled Penny to meet and have conversations in one location with the many people she was targeting. It was a stately affair that took time and effort to prepare and host with excellence.

Since Mary Ann and Elijah assisted with this event, Leonard invited them over for dinner as a thank you for their help. I admired this couple for their wisdom and guidance, as they were elders in my church. I valued their judgement so I thought it would be great for them to get to know Leonard better and share with me their sentiments about him. We had a fabulous evening together, and they were very impressed with Leonard.

I was invited to present at the White House United State of Women Summit in June 2016. It was an exciting one-day event that was held at the convention center in Washington. I spoke at a session focusing on programs to increase the number of women and girls in STEM. It was moderated by the nation's CTO at the time, Megan Smith. I gave an overview of the numerous programs in which I have been actively engaged over the years. This included programs for women and girls in STEM from secondary education to graduate students and professionals. It was well received.

I also met other great contacts while being there, including Dr. Patricia Bath. We discussed our mutual passion for serving communities in Africa. I later learned that she was a respected ophthalmologist and inventor of the laserphaco probe, a device and technique for removing cataracts. Dr. Bath is the first Black woman to hold a medical device patent and has contributed to the advancement of cataract surgery and noninvasive procedures. She is also a member of the National Inventors Hall of Fame.

I was also able to attend the general sessions and some of the parallel sessions of the Summit. This included talks by President

Obama, Vice-President Biden, First Lady Michelle Obama, and many notable people aggressively pursuing the rights of women. It was a fabulous day of learning and networking.

I had reached out to one of my mentees, Afua, prior to my trip to Washington. Afua was the Executive Director for the National Science and Technology Council with the Office of Science and Technology Policy. I reached out to schedule lunch with her during my stay. Not only was she willing to connect for lunch, but she also arranged for us to go on a White House tour. I was galvanized by the tour. During my past trips to Washington, including tours to the various museums and monuments, I had not toured the White House. Afua and I met for lunch at this restaurant with made-to-order fresh salads just across from the White House. It was so good to connect with her and to see how successful she has become. I am so proud of her.

After waiting in line and going through security, we had a fabulous tour of the White House. I was surprised by my level of excitement. I was like a child looking around at portraits, pictures, and the various rooms. It was like a dream and a wonderful, heartwarming day.

This Washington trip was several days after the reception Leonard hosted for Penny, who also had meetings to attend in Washington during the week of the Summit. I connected with her for dinner the night before we both departed Washington. It was a great way for both of us to get to know each other, and Leonard's broader family, better. It was a memorable evening where we had an enlightening girl talk. It was very relaxing as we were unwinding from a few hectic days before going back to our homes to continue our life's work.

Back in North Carolina, Leonard and I started seeing each other exclusively and fell in love. It was an exciting and magical time in my life, one that was completely unexpected. Lenore had graduated from high school and was planning to attend UNC-Chapel Hill in the fall. As Leonard and I discussed our future together, he wanted to ensure that Lenore had the strongest foundation for a successful future. Our discussions led us to decide to marry after her college graduation and the securing of a career-building job.

In the meantime, I continued to focus on my fintech startup plans. I had an initial team of executives I worked with to brainstorm on strategy and operations. That did not work out well, which happens in this space from time to time. I applied for, and was accepted into, the Venture Mentoring Service, a program sponsored by the Council for Entrepreneurial Development in Research Triangle Park, NC. I effectively created a board composed of these mentors who were primarily retired executives who volunteer to assist start-ups. We met regularly as I enhanced my business plan and strategy. They provided valuable guidance and insights for me throughout the process.

During my startup work and my relationship with Leonard, MaMe called me on a Saturday morning in April 2019. She asked for my assistance with an issue she had just learned about. She said a man called her from Pittsburgh and told her they found Kimberly dead in her apartment. Kimberly had MaMe's contact information on her, hence the man's call to MaMe. She said he was asking her questions that she could not really answer. She wanted me to call and talk to him. *What!?!?! Is she telling me Kimberly is dead? She wants me to call the coroner. Is she really that calm about this, talking to me as though this is a business request, this is her daughter!?* While my mother was very cool about this news, I was very upset.

I knew Kimberly was very ill. She and MaMe visited me the previous summer. Kimberly was rushed to the ER multiple times during her visit. I was with her and watched the doctors review her records and watch in amazement. I learned later that they were trying to understand why she was still alive. Kimberly had complications from severe diabetes that were life-threatening. She knew her time on the earth was limited and told me that she was desperately trying to live one day longer than MaMe. She did not want MaMe to experience the pain of losing another child. After having witnessed her numerous ER visits, I believed her. She also explained that she deliberately chose to live in a place that had a world renowned medical center, the University of Pittsburgh Medical Center (UPMC), and where the cost of living was relatively low.

I contacted the coroner and answered his questions. Kimberly was found in her apartment on the floor after the police were called due to the stench. The coroner asked medical-related questions as part of his investigation to ensure it was her. I then spoke to Kimberly's landlord and planned to travel to Pittsburgh to clean out her apartment and handle her final arrangements, on MaMe's behalf. I spoke to Darlene, Leonard, and other relatives and friends about Kimberly's demise. That Saturday evening, my friend Pat took me out to a local restaurant that we frequented. We sat at the bar and had our favorite beverages and appetizers. It really helped me as I came to terms with the news of the day and pending arrangements for Kimberly. It was medicinal to have a great conversation with a good friend.

We asked the bartender for the check when we were done and ready to go. He informed us there was no check for us because the bill was already paid. *What?* There was a guy sitting at the other end of the bar with his girlfriend. The bartender pointed to him as the one who covered our check. Neither Pat nor I knew this guy or had ever seen him or his girlfriend before. I was so moved by this gesture that I went over to him to thank him. He said he just had a strong urge to pay for our drinks. His girlfriend was right there with him, smiling and shaking her head in agreement. BTW, no one had ever done this for me or Pat before. I was so thankful to both and thanked God for sending me this angel with this small gesture to help with my grieving process.

As I prepared for my trip to Pittsburgh, Leonard came to me and volunteered to go with me to help and provide support. I was so grateful and accepted his offer. We flew to Pittsburg a couple of days later and went straight to Kimberly's apartment. On the way in, her neighbor stopped by and introduced herself. She and her son were the last to see Kimberly alive. They told me that she had gone to the store to buy groceries. She was feeling so bad that she could not go up the two steps to her front door and open it. She knocked on their door and asked for help. Her son helped Kimberly by opening her door and helping her up the steps. Kimberly closed the door, and the neighbor went back to his apartment. His mother was the one who called the police a few days later. When they arrived, Kimberly's door was unlocked, and they found her in the hallway with her groceries on the floor next to her. She had not made it to the kitchen.

This was extremely hard for me to hear. I was in her apartment, with the windows still up due to the stench a few days earlier, no stench now. I charged up her mobile phone. I went through her things, deciding what to keep, what to give away, and what to throw away. Once the phone was charged, it began to ring. Kimberly and I sounded alike when talking on the phone. There were times when MaMe could not tell us apart when on the phone with her. So many of her friends thought I was Kimberly when I answered her ringing phone. I spoke to friend after friend to share the unfortunate news, knowing none of them prior to this. I learned a fair amount about Kimberly and her life in Pittsburgh. It was shocking to learn about her world and how she lived. It is a mystery as to why. I was grateful to Leornard for his support. I could not have done that alone.

I arranged for Kimberly to be cremated after her body was released. During that time, cremation was in high demand and the funeral home was not sure they could get it done in my short time frame, but they did. While we waited, we cleaned out Kimberly's apartment and toured Pittsburgh. We found the local Goodwill store and donated much of what we, or her friends and neighbors, did not want. We toured the campuses of Carnegie Mellon University (CMU), the University of Pittsburgh, and UPMC. We also drove all around the city. Finally, we picked up Kimberly's remains and brought them back home with us.

Several days later, I flew to Lake Charles for Kimberly's final journey home. We had a marvelous memorial service for her at the funeral home, a block from MaMe's house, Fondel Memorial Chapel. We put together a wonderful display of Kimberly's pictures and placed them adjacent to her ashes. It was well attended by family members and friends. After the service, we brought Kimberly's ashes back to MaMe's house, then went to a local restaurant with family members and friends for repast. We had a lovely time reminiscing about our interactions with Kimberly during her life and discussed the latest events in our own lives. It was a great way to honor Kimberly and to assist in our grieving process. Most of the family left by the end of the day. I stayed a few days with MaMe before returning home, ensuring that her close neighbors would keep an eye on her while we were away.

I became concerned about MaMe, having shown no outward signs of grief, except a few tears at Kimberly's memorial service. I went back to Lake Charles to help her celebrate her 83rd birthday a few months later. MaMe loves to go shopping so we went on a few shopping sprees, and I took her to a nice restaurant to celebrate her birthday. We even bought her a new refrigerator, and she was excited about this. Still, MaMe was showing no signs of grief. I went back home to NC and celebrated my birthday the next month. I had planned a half-day of spa activities, then a nice dinner with Leonard. I turned my phone off during the spa services.

Once I turned it back on, there was a message from MaMe pleading for my help. She was having some type of medical issue that required urgent care. I called her and had difficulty understanding her slurred speech. I knew my cousins, Arnold and Tanya, were in town visiting their father. I contacted Tanya and asked her to go check on MaMe. She eventually took her to the hospital, where she was diagnosed with Bell's Palsy. They gave her medication for this and then sent her home.

I had installed video cameras inside and outside MaMe's house, with her permission. This enabled me to monitor her from NC. She was very comfortable in the house knowing that I was watching her. It enabled her to stay in her house. However, I started noticing some strange behavior. I would call her, but her slurred speech made it difficult to understand her. I eventually called Arnold to go check on her. Arnold discovered that she took too many of her prescribed pills. He took the pills from her, and she insisted that she was okay, so Arnold went home. MaMe was up all night, then fell out of bed early the next morning. I called Tanya who came and got her off the floor. She stayed with her for a while. I called Darlene and asked her to go and get MaMe and bring her to Houston. Darlene and Gary traveled to Lake Charles, went to MaMe's house, packed a few of her belongings, then took her to Houston.

I did some research on the medication and learned that her behavior was typical of an overdose. Darlene took her to urgent care, and they confirmed this. They encouraged Darlene to monitor her, and she would be fine when the medication wears off. We found a geriatric care physician for her and set up an appointment several days later. I was lecturing during a class at UNC-Chapel Hill on blockchain technology and cryptocurrency, during the time of the appointment. On my way home after the lecture, I listened to the voicemail left by Darlene.

MaMe was severely dehydrated and was being hospitalized to address this issue. I was not familiar with the hospital Darlene mentioned but was not concerned because it was to address MaMe's hydration. However, after a few days of talking to Darlene about the treatment, it appeared as though they were not focusing on hydration. They only gave her small bottles of water with her meals, and she refused to drink the water. As far as Darlene could tell—with her own eyes and when questioning the doctors—they were not giving her any type of liquid intravenously. At that point, I got on the first plane to Houston.

When I arrived in the city, and walked into the hospital lobby, my first thought was oh no, she's not staying here. I was not comfortable with the facility, call it intuition. After a couple of days' talking to the doctor and discerning that absolutely nothing was done to care for MaMe's issues, she began to get worse. That is when I informed the staff that I wanted MaMe transferred to another hospital, the Houston Methodist Hospital at the Texas Medical Center. Then the staff started gaslighting me. They tried to convince me that nothing was wrong with MaMe, who by this time was deteriorating to the point where she was constantly talking out of her head. I knew I had to get her out of there quickly.

They tried everything to convince me to keep her there. I was unrelenting, she needed to go, and she needed to go today! Once they realized I was serious, they started working with me on her transfer. Then, they tried to convince me to delay her transfer to the next morning, saying the ER at Methodist was so busy that she would be there all night before they would treat her. I was steadfast, saying she is leaving this hospital today, right now, I will drive her there myself if I must. They would not discharge her unless I signed a form releasing them of any legal liability for what I considered to be their gross incompetence. Knowing there are other ways to get the word out about this facility, I closely examined the document, and there was no indication preventing social media posts, or writing a book about it, so I signed it. I do not believe they knew who they were dealing with.

By the time MaMe was placed in the ambulance and transferred to Methodist, she was speaking gibberish constantly. Once we arrived at the ER, they started working on her immediately. They asked me lots of questions and the EMT folks gave them MaMe's record. The Methodist hospital staff and I learned later that they had given the EMT folks and me different records for MaMe. I gave them a summary of what happened, and it was like "say no more". I was just happy that MaMe was now at the best hospital in Texas and one of the best in the country.

The nurses and the entire staff were highly competent and professional. Several doctors came to see her. They ran tests all night long. Darlene and I stayed with MaMe during the entire ordeal. They moved her to another part of ER while they continued to run tests. Finally, after an EEG, we had a diagnosis. The constant gibber-ish, all night long, with no sleep was the result of a stroke. MaMe was having a series of strokes, one after the other, which caused this behavior. As a result, she was placed in a drug-induced coma to relax her brain while they determine the root cause of this behavior. She was transferred to the Neuro Intensive Care unit and placed on a ventilator. The neurologist explained to me what they knew at the time, the procedure for the ventilator, and all possible issues that could occur in the procedure. I signed the paperwork, and we waited. After a successful procedure, we were able to see MaMe for a few minutes before we went home, completely exhausted.

It was traumatic to see MaMe unconscious, on a ventilator, with all types of medical machines and devices filling this large ICU room. All of them were beeping and making other noises. While the coma addressed the constant strokes, we needed to determine the root cause. In the meantime, I called all my prayer warriors across the nation to pray for MaMe while she went through. I also prayed for her every day. Darlene and I talked to her and spent alternate nights stay-ing in the room with her while the doctors ran tests. I asked detailed questions about everything, then looked up more information about what the doctors shared. I wanted to be fully knowledgeable and engaged with the doctors to be the best advocate for MaMe.

After a couple of weeks, we learned the root cause. Some people have a low threshold for strokes. For example, an infection for some-one who is dehydrated can cause a stroke for those who have such a low threshold. Apparently, one only discovers their stroke threshold once they have a stroke. In MaMe's case, she had a bladder infection. That, coupled with the dehydration, resulted in the strokes. Since she had been given antibiotics for the infection, the doctors felt that MaMe's issues with the strokes were addressed. She will be on anti-stroke medication for the rest of her life.

They stopped the drugs inducing the coma, and over the course of a few days, she woke up. However, they were unsure if she would be at the same level, in terms of cognitive ability, given her ordeal. In addition, MaMe went from having the tube through her throat to get-ting a tracheostomy, another procedure that required my signature. This is due to the potential for an infection with the tubes. Also, she had been on a ventilator for two weeks, and it would take some time to ween her off this equipment. Once she awakened, she was able to respond to us nonverbally when communicating. We played music for her, and she would move her head from side to side to the beat.

During this ordeal, Darlene and I visited MaMe every day. We would have lunch and dinner in the medical center before one of us would go home for the night. Sometimes we would go out to a nice restaurant for breakfast or take a break to relax for a day. During one of our days driving to the hospital together, Darlene mentioned to me in a soft, sad voice, "It's my fault. I was the one that had her in that awful hospital, and they were just waiting for her to die there". I was surprised to hear her talking in this manner. I responded by saying, "let's not worry about what that awful hospital tried to do, let's just focus on ensuring MaMe has the best care now so she can fully recover".

She was transferred to a long-term acute care (LTAC) facility in the Texas Medical Center, Kindred Hospital. This was primarily to ween her off the ventilator and to get her walking again. She was at Methodist for two weeks, then another four weeks at Kindred. I was in Houston for most of those six weeks. However, I did take a break to go home to North Carolina. I used that time to relax for a couple of days and to find rehabilitation facilities for MaMe. While at Kindred, MaMe informed me, via writing on paper, that she wanted to come and live with me. I chose the Duke University Hospital Rehabilitation Center for MaMe's next visit. After six weeks, we took a private medical jet to Duke's rehab center. It was a couple of days before Thanksgiving.

I typically have Thanksgiving with my good friend, Shirley, and her family when I am not visiting my family for the holiday. That day, Shirley invited me over to fill two plates with a Thanksgiving meal for MaMe and I. I was able to stop by and quickly say hello to Shirley's family before going back to the rehab center when I had my Thanksgiving meal with MaMe. Her rehab was not going as well as expected because she was a difficult patient. The staff there were used to this and were very accommodating. I decorated MaMe's room for the Christmas holidays and asked many of my friends to stop by and visit her. Several friends stopped by, including Leonard who was very supportive. Just before Christmas, MaMe was discharged and came home with me.

Prior to MaMe coming home, I had to build a ramp at my house to enable MaMe's wheelchair to easily get into and out of the house. I set it up in my garage. In addition, the rehab staff taught me how to place an individual into a car from a wheelchair and vice versa. I also became a little apprehensive about taking care of MaMe. She was a difficult patient, having her own opinion, which many times was diametrically opposed to the doctor's and therapist's orders. This was a life-changing experience for me, something I was willing to do for MaMe, and I took it very seriously.

Once home, we had a routine. I would fix her meals and make sure she was comfortable during the day. It was very challenging for me, as she was very demanding. Yet I persevered to help her. I worked from home, which made it feasible to do this. Leonard and other friends helped me when I needed to handle anything away from the house. MaMe had no recollection of the serious health issues she had just overcome. I shared with her exactly what happened and the root cause, dehydration. Despite this, I had difficulty getting her to drink enough water daily. After a few weeks, she appeared to be less responsive, especially since she was not drinking water as strongly recommended. I became concerned and spoke to a nurse. She suggested I take her to the ER. I called an ambulance, and we went to Duke University Medical Center.

Not only was MaMe dehydrated, which they were able to quickly address, they also found a huge blood clot adjacent to her heart. They believed it had traversed to that location from her leg due to inactivity. The medical staff told me she may not have lived through the night had I not brought her to the hospital. She stayed in the hospital several days to address this issue. She was released a couple of days before Christmas. I had no time to prepare for the holidays; however, a good friend and former neighbor in Lake Charles, Cathleen, and her family came to visit us. (Cathleen was the valedictorian, whose high school graduation I attended so many years before when her school's commencement speaker spoke of me during his remarks.) They brought enough food to last a week. We feasted and were so grateful. We had a fabulous time.

MaMe recovered via a slow process. Nurses and physical and occupational therapists visited her at the house regularly. They also endured challenges working with her. MaMe did not like living in NC, although she initially requested to come and live with me. She became more vocal about it as time progressed. I started looking for adult daycare programs for her, but she was passionately against this. I recalled the conversation Kimberly and I had with her years earlier, when we asked her if there came a time when she could not live alone, would she prefer to live with Sandra or an assisted living facility. She chose assisted living. I started looking for assisted living facilities in the area. However, MaMe was adamant about leaving NC and moving to Houston.

I started looking for opportunities in the Houston Area. I shared a few options with Darlene. She and Gary went looking at a few facilities and selected one that was close to them and very nice and accommodating. I initiated the application process for this facility. She was accepted shortly afterwards, and in a couple of months, MaMe and I planned to fly to Houston so she could move into her new apartment. I was in constant communication with the facility while watching the news about this deadly virus, COVID-19. It appeared to be a very serious issue. I watched as more and more experts suggested that a closing or shutdown was needed to address this public health issue. I became concerned about whether we could get MaMe to her new home before such a thing happened.

I scheduled and confirmed the arrival date with the facility, it was a go. The evening before we were scheduled to leave, the facility called and told us MaMe could not move in. I explained to them that she had already moved in, and MaMe's things had been moved into the apartment. I told them we were taking an early flight in the morning, and MaMe would be in her apartment by noon the next day. They told me that they would call me back; they never did. So MaMe and I flew to Houston the next morning.

It was a great trip. After having a nice breakfast on arrival, I drove to the facility, it was nice. Darlene and Gary met us there. They were happy to see MaMe, as it had been a few months since they last saw her. It was a seamless move in. This was March 2020, literally a couple of days before the US shutdown.

I was monitoring the news closely and knew I had to get out of Houston ASAP. Once I knew MaMe was safe and comfortable in her new home, I left for NC. The plane was completely full, and I was praying that I would not catch the virus from someone on the plane; I thank God I did not. I made it safely home. The next day, the US shutdown happened.

8

Keep Rising

CHAPTER 19

New Opportunities

W HILE I WAS STILL AT THE KINDRED Hospital in the Texas Medical Center in Houston with MaMe, I received an email from a friend. She informed me that she was on the board of a local high school for the gifted in North Carolina, along with the Senior Vice Provost (VP) of North Carolina A&T State University (NCAT). The VP was looking for someone to lead NCAT's new Center of Excellence in Entrepreneurship and Innovation. Specifically, she was looking for someone with a business background, an entrepreneur who had an earned Ph.D. My friend suggested me and proceeded to introduce us via email. I communicated with the VP about the opportunity, I was intrigued. I informed her of my mother's situation in Houston. I knew I would be traveling home shortly to find a rehab center for my mother, so we made plans to meet during my trip back to NC.

I had a great day meeting with the VP and members of her team. She realized when I first told her about my mother's situation that leading the center was not a viable option for me; however, she wanted me to be involved in the center in some capacity. After some brainstorming in her office, we created a plan to have me come on board part-time as a Visiting Scholar. I would collaborate with university contacts to develop seminars and webinars related to entrepreneurship and success in business environments; create an IP clinic to provide the background for inventors, startup founders, and others in the NCAT community to file patent applications; work with the center's leader on its activities; and other similar projects.

DOI: 10.1201/9781032724270-27

I was excited about the opportunity and began my work a few weeks before the COVID-19 shutdown. I would spend one day a week on campus with this project. I was able to do this by hiring a home health care worker to spend the day with MaMe while being on NCAT's campus in Greensboro, NC, about an hour away. I started one month before MaMe moved into her assisted living apartment in Houston.

I was exhilarated on my first day on campus. I felt as though I had come home to a big family on this HBCU campus. I quickly connected with NCAT contacts and soon had several webinars scheduled. This was despite the shutdown. Through the center, I invited entrepreneurs, inventors, IP attorneys, and others to speak on topics relevant for entrepreneurs. I also spearheaded the founding of NCAT's IP Clinic. I worked to get funding for a few projects during my two-year tenure and worked closely with the Interim Director on innovative projects to assist student entrepreneurs.

In addition, I received an email from a headhunter while MaMe was still in the neuro ICU at Houston Methodist. She was working on behalf of a public company seeking a new board director. She found me via my LinkedIn social media page and explained that my background and experience matched what the company was seeking in a director. She suggested that we have a conversation if I was interested.

Over the years, I often thought about working on a corporate board, but for the most part it was a low priority. As I approached the end of my IBM career, I thought about it more frequently, conducting due diligence on specifics. I had an acquaintance who had been encouraging me to pursue opportunities for years. When I left IBM, I reached out to her, took her to lunch, and asked her about directorship. She shared her thoughts and experiences. I learned a good deal but still was not convinced it was something I should pursue. She introduced me to the membership contact of the Research Triangle Park (RTP) chapter of the National Association of Corporate Directors (NACD). I met with him and his team one weekday afternoon. While they were very cordial and businesslike in their approach, their body language reflected some hesitancy and coolness about me as a potential director.

I want to reiterate that I am not one to allow individuals to marginalize me. I am a fighter, but I choose my battles. In fact, in most instances, I am energized by people who attempt to minimize me. In this instance, I was running two businesses, and most of my time was focused on that. I was not interested in adding another work-related project to my full plate. This was not a battle I chose to fight.

A couple of years later, I received an email from one of the NACD RTP chapter's membership contacts. He invited me to a local event focusing on acquiring the right board directors for your tech startup. I was more interested in the subject matter than NACD, so I accepted the invitation. The event was informative and educational. I absorbed valuable information that I leveraged in my own tech startup. I also networked with other attendees and made some valuable contacts. The event occurred on my birthday, so after it ended, I went to the spa for half-day of services. I had my mother's call waiting for me when I was done.

This brings me back to the email in my mother's hospital room. I thought about whether I should respond to the headhunter in the affirmative. Since I was just working in my MaMe's room while they were trying to determine the root cause of her issues, I had time for a call. Once I spoke to the headhunter and gave her a summary of my background, skills, and experiences, she became more animated and stimulated. She informed me that I was exactly the type of person this company was looking for. She said with my permission, she would pass my information on to the primary contact at her search firm who was working with this company. She would also send me an overview of the company, its board and executive management teams, the type of director they were looking for, and other relevant information. I gave her my permission.

Once I received the information, including the specifics of the company and what they were seeking in a new director, I was astonished. I checked every box, and the company, Regional Management Corporation (NYSE:RM) was very attractive. I decided to pursue this opportunity. I scheduled a virtual meeting with the primary headhunter contact for RM. By the time it was scheduled, MaMe had been transferred to Kindred Hospital in the Texas Medical Center. I could not find a meeting room that was appropriate for the discussion. However, on the morning of the call, MaMe was moved to the lobby of her floor, near the nurse's station. They wanted her out of her room so she could sit and enjoy her surroundings and not lie in bed.

I tried to prepare a professional setting for the call. I knew there would be no visitors in MaMe's room while she was in the lobby, so I decided to have the call there, by the window. They would see the window as background and not know I was in a hospital room. However, I forgot about the get-well balloons in the window, visible to the people in the virtual meeting. They inquired about the balloons after our initial greetings, asking if I was in a hospital room. I was so embarrassed, thinking this was unprofessional. They had a different perspective. I explained why I was in such a room. They thought it was admirable. (I later learned they felt this character trait was a good cultural fit for the RM board.) We discussed my skills and years of experience as a global technology leader, including my CTO experiences, and many other exposures relevant to board work. I learned more about RM and became more interested in this opportunity. My contact would move forward and share my information with the board's Corporate Governance and Nominating Committee.

The board was interested and invited me to a face-to-face interview with the full board, a couple of months later. The headhunter set up a call to prepare me for the interview. He discerned that I would be a great fit for this board and encouraged me to be my authentic self. The interview was scheduled for February 2019 in Miami. My mother was staying with me, and I had yet to find a permanent person to take care of her while I was away. I arranged to fly to Miami mid-morning, have the interview, then fly back to NC later that day. I would be away about 12 hours. Mary Ann, Shirley, and Leonard committed to spend four hours, each, with MaMe. I arrived back home shortly after Leonard, who had the last slot, left my home. I had cameras in the house to monitor MaMe so I was able to see her during my entire trip away, except during the interview and the flights.

It was a great interview. We briefly discussed my credentials, skills, and experience. However, most of the time was spent getting to know me. They shared a couple of scenarios, and we talked through how I would address them. In addition, they assessed whether I would be a good cultural fit. Likewise, I had a few questions for them, assessing whether this would be a good fit for me. A high-performing, aspirational board has a good governance foundation and sustained effectiveness in guidance and oversight via educated directors operating with cultural cohesiveness. This potentially would be a long-term marriage between me and the board and company. I chose my questions carefully and closely listened to and monitored their responses, as they did. I walked away from the interview feeling it was very good. The headhunter, who escorted me into and out of the interview, was ecstatic.

It was a great match, and the board appointed me as their new director a few months later. I was delighted about the opportunity and was ready to work. I went through the onboarding process, learning about the specifics of the company and its executive team. I also conducted due diligence on the company and directorship in general. I took online courses in corporate finance and accounting to be a more effective director in providing wholistic guidance and oversight, not just for technology.

My board interview was about a month before the COVID-19 shutdown, and my appointment was after the shutdown. Therefore, my first board meeting and those for the next two years were virtual. It was a challenge to dive into this new experience, getting to know the management team, my fellow directors, and the company virtually. I was diligent and persevered, diving in to learn about all aspects of the company. In addition, I pursued many educational opportunities to learn about director responsibilities. I joined NACD and other professional director organizations. I later learned about Stanford Women on Boards (SWB) and Black Women on Boards (BWOB, an amazing, supportive organization cofounded by Merline Saintil and Robin Washington). I became actively engaged in these organizations. I became certified in board-related areas of expertise, *i.e.*, NACD Directors Certification, Diligent Climate Certification, and Diligent Cybersecurity Certification and attended conferences, webinars, and seminars. It is my intention to make an impact at the board level for many years to come. I will be a lifelong learner for such requirements and responsibilities.

Three years later, the Chair of RM's board recommended me as a new director for a private insurance company, Pan American Life Insurance Group (PALIG). I spoke to the CEO and Chair of the company, who then invited me to New Orleans, PALIG's corporate headquarters and one of my favorite cities, for interviews. It was a successful experience, and they appointed me as a new director starting June 2023. The onboarding process was virtual and over the course of a few days. It enabled me to learn about the company and executive team. It is a great cultural fit, and I am enjoying my work on this board as well.

I wanted to find one more board opportunity. I'm interested in making an impression with pre-IPO companies. I'm excited about the potential of assisting such a company in preparing to become a public company, providing guidance and oversight before, during, and after the IPO. I look forward to the journey.

Board directorship enables me to make an impact at the highest level of a company. It has been a wonderful journey to get to the table, having the influence to provide guidance and direction to corporations. It has been one of the destinations of my career journey, even though I was not aware of this most of the time. I am grateful that I had the right type of visibility via social media, board contacts, and a community of men and women who are passionate about board governance. In the true spirit of aspiration, now that I am at the table, it is time to prepare for chairing a committee and ultimately sitting at the head of the table as board chair. The new journey has begun.

CHAPTER 20

A New Life

THE RECEPTION LEONARD HOSTED for Penny while she was in town was held a few days before Lenore's graduation. Penny and Mweenda, Leonard's youngest sister, arrived about a week before the event. It was a pleasure to meet them. Penny is a very knowledgeable elder statesman full of wisdom, humility, and a touch of wit. Mweenda is outgoing and likes to enjoy a life of adventure. All of us, including Penny and Mweenda, planned the reception. We planned everything ourselves, including the menu and cooking. We went shopping for decorations and menu ingredients, solicited additional cooks to prepare, and sent invitations to distinguished guests and experts. We reached out to Lenore's friends and others to serve as hosts to escort the guests to various sections of the house and as parking attendants.

It was a magnificent reception attended by several dozen people. Many were excited about meeting a "celebrity", an advisor to the president of a country. We had a fabulous meal, full of grilled meat, a cultural staple for Namibia. We used Leonard's formal place settings for the event. Penny gave a few remarks, thanking us, and the American people, for our generosity in supporting Namibia. Her comments demonstrated her mastery of the highest level of diplomacy, esteemed delivery, and gratefulness.

This was followed by a few group meetings between Penny and a subset of our invited guests, facilitated by Leonard and me, to discuss some of the specifics of Penny's assignment. We also planned subsequent one-on-one meetings with a small number of people

DOI: 10.1201/9781032724270-28

who were unable to attend the reception. Overall, the reception and group meetings were a success. Once the guests left, Leonard, Penny, Mweenda, and I spent hours cleaning the dishes and the kitchen. It was a most humble ending to an outstanding day.

Lenore's graduation program was a few days later. It was a memorable event, where Leonore gave outstanding remarks during the program. Unfortunately, I was not in attendance as I was participating in the White House United State of Women conference in Washington.

I continued working with my fintech startup. Also, from time to time, I did small projects with my consulting company. My relationship with Leonard was blooming. I continued to do community service work through DST's Raleigh Alumnae Chapter. I was happy and in a good place. Soon, Leonard and I began to discuss marriage. Lenore was now in college, at the University of North Carolina at Chapel Hill (UNC-CH). We started to discuss our lives after Lenore's graduation. We were still on track with our plan to marry once Lenore graduated from college and was secure with her first professional job. In the meantime, Leonard and I spent more time together and got to know each other better.

It was a wonderful time in my life. Throughout the health challenges with MaMe and Kimberly's death, Leonard was right there with me, my strong support. I am so appreciative that he was with me during those difficult days. Then there was the COVID-19 shutdown. We were confined to our separate homes, communicating via telephone or zoom. After many months of confinement, we began to go on walks together, wearing our masks. We would meet at the start of the walking trail, do our walk, then go to our separate homes. While there were some relaxing of the shutdown requirements during that time, we were very careful not to encounter others during our walks. We chose walking trails that were not heavily used during that time.

I really enjoyed those walks. Lenore was months away from graduation, so we talked through the specifics of how our marriage and subsequent new life would unfold. For example, Leonard asked my thoughts about him selling his house and moving in with me, me selling my house and moving in with him, or both of us selling our houses and buying a new house. Leonard had just bought a new house several months earlier. I actively participated in his house hunting journey before he bought the fantastic house. My house was 15 years old, and I had been in it for over 10 years at the time. It was a great house that I loved, but it wasn't new. To me, this was a no brainer. I told him I would sell my house and move into his new house. This would become our home.

I also asked Leonard his views on prenuptial agreements during one of our walks. Given my experiences with my first husband, I had this mantra for years after I divorced him: *pre-nup or no nup!* Leonard's response was "I don't believe in chances". Leonard wanted a prenuptial agreement as well. For several walks, we discussed the specifics of an agreement. We were on the same page and had very enlightening and cordial discussions on the matter. We conducted research on the topic to ensure we covered everything. Once we were happy with our prenuptial plans, we each consulted separate attorneys to draft and review the legal document. We signed it several months before we told anyone we were getting married. We wanted the focus to be on Lenore's graduation.

Unfortunately, COVID-19 prevented the traditional commencement exercises during the time of Lenore's graduation in 2020. Her ceremony was online. Leonard also hosted a Zoom party for her. It was superb, attended by relatives and friends from the United States and Namibia. She has a recording of this exciting event that she can cherish throughout her life.

Lenore secured a job as a consultant with Accenture, based in Washington, DC. However, due to COVID-19, she did not initially move to DC. She worked from home in NC for about a year before moving to DC. When the time came, Leonard and Jamie McDaniel, Lenore's older brother, helped her move. Lenore prepared for months leading up to the move. She and Leonard went on an apartment hunting trip, and she found a great apartment in the city. She spent time buying furniture and other necessary household items before the move. The excitement began to build, and eventually the day arrived. They rented a U-Haul truck, packed up Lenore's things, and drove to DC. I was there to help with the packing and wish Lenore well on her new journey.

When Leonard returned, we started planning our wedding. We went shopping for wedding rings. I found the engagement and wedding rings I wanted, and Leonard found a matching wedding ring. We were delighted about planning our new life together! We finally told our family and friends we would be getting married in a few months, on August 7, 2021. We wanted to have a small wedding with a few guests. We did not want to have this at a large public venue as we were still uncomfortable with that type of setting at the time. When we shared the good news with some of our closest friends, Edwin and Minnie, the couple that interviewed me when I first visited Leonard at his house in Chapel Hill, they offered their house as the venue. This was something Leonard and I did not discuss and did not expect, we were surprised. However, we looked at each other when the offer was made and decided to accept it.

We wanted no more than 12 people at the wedding. I worked with Mary Ann to plan the event. She had planned corporate events for her company for years and still knew the contacts for flowers, decorations, and other details. We spent weeks on regular Zoom meetings with Minnie to plan the affair. I wanted a classy affair with ivory and champagne gold as our wedding colors. Both Leonard and I focus on healthy foods, so we were particular about finding the right caterer for the event. We settled on one of our favorite restaurants in the area, but they were unable to bring the food and serve it. We settled on this restaurant, then went looking for people to pick up the food from the restaurant and prepare and serve it to our guests. We did not have to look far. One of my church members, Monica, is a caterer. She was more than happy to pick up the food from the restaurant, bring it to the house, and lead the effort to prepare and serve it to our guests. I solicited the help of a good friend, Sigmon, to work with Monica.

We learned that many couples were planning their weddings on this day. There was pent-up demand following the COVID-19 restrictions. In fact, it was difficult to find a good florist because they were booked with so many weddings. I finally found one that was fabulous.

Also, I learned from a former IBM colleague, Sheila, that another IBM colleague, Donald, had taken some fabulous photos of her grandchildren. Donald was an engineer, not a professional photographer. However, I knew that Sheila's work is always excellent; she has discriminating tastes. If she says Donald's photos were excellent, that was good enough for me. I had also worked with Donald and knew everything he did was in the spirit of excellence. Leonard was okay with this, so I contacted Donald. He was happy to be the photographer for our wedding. Mary Ann also secured the services of another church member to provide the cake. This woman was unaware that she was making a cake for my wedding. Leonard and I wanted our wedding to be small and drama free. We limited the number of people who knew we were getting married.

In fact, I only told my pastor a couple of months before we married. When I told him I was getting married, his response was "to who?". He had never seen Leonard and I together, and I never mentioned Leonard to him during our discussions. I asked him to keep it confidential, and he did. We scheduled a few premarital counseling sessions prior to our wedding. During our first session, my pastor, a native Ghanaian and fellow African, fell in love with Leonard. They had this bromance going on in the middle of our counseling sessions. It was interesting to witness. I had to remind them a few times of the reason for our sessions.

My maid of honor was my good friend, Shirley. Leonard's best man was Jamie, his son. We asked Lenore to recite a poem of her choosing at our wedding. These people and my pastor were the official participants in our wedding. Jamie's wife, Petrina, was the only other family member present.

Mary Ann and I worked on the decorations and logistics of the event. Leonard and I wanted to use our own formal place settings for the event. We also used our own tablecloths for most of the tables. Minnie and Edwin provided some tablecloths and dishes as well. We wanted the wedding to be outside but included an alternative plan if it rained.

Amid planning my wedding and working as the founder and CEO of a fintech startup company, I planned to sell my house and move into my new home with Leonard. I did not want to go through the traditional house-selling process. During my afternoon walks through my neighborhood, I saw many homes for sale via Opendoor. I conducted research on that company as well as Offerpad and Zillow, their competitors. These companies buy houses outright, as is for the most part. They do not require that you clean the house, but I had to at least leave my house clean for them. The thought of selling my house as is, with no painting or trimming, etc., was a dream. It was just what I needed. However, I wanted to cover all my basis and contacted a couple of real estate agents as well. I pitted everyone against each other for the best offer.

I began packing up for the pending move. I had a five-bedroom house. The closets of four bedrooms were full of boxes I accumulated over 20 years of moves. Every time I moved; I did not unpack all the boxes. This time I was determined to unpack everything before my move. I did not want to bring any baggage into my new home. It was a grueling process, especially in the middle of planning a wedding and running a startup company. For example, I took discarded paper to a commercial shredder. It took two trips, filling up my car each time. I had over 500 pounds of paper shredded. I had hundreds of items of clothing, as well as hundreds of other items, donated to Goodwill. It was a very challenging time doing all of this at once. I would not recommend this to anyone.

Zillow was the winner of my quest to sell my house. They made me an offer I could not refuse, so I didn't. I signed the contract the night before my wedding. I just needed a few days to move the furniture I was taking with me to my new home, have an estate sale to sell everything else, and another mover to take away anything that did not sell. I was able to get all of this done shortly after our wedding. I closed the sale a few weeks after getting married. I had also finished packing up most of the things in my house by that time.

In the days leading up to the wedding, I was excited and nervous. This was a big commitment. I could not believe that after over 20 years as a single woman, I was getting married to a wonderful man. I was not even looking, did not actively seek this. But Leonard is so amazing; he came into my life and completely changed it. I was in a good place when we met; I was happy and confident in who I was, ready for anything, including a relationship I did not seek. After dating for five-and-a-half years, I was ready.

We knew by August 5 that it was more likely than not to rain on our wedding day. We therefore planned for an indoor ceremony and luncheon afterwards. We set up the luncheon table, including the tablecloths, China, utensils, *etc.*, in Edwin and Minnie's dining room. Lenore arranged the napkins in a fanciful decoration. August 5 is also Leonard's birthday, so we took a break from decorating to celebrate his special day. I bought some of his favorite Mediterranean food for the event. It was a fabulous affair. We then completed our decorating tasks and celebrated some more.

It rained on the morning of our wedding but stopped before it started. We had the ceremony inside. It was a beautiful affair, and my heart was full. Leonard looked so handsome in his attire. My pastor did a beautiful job performing the ceremony. We set up a Zoom meeting for the event which we recorded. Our relatives from across the United States and Namibia were able to view the wedding. Afterwards, we spoke to them while Monica and Sigmon prepared our luncheon. We celebrated the occasion by dancing on the floor with our invited guests. Donald was everywhere taking beautiful photographs.

The wedding luncheon was very intimate. Monica set up the food buffet style. We served ourselves, then she and Sigmon picked up the plates and served us the wedding cake and champagne. Jamie's toast was so loving and heartfelt, it brought most of us to tears. He said something along the lines of "how does a Best Man toast the best man?". Shirley was a little apprehensive, having to follow Jamie, but her toast was fantastic. We then ate cake and had a fabulous conversation. It was so heartwarming for Leonard and me, a day we will cherish forever. After lunch, Leonard and I quickly changed into casual attire for our short honeymoon trip to the Outer Banks of North Carolina, specifically, Kitty Hawk. Monica, Sigmon, Shirley, and Mary Ann stayed behind to clean and pack up our dishes, tablecloths, and everything else we owned. We wanted to leave Edwin and Minnie's house in the same condition it was in prior to our event.

The rain had stopped, resulting in a wonderful drive to Kitty Hawk. Neither Leonard nor I had been therefore before. It was a memorable honeymoon. We were grateful for the time we had together, the intimacy, the conversations about the day and our future, the walks along the beach, they were all perfect. We spoke about coming back to the Outer Banks, renting a house right on the beach, and enjoying those peaceful, soul-transforming walks in the future. We also visited the Kitty Hawk Museum showcasing the Wright Brothers and their first flights. We toured all around the Outer Banks, relaxing and having a great time. After a couple of days, it was time to go back home. We arrived home and started our life together.

Two days later, the movers came to my house to move the furniture into my new home with Leonard. I began the task of unpacking, which took months. Two days later, I flew to Houston for my mother's 85th birthday party. I promised her I was coming to her party. I don't think she believed me until I arrived. MaMe had invited family members to the event, some we had not seen in decades. It was an amazing affair, and a party fit for a queen. MaMe was so happy! Then it was back to NC to complete my house-selling process.

In the ensuing days upon returning to NC, I had an estate sale and moved everything out of the house that did not sell. After numerous trips to Goodwill to donate items, and to the dumpster to remove unwanted items, I did minor cleaning. Then I left the key for the new owner, Zillow. After encountering some minor obstacles, we closed. I had completed the process of selling my house and was now fully engaged in unpacking everything and putting the woman's touch on our new home together.

I soon learned that Leonard had plans for adding to our property. Over the course of a few months, we added a second deck and a patio with a fire pit and grill. I worked with him to transfer the house from a male place with dark furniture, floors, and cabinets, to a bright place. I added sunny window treatments, after explaining to Leonard exactly what that was, new sunroom furniture (the furniture previously in the room went to the upper deck outside), and bright and sunny outdoor furniture for the lower deck and patio. I turned the game room upstairs into my office and a lady's room, strictly for my entertainment. I now spend most of my time in the bright portions of the house, especially the sunroom.

We technology-enabled the house, with IOT devices everywhere, controlling lights, doors, thermostats, fans, you name it. Given that we are both technology experts, of course we would do this. For several weeks after our wedding, when Leonard would come home after a walk around the neighborhood, he would come back with an additional item to add to our list of home improvements. There were so many that I became apprehensive about his walks, fearful that he would come back with something else to add to the list. He was the dreamer; I was adding up the cost in my head as we talked. We completed most of the tasks after several months. It has been a great transformation, but I have learned from Leonard that there is always more work to do. He walks through the neighborhood every day.

We have since adjusted to a wonderful life together. We both work from home. Leonard's office is on the ground level while my office is in my lady's sanctuary on the second floor. We spend every day together in the same house, although we work on different levels, so we see each other when we have lunch or take breaks. Most of the time we cook from home but regularly go out to dinner. We frequently entertain guests; what are two decks and a patio for anyway. Marriage also came with wonderful, grown children as well as grandchildren who call me Grandmama. I am not getting tired of this. In fact, this is so awesome for me. I am living my best life!

In the late 2010s, I added an item to my things-to-do list to visit all states that I had yet to visit. I have traveled to many parts of the world but have not yet traveled to all 50 US states. I put together a list of the states I had yet to visit, around ten. Although Kansas was on this list, I previously crossed over into the state during a visit to Kansas City, Missouri. I planned to travel to some of those states in 2019, then make subsequent trips in the ensuing years until I visited all of them. I shared my plans with Leonard, and he asked if he could join me on these trips. I said yes, I was happy to have a traveling companion, especially Leonard.

Our first trip was to the Midwest and part of the great plains. We flew to Chicago, then rented a car to travel through Illinois, spending the night just outside of Chicago. We then got up for a drive through Iowa, stopping in Des Moines for lunch and a visit to the state capital. I have never seen as many windmills in my life as the numbers in Iowa. It was amazing to see. We drove on to Lincoln, Nebraska, for the night. We toured the campus of the University of Nebraska, then visited the capital building. We traveled through Nebraska to Omaha and on to a glimpse of Sioux City Iowa before reaching South Dakota and a long drive across the state to Rapid City.

While we were there, we toured Mount Rushmore and the Crazy Horse Memorial in the Black Hills. It was an educational experience. Rapid City is close to Wyoming, so we took a quick ride to the first town in Wyoming over the border, bought some snacks, then went back to Rapid City. We enjoyed walking around the city, seeing the statues of American Presidents around downtown. We also enjoyed dining out the two nights we were there before heading back across this vast state to Sioux Falls.

The speed limit on the interstate in this part of the country is 80 miles per hour. It was sheer excitement to drive that fast on a lonely highway with fantastic scenery. We arrived in Sioux Falls in the evening. We met a friendly worker at the hotel who volunteered to take us on a short tour of the city. It was a glorious way to see the city, including the beautiful waterfalls for which the city is named. We walked around the park near the falls and enjoyed a great summer evening taking it all in. We later went to dinner at an Ethiopian restaurant that we enjoyed. Then it was back on the road the next day, on to Minneapolis/St. Paul, Minnesota. We visited the capital building in St. Paul and found a nice restaurant for a great meal in Minneapolis. We then headed to Rochester, Minnesota, and had a great meal in a local restaurant near the world-famous medical center.

Next, we traveled to Madison, Wisconsin, to visit the state capital building and the campus of the University of Wisconsin at Madison. We spent the night there, then on to Illinois and Chicago where we flew back to NC. It was a wonderful trip. I enjoyed Leonard's company during our journey. We drew closer during and after this fantastic vacation.

We were planning to take another trip to the Great Northwest a couple of years later, but the shutdown delayed the trip until 2023. However, we did take the trip in the summer of 2023, flying into Salt Lake City and spending the night there. The next morning, we visited the Utah state capital building, then drove through Idaho to reach Butte, Montana, where we had a nice dinner and spent the night. We toured the city the next day, then drove to Helena to visit the state capital building. Next, we drove to Billings, Montana, for the evening.

The next stop after Billings was Yellowstone National Park, entering from the north. It was a marvelous place to visit. The drive through sections of the park, the walks in various parts of the park, the fresh mountain air, it was fantastic. We stayed at the Old Faithful Inn with a window view of Old Faithful, the world-famous geyser. We first saw the periodic eruption from our hotel room, then the next time and the next. It was a dreary day, so we stayed inside and had a nice dinner. The next day was much better. We spent time walking around the area, viewing many other geysers that erupted occasionally. We saw the full force of Old Faithful outside. It was simply magnificent.

We continued driving through the park after our Old Faithful stay, driving south to exit. Once we left Yellowstone, we entered the Grand Teton National Park with stunning views of the majestic Teton Range. We were taken away by the beauty of the park. We continued our drive to Casper, Wyoming. After spending the night there, and touring the area the next morning, we hit the road again for Chyenne. We spent the night there, then visited the Wyoming state capital the next day. We also toured the city and later had a short afternoon visit to Fort Collins, Colorado. It was a lovely visit with the beautiful Rocky Mountains in the background. We spent the night in Cheyenne before driving back to Salt Lake City. After spending the night there, we flew back home the next day.

It was an amazing trip. The people, the places, the visual images; all of these and more, I will vividly remember over the years. We have a few more states to go, then on to other parts of the world. We have a global society we continue to explore!

Over the years, I have been recognized many times, in various capacities, for my professional and community contributions. I pursue my life's work with a passion and a joy to deliver, to make noteworthy contributions, and to encourage and inspire others. Awards and other types of recognition are not something I have generally sought. In fact, in many instances, I am pleasantly surprised and honored. I received two unexpected communications early in 2023. They were notifications of awards to be presented to me later that year. The first was a Rice University Laureate Award, a Distinguished Alumni Award. This is one of the top awards bestowed on an alumnus and presented by the Rice Alumni Association. It was to be presented in a formal awards ceremony in May. The second was a notification of a local award, the Emerald Award, presented by the Raleigh Chapter of The Links, Inc. The award was to be presented for my outstanding work provided to the community in International Trends and Services. In both cases, and unknown to me, I was nominated. Both were pleasant surprises.

Regarding the Distinguished Alumni Award, presented on May 4, 2023, I had planned to travel to Atlanta, then on to Tuskegee to attend my niece's graduation from veterinary school on May 6. (We are so proud of Brianna. A new generation of doctors, a veterinarian, is now in the family!) Leonard and I decided to do both; travel to Atlanta a couple of days earlier, fly to Houston for the awards ceremony, fly back to Atlanta the next day, then travel to Tuskegee early that Saturday morning to attend Brianna's graduation ceremony.

I learned about the Emerald Award a couple of months later. As a result of these experiences, and others the same year, I became very excited about regularly reading my email. At this point, anything was possible.

The opportunities kept coming! In the Fall 2022, I received an email from one of my former protégés, Chanceè. We had not communicated in some time, although I had been keeping up with her life events via social media. I had recently reached out to her as a potential panelist for a climate change panel, hosted by my local DST chapter, Raleigh Alumnae Chapter. I assumed she wanted more information on this. However, when we connected it was about something else.

She informed me of a nationally known community activist, LaTosha Brown, with whom she had been working on a historic project. LaTosha had a vision of creating an Executive Education program at the Harvard Kennedy School on Power, Innovation, and Leadership. It is designed for leaders who are working to empower Black women and girls in the south. It is sponsored by the TruthSpeaks Innovation Foundation, in partnership with the Harvard Kennedy School. Chanceè asked me if I would be interested in participating as a member of the first cohort. The program was targeted to begin in January 2023. I was happy and excited to say yes. Shortly thereafter, I received a link to an application for the program, which I completed. As a result, I was looking toward 2023 with great anticipation. I also had a strong sense that more was coming, but I did not know what.

Two weeks later, I received an email from BWOB inviting me to participate as a cohort member of their next board accelerator program. It was a six-month program of educational and other activities, including workshops, coaching, and other similar events. In addition, at the end of the program, the cohort would be treated to a trip to the big island of Hawaii. Of course, I accepted. My first thought was, after the excitement died down a little, *I knew it!* I sensed there was more to come. In fact, even with this new project, I sensed there was more.

I checked my email one last time late one evening in early January 2023 and saw an email, again from BWOB. This time it was an invitation to attend a BWOB event hosted by the New York Stock Exchange (NYSE). To help commemorate the Black History Month in February, the NYSE invited BWOB to come and help ring the opening bell on Valentine's Day. My reading glasses were a little dirty, so I got up to clean them, as I wanted to make sure I read this correctly. Yes, that's what the note said.

The NYSE event would end around 1:30 PM on February 14. I informed Leonard that I would have time to fly back to NC so we could have a nice Valentine's Day dinner together. We were still newlyweds, having been married for 18 months at that time. Leonard's response was, "why do we have to have dinner in NC . . . can't we have a Valentine's Day meal in NYC?". Well then, we decided to make dinner plans in NYC. In addition, during the years I had lived in Westchester County, New York, I had always wanted to do a carriage ride in Central Park. My husband at the time would always say, yes, but we can do it later. We never did. I told Leonard that a carriage ride in Central Park was something I always wanted to do. His response was, let's make it happen. I was so excited! We made plans.

So, the first few months of 2023, I attended a Power, Innovation, and Leadership program at Harvard University Kennedy School of Government (HKS); participated in a BWOB board accelerator cohort with a graduation in Hawaii; and walked onto the floor of the NYSE, helping BWOB's cofounders, as well as about ten students from Spelman College, ring the opening bell on Valentine's Day. The servant leadership of the BWOB founders and their "lift as we climb" mantra were on full display. From the first Black woman to be appointed to a Fortune 500 board, Patricia Roberts Harris with IBM in 1971 to Valentine's Day on February 14, 2023, it was a clear display of progress on representation on public corporate boards. Representation that provides guidance and oversight, which is the foundation for board seats. It was truly a historic day for a historic institution. Never had 100 plus Black women, those on public boards and those with aspirations, been represented and acknowledged on the floor of the NYSE. Here I was again, part of a history-making event. It was so exciting for all of us, especially the young students from Spelman. What an incredible opportunity!

Leonard and I arrived the night before. We quickly checked into the hotel, then rushed to a magnificent dinner with Caroline and Jacques, a friend previously mentioned and former IBM colleague and her husband, at this incredible Turkish restaurant a couple of blocks from Central Park. After the tasty meal and a delightful conversation, off we went to Central Park to commence the carriage ride. We rode through Central Park and along 5th Avenue before making our way back to Central Park. It was a relatively mild winter night but cold enough for a coat. We rode in a purple carriage, driven by a horse named Mama, with purple blankets, which we used; they were very much needed. It was a magical romantic evening that I will cherish for a lifetime. My thinking at the time was, yes, the NYSE event was good, but this was unforgettable, an evening to cherish always!

The Harvard Executive Education program was incredible. The two-month program challenged me to think differently about power, innovation, and leadership. We had two face-to-face sessions, one at the beginning of the program, the other at the end. The closing event included a wonderful dinner with well-known invited guests and a graduation program. I learned some techniques that I immediately started to use in my professional and personal life. The professors were top notch, as expected. I was grateful to have the opportunity to participate in an amazing program and to have met exceptional Black women in our cohort. We bonded in a manner that will stand the test of time, and we made an impression on Harvard's campus with our cultural, southern traditions and activities.

The BWOB accelerator program was very informative. I added to my board expertise due to the online webinars and the final face-to-face meeting on the Big Island of Hawaii. I connected with an incredible cohort of highly successful and accomplished visionary leaders and executives. We met some amazing, successful, and powerful high-level executives who shared with us words or wisdom on successful board directorship. It was awe inspiring. I will certainly leverage these Black women in my future pursuits, be it collaborating, providing, or seeking advice, connecting people, supporting each other, or just getting together with a sister girlfriend to relax and enjoy. I am hopeful about my expanding network of support.

I had a quiet New Year's Eve with Leonard, celebrating the ensuing year, 2023. He is a morning person and went to sleep early, asking me to wake him up just before midnight, which I did. I watched the New Year's Eve celebrations on television and eventually viewed my church's streaming New Year's Eve program online. I awakened Leonard around 11:45 PM. We prepared the champagne we bought earlier in the day, as well as some great cheese and crackers. We watched the countdown on television. At the stroke of midnight, we had our traditional romantic kiss to ring in the new year, as well as the champagne and cheese. Leonard enjoyed himself so much that he suggested we have champagne and cheese in the middle of the night on many occasions in the future. I was in total agreement!

Just in 2023, from Harvard's Executive Education program to the NYSE, the Central Park carriage ride, the networking and educational opportunities with the BWOB accelerator, the awards and associated programs, a new board appointment with an incredible company, a wonderful vacation in the great Northwest, and it's only the summer!

It has been an incredible life thus far, and I sense *all* have been preparation for what happens next in my life's journey. From the encouragement of MaMe and other family members in my early years, to my unexpected wins in high school and academic successes as an undergraduate, I have been preparing for this. From my difficult and challenging graduate school experiences to my experiences in corporate America, from good to bad and ugly, I have been preparing for this. From my personal experiences with relationships to my wonderful new life with Leonard, I have been preparing for this. From my experiences as an entrepreneur to my corporate board impact thus far, I have been preparing for this. Throughout this journey I kept focusing on my future impact. Even when it was difficult to do, when I didn't really see how, with my strong faith, I focused on the future.

I dreamed of a world of travel as a young teenager. I dreamed of having a career that would enable me to afford a dishwasher. My life has been exceedingly, abundantly above everything I could ever ask or think about. If I, who tragically lost my father at the age of two, can do this, then so can you.

My way out of living a lower class, challenging but happy life was through education. It was the unlocking of my mind that holistically broadened my views about life. It has been through education that I learned about our global society, people, systems, structures, and life. It was through education that I transitioned from living in a financially challenged household, raised by a single mother of four children, to professional success and financial independence. This is my story, and it's just the beginning! I am no longer in a place where I am just tolerated, or worse. I am in a place where I am celebrated for my skills, abilities, passion for delivery, desire to touch the lives of millions, and make a difference. It is through a continued, lifelong, educational process that I will continue to live life to its fullest, to make an impact on this global society, and to encourage millions to aspire to attain their God-given greatness! Be encouraged, be strong, your life is but a journey. Make it a good one.

I sense I am on the precipice of fulfilling a grand assignment in this new life, one with a significant global impact. All my life's work has prepared me. My vision is not only to continue with these pursuits but also to passionately work to encourage and inspire those who aspire to make a difference globally, leveraging technology. To assist tech entrepreneurs of the Africa Diaspora, and others, to become technology billionaires, or just billionaires. And with this comes the power and influence to positively impact our global society.

Along the way, I will continue to innovate and invent, to be creative, to learn about and advance new technologies to improve our lives for the future, to be the technology and business voice for sub-Saharan African nations, and to continue to sit at the table on corporate boards and make a difference. It has been my life's desire to encourage and inspire the generations to be the best they can be, to leverage their God-given talents to the utmost. I am excited about influencing at the highest levels. Yes, my work has just begun. My new life has begun. I am ready for the journey!

Index

A

Accelerated Strategic Computing
Initiative (ASCI) Blue, 156–159
accelerator programs, 255–257, 259, 300
Adams, Howard, 61, 64, 73, 80
Adams, Yolanda, 201
Adamtey I, King (HRM), 202–203,
207–210, 212, 215–216, 221
Adkins, Rod, 190, 194, 198–199, 225
Africa
Elmina Slave Castle, 203, 219–221, 245
foreign direct investment (FDI),
233–234
Ghana, 202–203, 209, 218–221
IBM CEWA division, 239–240
mobile phone service, 251–252
Nairobi, Kenya, 240–241, 243
Namibia, 266–267
remittance market, 254–255
Tanzania/Zanzibar Archipelago,
244–245
technological development/
emerging markets, 232–234
technology parks, 211–215, 227
African Technology Conference (2008),
215
AIX operating systems, 183
Allen, Fran, 121, 159, 179, 181
Alpha Chi (honor society), 78
Alpha Kappa Alpha Sorority, 51
Alpha Kappa Mu (honor society), 78
Alpha Phi Alpha Fraternity, 51
Anderson, James, 65
angel investors, 256, 259
Antioch Baptist Church, 133

Arab Spring, 225–226
Association for Computing Machinery
(ACM), 147, 218

B

Bailey, Mona H., 79
Bailey, Philip, 62
Barcelona, Spain, 144–145
Bath, Patricia, 268
Baton Rouge, Louisiana, 37
Battle, Kathleen, 150
Bayou Classic, 55, 62, 72–73, 80
Bell Laboratories, 61, 87–88, 116–117
Cooperative Research Fellowship
Program (CRFP), 61, 82, 83–84,
93, 94
Benveniste, Caroline, 130, 131
Biden, Joe, 269
Black Collegian, The (magazine), 140
Black Engineer of the Year, 215
Black Enterprise (magazine), 160, 169
cover story (March 2001), 172–173
Black Family Technology Awareness
Week, 184–185
Black Women on Boards (BWOB), 285,
298–299, 300
blockchain technologies, 252
Borg, Anita, 146, 160
Bourne, Massachusetts, 4
Boyd, Gwendolyn E., 173–175
Briggs, Fayè A., ix–x, 103–104,
110–111, 112, 118, 119, 124
Brown, LaTosha, 298
Brownie (pet dog), 12, 14–15
Burlington, Vermont, 68, 69–70

Burrus, Sidney, 116
Bush, George H.W., 77
Business of Blockchain
Commercialization Lab, 257

C

cache coherence protocols, 113–114,
131–132
Calacanis, Jason, 256
Cancun, Mexico, 145
Careers and the Engineer, 140
Carter, Jimmy, 27, 30
Center of Excellence in
Entrepreneurship, NCAT, 281–282
Chennault Air Force Base, 3
Coalition to Diversify Computing
(CDC), 160
Committee on the Status of Women in
Computing (CRAW), 147–148, 160
Communications of the ACM, 147
computational fluid dynamics (CFD),
114
Computing Research Association
(CRA), 146–148, 160
Computing Research News, 147
Taulbee Survey, 148
Cooperative Research Fellowship
Program, Bell Labs (CRFP), 61,
82, 83–84, 93, 94
Cordoza Law School (Yeshiva
University), 254
Council for Entrepreneurial
Development, 270
COVID-19 pandemic, 278, 282, 285, 288,
289

D

Darden, Christine, 114
Dean, Mark, 179–180, 189–190, 200, 239,
243
Deep Blue machine, 146
Deloney, Thurmon, 106–107
Delta Sigma Theta Sorority, 51, 60, 72,
74–75, 76, 83, 88, 115–116, 166, 298
social service, 78–79
Westchester Alumnae Chapter, 133,
148–149, 168, 216

Diversity (magazine), 160
Divine Nine (Greek-letter
organizations), 50–51
Dubai, 225, 236–239

E

Earth, Wind & Fire (musical group), 62
electrical engineering (EE) curriculum,
55–56, 57–58
Elmina Slave Castle, 203, 219–221, 245
Emerald Award (The Links, Inc.), 297,
298
Engineering Horizons, 140
Engineering Summer Institute (ESI),
Southern University, 35, 37–39
Essex Junction, Vermont, 67
Eta Kappa Nu (EE Honor Society), 75, 78

F

Feinzaig, Leslie, 255
Female Founders Alliance (FFA), 255
Ford, Gerald, 27
Founder University, 256–257
Fukuoka, Japan, 3

G

Garriett, Lisa, 12
Garriett, Michelle, 12
Garriett, Renee, 12
Gaudi, Antoni, 145
geeRemit, 252–253, 254, 258, 259–260, 261
Geingob, Hage Gottfried, 268
GEM (National Consortium
for Graduate Degrees for
Minorities...), 61, 73, 75, 80
Ghana, Africa, 202–203, 209,
218–221
Global Mobile Finance, Inc. (GMF),
254–261
Google, 199–200
Grace Murray Hopper Celebration of
Women in Computing, 160, 169
Graduate Research Program for
Women, Bell Labs (GRPW), 61
Grambling State University, 55, 62
Greek-letter organizations, Black, 50–51

Gregory: The Life of a Lupus Warrior (Johnson), 156
Griffin, LaVerne, 12
Griffin, Lionel, 12
Griffin, Paul Wayne, 12

H

Halabi, Mitri, 96, 99–100
Halifax County, Virginia, 3
Halifax Training High School, 3
Hango, Lenore, 263, 269, 287–289
Hango, Leonard, 263–268, 269–270, 284, 287–295, 299, 300
   Mweenda (sister), 268, 287–288
   Penny (sister), 268, 287–288
Hannah, Marc, 107
Harris, Patricia Roberts, 299
Harvard Executive Education program, 300
Harvard University Kennedy School, 298, 299
Hidden Figures (Shetterly), 114
High-Performance Computing Conference, 157
Hill, Harlin, 67
Hinton, Shirley, 188, 216–217
Home Node Migration for Distributed Shared Memory Systems, 157
Hong Kong, 137–138
Honsinger, Paul, 28
Hughes, Langston, 154
Hughes Aircraft Company, 80–81

I

IBM (technology corporation), 67–68, 120–121
   Academy of Technology, 179–182, 217
   Accelerated Strategic Computing Initiative (ASCI) Blue, 156–159
   advertisements/publications featuring Johnson, 140, 160, 169, 175
   African focus, 224–225
   Austin Black Diversity Network Group, 218
   CEWA (Central, East and West Africa), 239–242
   Corporate Technical Recognition Event (CTRE), 217
   Deep Blue, 146
   Global Innovation Outlook (GIO), 215, 224
   Global Sales School, 232
   IBM Academy, 224
   IBM Research, 129–139
   Innovators Tour, 184
   internal review process, 132
   Java Server Performance (JASPER) team, 168–169
   Linux Technology Center, 175–176
   Research Staff Members (RSMs), 129–130, 134, 141–142
   Senior Technical Staff Member (STSM) position, 179, 183, 185
   Silicon Valley Lab (SVL), 170, 171
   Systems and Technology Group (STG), 183, 217
   T.J. Watson Research Center, 123, 143
   Vesta Parallel File System (VPFS), 142–143, 145–146
IBM Systems Journal, 143, 159
"I Gotta Believe" (Adams), 201
Inspirational Nuggets (Johnson), 208
Institute of Electrical and Electronics Engineers (IEEE), 60, 65, 72, 75, 78, 82–83, 147, 185–186, 192, 210
integrated circuits (ICs), 68
International Conference on Parallel Processing, 131
International Conference on Supercomputing, 134–135, 143
International Journal of High-Speed Computing, 134
International Parallel Processing Symposium, 143
I/O (input/output) performance, 142–143
Iota Phi Theta Fraternity, 51

J

Jackson, Alvin, 50, 55
Jackson Street Elementary School, 9
January, Wanda, 22–23

Java server performance, 159
Java Server Performance (JASPER)
    team, 168–169
Johannesburg, South Africa, 232–233
Johns Hopkins University Applied
    Physics Laboratory (APL), 75
Johnson, Donald, 41
Johnson, MaMe (Gloria Dean), 4, 111
    85th birthday, 293–294
    illness, 283
    Kimberly's death, 270, 272
    Lake Charles, 5–6
    medical issues, 273–278
    during Sandra's childhood, 6–11, 12
    as supportive mother, 13, 20, 28, 71,
        86, 98, 122, 133, 226
    widowhood, 5
Johnson, Mikel, 52
Johnson, Sandra K.
    Africa, travels in, 233–239
    African technology consulting (SKJ
        Visioneering), 244, 251–262
    African technology projects,
        212–215, 224–225
    birth and family background, 3–4
    Brownie (pet dog), 12, 14–15
    childhood, early, 4–11
    college, first two years, 47–66
    college, last two years, 71–88
    Delta Sigma Theta Sorority
        leadership positions, 148–149,
        216–217
    dissertation, 117–119, 122–123
    Dubai, move to, 225–233
    fertility issues/pregnancies, 151–154
    Ghana trip (2007), 218–221
    Google interview, 199–200
    graduate school, Rice University,
        109–125
    graduate school, Stanford
        University, 91–108
    high school, 24–43
    high school sweetheart, 30–34,
        35–37, 38–39, 40, 41, 42, 43, 52–53,
        70, 175–176, 187, 195
    husband/marriage, first, 116, 122,
        129, 132–133, 136–137, 144–145,
        151–152, 169–170

husband/marriage, Leonard
    Hango, 263–268, 269–270, 284,
    287–293
IBM, CEWA leadership, 239–242
IBM, DE application/rejection,
    189–199, 222–223
IBM, internal promotions, 165–170
IBM, Small and Medium Business
    (SMB) role, 186–187, 217
IBM internship, 67–71
IBM Linux Technology Center
    (LTC), 176–177
IBM Silicon Valley Lab (SVL),
    171–172
IBM STSM position, 183–184, 185
junior high school, 12–23
leadership roles, school days, 7–8,
    20–21, 27–33
leadership roles as adult, 149–150,
    160–161
music lessons, 10–11, 17–18
North Carolina, move to (2007),
    216–217
patent applications/patents, 144,
    157, 158–159, 172, 177, 178–179,
    217, 222, 254
personal finance, 62–64, 119
racism and prejudice experienced,
    95, 100, 102, 112, 194, 217,
    222–223
as role model/mentor, 140, 177–179,
    198, 298
spiritual faith, 99, 150, 182, 187,
    197–198, 200–201, 204
Tokyo, Japan trip (1991), 135–137
travel, love of, 135, 144–145, 184,
    217–218, 242, 295–297
Johnson, Sandra K., family
    Arnold (cousin), 10, 12, 72, 75, 273
    Aunt Gertie, 18
    Aunt Mae Ruth, 5, 6, 13, 21, 24, 27,
        66, 122, 133
    Aunt Rosa Bea, 13, 20, 24, 25–26, 49,
        122
    Aunt Roy Lee, 5, 105, 122, 133
    Aunt Yvonne, 25
    Big Daddy (paternal grandfather),
        8–9, 15–17, 23, 25, 154–155

Big Mama (paternal grandmother), 8–9, 15–17, 23, 25
Brianna (niece), 198, 297
Bryan (cousin), 14
cousins, closeness with, 13
Darlene (sister), 3–4, 10, 12, 13, 19, 21–22, 110, 115, 122, 154, 155, 188, 198, 273–276, 278
Dottie (cousin), 110
family support, 104–105, 115–116
father, 3, 4
father's family, 8, 15–17, 23, 25, 76–77, 123–124
Gregory (brother), 4, 6, 9, 10, 12, 14, 19, 20, 57, 71, 77–78, 82, 107–108, 109–110, 154, 155–156
Kimberly (sister), 4, 5, 10, 12, 19, 20, 86, 122, 270–272
MaMa (maternal grandmother), 4, 133
Schirrell (cousin), 7, 14, 18, 24, 41, 47–48, 110, 115, 122
Tanya (cousin), 273
Theryl (cousin), 7, 41, 47–48, 69, 79, 160
Uncle Edward, 5, 13
Uncle Ernest, 7, 18
Uncle Leon, 25
Uncle Morris, 7
Uncle Noah, 13–14, 24, 122
see also Johnson, MaMe (Gloria Dean)
Jones, Cathleen, 42, 125
Jones, Rosemary, 48, 56, 57, 71, 86
Joyce, Dennis, 256

K

Kappa Alpha Psi Fraternity, 51
Kasparov, Gary, 146
Kinsey, Cassy, 91–92

L

Lackland Air Force Base, San Antonio, Texas, 37
Lake Charles, Louisiana, 3, 5
Lake Charles High School, 14, 24, 27–28
Wildcat Nation, 27–33
Lake Placid, New York, 69

Lawrence Livermore National Laboratory (LLNL), 156–157
Lewis, Bryan A., 124
Linux operating system, 183, 199
Linux Technology Center (LTC), 176–177, 180
Los Angeles, California, 13–14
Louisiana State University (LSU), 50
Lyman, Richard, 105–106

M

Marks, Faye, 108, 119
McClurkin, Donnie, 201
McDaniel, Jamie, 289, 291, 293
McDaniel, Orlando, 50
McLaughlin, Charlie, 60, 62, 72, 73, 74, 77
Middle East, 225
Minerva's Machine: Women in Computing (documentary), 140
MIT (Massachusetts Institute of Technology), 69
Mitchell, Joan, 182–183, 185–186, 192, 222–223
Mohanty, Rama, 58–59
Montreal, Canada, 69
Mt. Kisco, New York, 123, 129, 151
Museveni, Yoweri, 235

N

Nathalie, Virginia, 4, 8, 15–17, 25
National Association of Corporate Directors (NACD), 282–283, 285
National Inventors Hall of Fame, 268
National Science Foundation (NSF), 160, 259
National Society of Black Engineers (NSBE), 135, 160, 169
New Emmanuel Baptist Church, 5–6, 9–10, 18–19
New York Stock Exchange (NYSE), 298–299
North Carolina A&T State University (NCAT), 281
North Carolina Central University (NCCU), 253

O

Obama, Barack, 268–269
Obama, Michelle, 269
Omega Psi Phi Fraternity, 51
Opelousas Street Elementary School, 9
*Optimum Write-back Strategy for
    Directory-Based Cache Coherence
    Protocols,* 132
Ossining, New York, 151
Otis Air Force Base, 4
Outstanding Technical Achievement
    (OTA) award, 217

P

Palo Alto, California, 92
Pan American Life Insurance Group
    (PALIG), 285–286
parallel processing, 130–131
    Vulcan machine, 142
patent applications/process, 132, 210,
    223–224, 253–254
    Patent Diversity Project (Cardozo/
        Google), 254
Pearl Watson Junior High School, 14, 21
Performance Tuning for Linux Servers,
    177
Pete, Cathleen, 12, 87, 277
Pete, Renee, 12
Pete, Sonja, 12
Phi Beta Sigma Fraternity, 51
Plauche, Jimmy, 27, 29, 31–33
Porche, Isaac, 58, 65, 74–75
Poughkeepsie, New York, 121–122
Proctor & Gamble, 81

R

Raisin in the Sun, A (Hansberry), 40
Rankin, Raju, 67–68
Ready Set Raise (RSR) accelerator
    program, 255–256
Regional Management Corporation,
    283–285
Research Parallel Processing Prototype
    (RP3), 130–131, 141–142
Research Triangle Park (RTP), North
    Carolina, 177, 202, 254, 270

Rice, William Marsh, 111
Rice University, 103–104, 110–111,
    112–114
Rice University Laureate Award, 297

S

Saintil, Merline, 285
San Jose, California, 171
Sata, Michael, 235
school segregation/integration, 9, 14,
    27–30
Science (magazine), 140
Shabazz, Betty, 149
Shockley, William, 102
Sigma Gamma Rho Sorority, 51
Silicon Valley, 171
Simon, Cassandra, 125
Singh, Ajit, 79
single board computers (SBCs), 87–88
Single Program Multiple Data (SPMD),
    134
SKJ Visioneering, 244, 251–262
Smith, George F., III, 79
Smith, Megan, 268
Society of Women Engineers (SWE), 60
SoutheastCon (1980), 65–66
SoutheastCon (1982), 83
Southern University, Baton Rouge,
    Louisiana, 35, 37, 39, 47–48, 49,
    50–51
    College of Engineering, 140
    electrical engineering, 55–56, 57–58,
        71, 74, 84–85
    Human Jukebox band, 50, 54, 55, 61,
        72, 80
Spelman College, 299
SP machine (Scalable POWERparallel),
    145–146
Springboard Enterprises, 257
"Stand" (McClurkin), 201
Stanford University, 92, 94, 104–106
    computer coursework, 95–100
Stanford Women on Boards (SWB), 285
STEM fields
    brainstorming sessions, 144
    diversity and collaboration, 140–141
    impact of, xi

mentorship, 177–179
research culture, 143
STEM-focused students at
    Stanford, 93
Stewart, Nancy, 165–166, 167–168, 170
St. Michael's College, 67
Sunflower Baptist Church, 16–17, 25
Sun Microsystems, 118
Supercomputing, 93, 143
Systers network, 146

T

Tanzania, 244–245
technology parks, 211–215, 227
TruthSpeaks Innovation Foundation,
    298

U

United Arab Emirates (UAE), 225,
    235–236

V

Venture Mentoring Service, 270
Vesta Parallel File System (VPFS),
    142–143, 145–146
Vulcan machine, 142, 145–146

W

Wang, Kai, 103–104
Warner Robbins Air Force Base, 82
Washington, Earl and Leola, 101–102,
    106, 107, 187
Washington, Robin, 285
WebSphere Application Server (WAS),
    171
White, Maurice, 62
White, Verdine, 62
White House United State of Women
    Summit, 268, 288
Williams, Doug, 62
Winooski, Vermont, 67
W.O. Boston High School, 3
Women in Computer Science, 140
Women of Color Technology Awards,
    160, 165, 169

Y

Yeshiva University, Cordoza Law
    School, 254
Yorktown Heights, New York, 123

Z

Zanzibar Archipelago, 244–245
Zeta Phi Beta Sorority, 39, 51

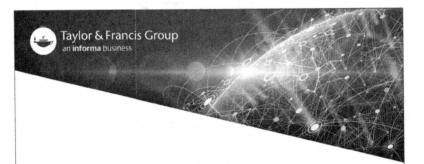

Printed in the United States
by Baker & Taylor Publisher Services